april 2017

Dear Gina,

What a pleasure to meet a sister in Christ who (truly) embraces the Sanctity of human life!

May this Book stand as a lasting symbol of (not only) 40 days (but also) 40 years (or) 400 years, however long it takes to overturn the murderous, Satanic Roe vs. Wade legislation,

Allutu continua (The Struggle Continues)

Sister Azariah

"The fruits of 40 Days for Life are simply invaluable to our cause. Every child saved, abortion-minded mother changed, and abortion industry employee converted becomes a shining witness to Life, another foot soldier working to build a Culture of Life in our nation. People of faith will be inspired and invigorated by this book."

Marjorie Dannenfelser, President, Susan B. Anthony List

"When the Word of Life is proclaimed in the Church, the People of Life then proclaim it on the streets! That is why I have strongly encouraged the work of 40 Days for Life from its very inception. The pro-life movement has long known that when God's people show up at abortion centers, miracles happen, and this book is evidence of that fact!"

Fr. Frank Pavone, National Director, Priests for Life

"*40 Days for Life* brings 2 Chronicles 7:14 into 21st century focus. As one human race, we become united in prayer. Glory to God!"

Dr. Alveda C. King, Niece of Dr. Martin Luther King, Jr.

"*40 Days of Life* is a testament of how God's amazing grace can bring healing and restoration, even in the midst of the horrific tragedy of more than 50 million deaths through so-called 'legal' abortion. These stories will not only inspire you, but also hopefully change hearts and minds to restore a culture where every life, from conception to natural death, is protected and affirmed."

Alan E. Sears, Esq., President, CEO, and General Counsel,
Alliance Defending Freedom

"40 Days for Life is so essential to the pro-life movement. And this book is one more example of their pivotal contribution. It was such an encouragement to read how hearts and minds were changed for life. It's important for us to remember that we are building momentum and seeing victories for life every day."

Charmaine Yoest, Ph.D., President and CEO, Americans United for Life

"*40 Days for Life* puts a human face on the agony of abortion. These uplifting stories remind us of the fear and confusion that drive women experiencing an unplanned or crisis pregnancy. The courageous people profiled in this book are examples of the power of prayer and the freedom and healing that come from choosing life."

Penny Nance, President, Concerned Women for America

"When historians look back at the end of abortion, they will write about the crucial role that 40 Days for Life played in its demise. Please read this vital book. I know no other book that is better suited to motivate a whole new generation of abortion abolitionists."

Kristan Hawkins, President, Students for Life of America

"This beautiful book will touch your heart and challenge and inspire you. *40 Days for Life* helps us to be spiritually aware of the need to pray for our unborn brothers and sisters, empowering us to be on the front lines of the pro-life movement, reaching out to mothers and fathers with a message of hope. There is no movement more important, and 40 Days for Life is leading the fight—spiritually and practically—in the trenches every day. This book will help you see how you, too, can take part in saving a life."

Lila Rose, President, Live Action

"*40 Days for Life* is one of the most inspiring books you will ever read. It is not merely a book, it is a life-changing experience, an exercise in sacrifice for the needs of others, an appeal to your heart to love the innocent, defend the helpless, and embrace the needy. I daresay you will find yourself participating in 40 Days for Life in your community. Don't deprive yourself of these words filled with hope, joy, and love—read *40 Days for Life*."

Judie Brown, President, American Life League

"The international pro-life movement recognizes 40 Days for Life as a powerful witness in today's secular society with its lack of respect for human life. *40 Days for Life* provides powerful inspiration at a crucial time in history. This book is a must read for anyone desiring to restore a Culture of Life worldwide."

Jim Hughes, National President, Campaign Life Coalition Canada

"For anyone who has doubts about whether God's blessings are still flowing, I commend to them the inspiring new book *40 Days for Life*. And for any who wonder what they personally can do to help restore righteousness and humanity, here is not just a handbook, but an irresistible invitation to join in."

Joseph Farah, Founder, Editor, and CEO of WorldNetDaily

"I was pro-choice and ran multiple abortion facilities. Now I am a pro-lifer committed to ending abortion. If God can change my heart and use me then he can use you too. Read *40 Days for Life* and discover how!"

Carol Everett, Former abortion facility owner

40 DAYS FOR LIFE™

DISCOVER WHAT GOD HAS DONE...IMAGINE WHAT HE CAN DO

True Stories from the Movement that Is

Changing Hearts and Saving Lives

One Prayer at a Time

DAVID BEREIT & SHAWN CARNEY
WITH CINDY LAMBERT

Cappella
Books

Nashville, Tennessee

40 Days for Life
© 2013 by David Bereit and Shawn Carney

All rights reserved. Published by Cappella Books.
No part of this book may be reproduced or transmitted in any form or
by any means, electronic or mechanical, including photocopying, recording,
or by any information storage and retrieval system, except for brief quotations
in critical reviews or articles, without written permission from the publisher.
For information write to Cappella Books,
P.O. Box 50358, Nashville, TN 37205. First Edition

ISBN 978-0-9882870-2-0

Unless otherwise identified, all Scripture quotations in this publication are taken from
the *Holy Bible, New International Version*® (NIV®). Copyright © 1973, 1978, 1984, 2011 by
International Bible Society. Used by permission of Zondervan. All rights reserved.

Cover Design by Matt Lehman
Author Photos by Lori Elizabeth Fowlkes

Manufactured in the United States of America

13 14 15 16 17 18 19 • 19 18 17 16 15 14 13 12 11 10 9 8 7 6 5 4 3 2 1

To our wives, Margaret and Marilisa,
whose examples first inspired us to get involved in this work.
To our children, who are daily reminders of why we do this.
And to all of the local leaders and participants
in 40 Days for Life campaigns around the world—
this is your story.

Contents

Foreword

"Does it really make a difference?"

"Are my prayers really working?"

I hear these questions from those who stand and pray outside abortion facilities, and all I can do is smile and say, "Yes, your efforts make a difference."

They made a difference in my life. I watched from inside the Planned Parenthood abortion center I managed while the first-ever 40 Days for Life Campaign took place. *What are they doing?* I wondered. *Do they really think this is going to work?* I asked myself those questions every day for forty days.

A few years later, they were still doing the same thing, but now as part of a nationwide movement. And then again. And again. Was it working? Yes. Clients were walking away from our Planned Parenthood facility and accepting information about alternatives from the volunteers. I couldn't stop thinking about the 40 Days volunteers in front of our facility who, every day, told me they were praying for me. That, too, was working, although I didn't realize it yet.

Five years after the first 40 Days for Life Campaign started, I found myself convicted to leave my job. It had taken *eight years* of prayer and outreach to me, a Planned Parenthood regional employee of the year. But how could I leave? Could I just walk away? What about the emotional whirlpool I found myself in? What about income? What about legal repercussions from Planned Parenthood? The simple answer is this: I wasn't alone. I had so much support from pro-lifers I had once seen as the enemy. The day I drove out of the Planned Parenthood parking lot for the last time,

40 Days for Life prayer volunteers were outside watching me leave. I remember looking in my rearview mirror and seeing one of them fall to his knees. He realized that, yes, their efforts had worked.

Today, nearly seven thousand babies (and counting) are alive because of 40 Days for Life. Abortion center workers have resigned, no longer willing to facilitate abortions. Women have found healing from their past abortions, and others never had to walk through that pain because they chose life instead. Prayer volunteers have seen the reality of abortion in the faces of women leaving centers in pain. They have seen the joy and relief on the faces of those who never walked in.

I admit that, at first, 40 Days for Life made me uncomfortable. And now I thank God for that. Being pro-life *is* sometimes uncomfortable. We are reaching out to people who have lost hope. We are restoring joy to those who felt like they would forever live in pain.

It does not feel good to pray outside abortion centers. It does not bring me joy to watch women walk out of abortion centers, faces filled with despair. But I go anyway. I go because when we show up to do God's work, he shows up. And let me assure you, rescuing those who are about to walk into or have walked into abortion centers is, indeed, God's work.

Sometimes I look at my life now and laugh. Me? Writing the foreword for a book about 40 Days for Life? That's just how God works. He is unexpected, unplanned, and yes, sometimes funny. I now stand alongside you in this 40 Days for Life movement.

It works.

Join David and Shawn in dedicating your next forty days to reading this book, meditating on the daily verse, and praying the daily prayer, and you, too, will be a part of this movement that is making a difference—and saving lives.

ABBY JOHNSON
Pro-life Speaker, Author of *UnPlanned*

The Wooden Table

David

YOUR LIFE IS ABOUT TO CHANGE.

That's a bold statement, I know, but it's accurate because forty days of prayer brings transformation. And though the circumstances, timing, and specifics for each of us who reads this book will vary greatly, there is one certainty concerning the forty days of prayer you are about to begin—God will hear, and, in his own way, he will answer.

Hearts and minds will change—because God hears and answers your prayers.

Lives of those affected by abortion will change—because God hears and answers your prayers.

You will change—because God hears and answers your prayers.

We invite you to dedicate yourself over the next forty days to reading a chapter a day, meditating on the daily scripture, and praying with us.

Why forty days? Throughout biblical history, we see the forty-day time frame come up over and over again. Noah was on the ark for forty days. Moses was up on Mt. Sinai for how long? Forty days. Jesus, at the launch of his earthly ministry, spent forty days in the wilderness in prayer and fasting. The apostles had forty days with our Lord following his resurrection. Over and over again, it's a time frame of transformation.

God repeatedly uses forty days to call his own people back to him, both to chastise and to encourage. He uses forty days to transform and prepare his people for the mission he has called them to do. He uses forty days to ready the world for the impact his people are about to have on their culture.

For the first thirty-six years of my life, I saw God's forty-day time frame as a thing of the past, a Sunday school lesson of biblical times long ago. But that was before 2004, and before a life-changing, world-changing one hour of prayer around an old wooden table.

The place—the modest little office of Coalition for Life in College Station, Texas.

The mood—desperate.

The need—well, first a little background ...

Five years before, in early 1998, Planned Parenthood had announced that it was opening an abortion facility in our hometown of College Station, Texas,[1] and the pro-life community in College Station was alarmed. I was there on the first night when more than four hundred concerned friends and neighbors from sixty churches and a number of local organizations and businesses gathered at a local church to discuss our concern and a possible response. (I confess that I somewhat reluctantly tagged along with my wife.) That night, a local pro-life organization was born: Coalition for Life. After three years of volunteering for this fledgling group, and defying all laws of probability, I left a lucrative career in the pharmaceutical industry to become its executive director in 2001. God was on the move.

Coalition for Life got off to a great start, but by 2002 our initial zeal had begun to wane. We'd had ups and we'd had downs, but the downs were lasting longer and coming more often. In 2004, things started to seriously erode. We had been working hard, and people were getting tired. They started getting back into their busy lives. It felt as if the pro-life movement was dwindling in our community just as Planned Parenthood was picking up speed. Abortion numbers were up, our momentum was running out, and frustration was setting in as life after precious life was lost to abortion and woman after woman was harmed—some physically, and many more emotionally and spiritually. We no longer had a clear idea of what we should do next.

I had a tiny staff: Shawn Carney, his wife, Marilisa, and a young woman named Emily. One scorching hot summer day, out of desperation, I gathered them together and said, "We really need God's help. Let's pray for God's direction, without interruption, for one hour."

The four of us bowed our heads around the old wooden table that served as conference table, lunch table, desk, mailroom, and had about a hundred other uses in our little office. We prayed, "God, we don't know where to go from here. Can you show us what we need to do next?"

For an hour we prayed. We prayed for direction, for ears to hear God's leading, for eyes to see the next step, for words that he would plant on our tongues, for wisdom to know his will, and for vision to carry it out. We confessed our own limitations, and we praised him for his unlimited love and power. For one hour we implored God, in every way we knew how, to give us his direction.

After that one hour of prayer, we all looked at each other.

And I said, "What about forty days?"

Immediately, the idea resonated with the four of us. Of course. Forty days. We can do almost anything for just forty days. We turned to Scripture and were inspired by God's amazing intervention in the biblical accounts of forty-day periods. So why not align ourselves with that divinely inspired time frame?

We saw that the forty-day events in Scripture were not easy—in fact, quite the opposite—but they were always meaningful and always transformational.

So we decided to do forty days of ... *something*. We had no idea what. But, believing that God was answering our prayers for discernment, wisdom, and leading, we asked ourselves, *If we poured everything we have into fighting abortion locally for forty days, what would that look like?*

And then the ideas began to take shape so fast we were literally talking over one another in excitement.

But the number-one task we kept coming back to over and over and that all four of us felt called to do was what our Lord did at the launch of his own earthly ministry—prayer and fasting. We would commit to forty days to pray and fast for an end to abortion. Prayer, because we know that with God all things are possible—even ending abortion. Fasting, because it's an act of humility before God, undertaken with a broken, repentant, and contrite spirit, to seek his face and his divine intervention in the events of our world. I had never fasted before in my life! I had grown up in a church that didn't emphasize it. But every Lenten season my wife, who is Catholic, would tell me a little bit more about it. The four of us realized that we'd never fasted for our ministry, let alone for lives to be saved or for the end of abortion. Two of the people at that table, even though it was uncomfortable, decided to do a bread-and-water-only fast for forty days. I wasn't ready for that. The other two of us gave up one type of food or a meal a day. We agreed that not only would we four pray and fast but that we'd also invite the entire local pro-life community to join us.

Then came a truly radical idea. The second thing we felt led to do was forty days of nonstop, around-the-clock peaceful prayer vigil outside our local Planned Parenthood abortion facility. Now that was crazy! How in the world could we possibly do that? Our ranks of volunteers were shrinking as it was. But immediately, Marilisa committed to being there, if we committed to do this crazy forty-day thing, from 7:00 in the morning to 3:00 in the afternoon every day for the entire forty days. As soon she made that declaration, the whole room changed, and the rest of us started making bold commitments as well.

We knew we were onto something. Where two or more are gathered in the Lord's name, he is present in our midst. Where is he more urgently needed than outside a place of such hopelessness and despair as an abortion facility? We knew from Coalition for Life experience that our presence praying outside an abortion facility awakens the conscience of the community. People drive by that abortion center day after day who either don't know or have chosen to ignore the fact that abortion is happening right in their backyard, but when they see people standing and praying in the public right-of-way, it becomes much harder to ignore. Even if reluctantly, they recognize that abortion affects their own community.

The third thing we felt led to do was grassroots community outreach. But what would that mean? We had already been reaching out to churches, asking people to get involved. But then Shawn had an idea. During his college years, he had sold books door to door to raise money for his school bills. He said, "I think, with a small team, I could hit every single household in this community—thirty-five thousand homes—in forty days. We could simply ask them to pray for forty days for an end to abortion."

I said, "There's no way you could do that in forty days!"

"Yes, we can!" he said. "We'd need a team of five or six people."

In addition to the door-to-door initiative, we also decided to engage in extensive outreach to local churches, inviting them to join the concentrated prayer effort for the forty days.

So, as crazy as it sounded, we agreed on the plan for this three-fold, forty-day initiative. Pray and fast, twenty-four-hour peaceful prayer vigil, and community outreach. Then we agreed we would each go home, pray more about it, and come back the next day to confirm this wasn't just something inspired by too much caffeine—that it could actually be from the Holy Spirit.

We returned the next day each convinced this was, indeed, the Lord's leading.

We started with the easy stuff, approaching close friends who were also pro-life volunteers. We were amazed at how many of them stepped up to the plate as soon as we'd outlined our idea.

Then we called a meeting with some of our local supporters. Their reaction wasn't quite as enthusiastic. When we announced that we were going to hold a twenty-four-hour vigil for forty days outside Planned Parenthood, the room fell silent. The expressions on their faces said they thought we were crazy. They reminded us that we were already having a tough enough time recruiting an adequate number of prayer volunteers to stand and pray outside the facility on abortion days one day a week, just during the hours the place was open. But doing a twenty-four-hour vigil for a full forty days? That makes 960 hours! Nobody in the room had ever participated in anything like that or even heard of it happening anywhere.

One close friend said, "You know, I'd like to see this happen, but I don't think it's going to. I don't think you're being realistic. This just doesn't seem possible. A forty-day vigil for twenty-four hours a day? No way."

We said, "Well, we actually already have volunteers committed for a number of the shifts." We told him of Marilisa's commitment. We told him that several members of the local Knights of Columbus council had already volunteered to take the overnight shift from 11:00 p.m. to 7:00 a.m. every single day and a few of the other shifts were already covered throughout the entire forty days.

Finally, we were so sure and passionate that we were following the Lord's leading, we told them we, the four of us who'd been around that wooden table that day—Shawn, Marilisa, Emily and I—were committed to filling any gaps and to go out at any moment of the day or night, no matter what, to make sure every single hour was covered.

After that, the room began to fill with confidence! But a few moments later, that confidence almost vanished. We announced that the first 40 Days for Life Campaign would begin in *two weeks*, on Wednesday, September 1. The air of confidence was suddenly stifled by a cloud of skepticism. I suppose they thought we were crazy to think we could pull off such a massive undertaking with only two weeks' prep time. But the four of us were sure this was God's undertaking, God's plan, revealed to us during our one hour of prayer.

One man, an eighty-year-old supporter who made time to pray outside Planned Parenthood whenever possible, sat quiet and expressionless in the front row. As a former Grand Knight for the Knights of Columbus, Emil Ogden attended every pro-life event and often said he had heard it all. But he had never heard anything like this. Mr. Ogden didn't say anything during the meeting, but at its conclusion he waited for almost everyone to leave before walking up to me. He shook my hand and said, "Good luck!" Into my hand, he pressed what looked like a note.

But it wasn't a note. It was a check for $10,000.

My faith grew. We had prayed and God had answered. And my faith has been growing ever since as I've had the great privilege of seeing God intervene in life after life after life—volunteers as well as those reached through our vigils.

Shawn and I have chosen forty (and it was hard narrowing down to just forty!) incredible instances of God's intervention through 40 Days for Life over the years since 2004. Each of these forty faith-building events have had a huge impact on our lives and on our spiritual growth. You are about to meet a diverse array of people who love not only the unborn but also the women carrying them and the workers in the abortion facilities. You are about to discover the power of showing up, standing, and praying.

Our prayer for you as you read this book is that you will be awed by what God has done within a community of people who stepped out in faith and committed themselves to forty days of praying to end abortion. We pray that you will be so awed that you'll join us in prayer and peaceful action.

So welcome to *your* forty-day experience! Pray with us for the next forty days.

Your life is about to change.

Love must be sincere.
Hate what is evil; cling to what is good.
Be devoted to one another in love.
Honor one another above yourselves.
Never be lacking in zeal,
but keep your spiritual fervor, serving the Lord.
Be joyful in hope, patient in affliction,
faithful in prayer.
ROMANS 12: 9-12

Heavenly Father, fill me with your zeal and fan the flame of my spiritual fervor, so that my heart is aligned with your heart. You are the God of life and the giver of life. You create life in the mother's womb. Every life is precious to you, fearfully and wonderfully made. For each of these next forty days, dear Lord, keep me joyful in hope and faithful in prayer for the unborn and for all those affected by the tragedy of abortion. Amen.

The Reluctant Volunteer

David

I SAW A CARTOON YEARS AGO THAT SHOWED MOSES WITH HIS staff, looking heavenward but pointing to a man a short distance off. The caption read, "Here am I, Lord. Send Aaron!"

I can relate.

How about you? Have you ever sensed God prompting you to do something but you were certain you weren't the right person for the job? I have! The good news is that we are in some mighty fine company—Moses, Jonah, Esther, Gideon, and Paul, just to name a few. God, it seems, delights in choosing unlikely characters.

When I first sensed that God was leading me to get involved in the pro-life movement, I knew just what to say: "I'm not the guy. That's controversial—and it's outside my comfort zone. I'm an introvert. I don't like getting in front of people. What use could I be in the pro-life movement?"

At best, you would have to say I was reluctant to attend my first-ever pro-life meeting. It would be more accurate to say I was flat-out disinterested in the entire issue of abortion. It was somebody else's issue, not mine.

But Margaret, my wife, saw abortion through very different eyes.

I was raised in a Christian home in Pittsburgh, Pennsylvania. I went to a little Presbyterian church. Every Sunday I was there with my family. Never in my entire childhood do I remember hearing a message on the sanctity of human life. Never do I remember the word *abortion* coming up in our church. Even in my home, a wonderful Christian home, it was never discussed. So for much of my youth, it wasn't on my radar.

Then I moved to Texas to go to school at Texas A&M. Suddenly I was in the Bible Belt, surrounded by Catholic and evangelical Christians on fire for their faith. I learned that the gospel message of two thousand years ago is relevant to the issues we face in our world today. The Christians around me taught me what abortion did to that innocent child made in God's image and likeness in the womb. They also helped me understand how abortion devastated the life of the mother, the father, the family. I thought, *Well, this makes sense, but I'll just be passively pro-life—I don't want to actually do anything.*

Then came Margaret.

I was in college when I met this delightful young lady. She absolutely captured my heart. I wasted no time declaring my love for her, and we married three years after we met. Twenty-plus years of marriage later, I love Margaret more than ever. She is my best friend and the mother of our two children, Claire and Patrick.

Margaret grew up in a loving Catholic family in Corpus Christi, Texas. Every Saturday morning, early, her parents would herd Margaret and her sisters into their family car. And they would join hundreds of other believers praying and standing vigil outside abortion facilities there in Corpus Christi, believing that it would make a difference for someone. They went in the heat of summer and the cold of winter, rain or shine, it didn't matter. Margaret and her sisters didn't always want to go—but that didn't matter either; they did it anyway.

And they watched as every single standalone abortion facility in Corpus Christi, Texas, one by one, went out of business.

We were living in College Station, Texas, after we got married, and Margaret shared these stories with me. I started to sweat a little. I could see that abortion was a problem, and I was glad there was a way people could be a part of the solution. Did that mean I had to do something? I looked around our community. There was no abortion facility. *Yes!* I thought. *I'm off the hook!*

Then in February 1998, news broke in our local newspaper that Planned Parenthood, which for twenty years had operated in an office in College Station without doing surgical abortions, was planning to build a stand-alone abortion facility in our community.

Lauren Gulde, a nineteen-year-old church secretary, heard this news and thought, *I don't know what to do, but something should be done.* Nervously, afraid of being rejected or looking like a fool, she called some friends and said, "Let's get together to talk about what we can do."

"David, we need to go," Margaret said when we heard about the meeting.

I said, "I don't know anything about this. I don't know how to articulate the sanctity of human life. I'm not sure I have anything to offer." But Margaret persisted, and I reluctantly accompanied her.

The meeting Lauren had planned for a few friends and neighbors who shared her concern about an abortion center coming to town was held at a local church. To everyone's amazement, four hundred people came from thirty different congregations. Lauren had never organized anything before. She had no grand plan. She was simply a young woman who felt that something should be done, so she did it.

As I sat in that church—as far back as I could get so they wouldn't get me involved in this stuff—I looked around the room and saw people who were sharper than me, people who had a lot of money, people who had political connections. I had none of that. I was a representative for a pharmaceutical company. I remember thinking to myself, *What can I do? How can I possibly make a difference?* But God spoke silently to me and placed a conviction in my heart. Even though I was scared, I knew I needed to get involved. I wasn't happy about it, but I felt God's call, and I couldn't ignore it.

Plans were made that night to pray at the site where that abortion facility was being built. I didn't want to go. I thought about who might see me while I was out there on the street. I was in sales— what if some of my customers drove by? Would they no longer do business with me because I'd been outed as an abortion foe? But Margaret said, "David, it doesn't matter. We need to do it anyway."

It was there on the sidewalk—first during the construction of the abortion center, and then after it opened and began performing abortions—that God began to really convict my heart, to show me I had a role in the pro-life effort.

A little organization was formed out of young Lauren's vision—Coalition for Life. They asked me early on if I would consider serving on their board of directors.

"I've never been on the board of anything," I said. "I don't know anything about pro-life work."

They said, "Are you willing to learn?"

Reluctantly, I said, "I guess."

I walked into my first board meeting, and they announced that the previous chairman of the board had just resigned. "We need a new chairman of the board before this meeting is over." Everybody else gave compelling reasons why they absolutely could not do it. I didn't say *no* fast enough.

I went home and said, "Meet the new chairman of the board."

I had no grand vision, no compelling drive to lead this mission. But I couldn't shake the inner conviction that had begun on that sidewalk. In my mind's eye I kept seeing the faces of the women I'd seen entering the abortion facility and their downcast eyes as they left. Everything about the place felt so wrong, and I had an inner sense that God wanted me to try to right that wrong.

Coalition for Life had started with zeal and passion. But over the three years I served on the board, we foundered. We struggled. We tried everything we could think of, and none of it seemed to be working. Abortion numbers continued to climb. Feeling like a failure, I decided to quit the pro-life movement. *I was right the first time*, I thought. *This is not my gifting. I've got to go do something else where I can see progress.*

I told the board. At our fundraising banquet in April 2001, it was announced on the platform that my term on the board was complete and that I'd be leaving. It felt like such a relief.

And then our speaker for the evening, Joe Scheidler, delivered the message God had laid on his heart. Joe talked about overcoming our fears. He talked about doing what we know we should do anyway, even when we don't feel like it. Joe said, "There's somebody in this room who is supposed to do this work full time, somebody who is supposed to take a leadership role in this work." I looked around the room, curious as to who it might be.

I walked out that night with a new stirring in my heart. Maybe I *did* have a role.

Several weeks later, while I was working my real job, my cell phone rang. It was Lauren, the woman whose concern had started Coalition for Life.

"David, today Planned Parenthood aborted ten more boys and girls." Her voice held such pain that it broke my heart. Ten abortions was a typical day at that abortion facility in College Station. Even so, June 26, 2001, was the day when my heart finally broke.

I said to Lauren, "Maybe I'm supposed to quit my job and do this full time, and give it everything I've got." I wasn't proposing it—I was just thinking out loud.

Lauren paused for a moment and then said, "David, why don't you?"

The light went on.

I went home and talked to Margaret. We talked to our pastor. We prayed fervently. As much as we knew we were giving up—the company car, the salary, the health benefits, all the bonuses, and fancy dinners out with the doctors—all we had to do was weigh that against the innocent children's lives and mothers' well-being at stake, and even though we were terrified, we knew this was God's call.

I quit my pharmaceutical job and threw myself into Coalition for Life with everything I had. Over the next few years we saw sixty churches join together to create a true coalition in that community. We saw hundreds of people from different churches commit to spending an hour a week in prayer in front of the abortion facility, eventually forming a prayer presence that covered every hour it was open.

We went through all kinds of growing pains. I recall my first

January as a full-time worker in the pro-life movement. I showed up at the office on January 2 after having New Year's Day off and went through the ledger. We had $2,200 in bills. Our bank account balance was $0. We had already called everyone about our financial needs. So our little staff grabbed hands around the wooden table in our office and we prayed, "God, we're trying to do this to the best of our ability. If you want this work to continue, it's in your hands, not ours."

The mailman showed up shortly after that prayer. There was $2,800 in the mail that day.

We were exuberant! God had acted again!

Those next few years were amazing yet challenging, energizing yet exhausting. It felt as if we took two steps forward, then one step back. But, as I described in yesterday's chapter, 2004 brought with it a serious slide backward.

And that led us to our "wooden table prayer."

I smile now, looking back. I can see God's fingerprints all over every one of those scenes, the good and the ugly! All in all, it was a shaky start for a fledgling group. We never had any idea what God was about to do and no inkling at that time of the global impact that would grow from our trial-and-error efforts.

But we knew one thing. Abortion was killing children and harming women—and men—in our hometown, and just like Lauren, that nineteen-year-old church secretary, we could each say, "I don't know what to do, but something should be done."

Is God stirring your heart to do *something*? You don't need to know how the future will turn out to take action today. You simply need to take a step forward and do something. Over the next thirty-eight days, you'll be reading the stories of those who did just that and how God multiplied their efforts exponentially. May God stir your heart to *do something*.

Certificate
of
Authenticity

PREMIERE

Collectibles

Your Exclusive Source for Autographed Books

www.premierecollectibles.com

**We certify that this autographed book
has been personally signed by the author.**

Duane Ward, *President*
PREMIERE COLLECTIBLES
www.premierecollectibles.com

*Therefore if you have any encouragement
from being united with Christ, if any comfort from his love,
if any common sharing in the Spirit,
if any tenderness and compassion,
then make my joy complete by being like-minded,
having the same love, being one in spirit and of one mind.
Do nothing out of selfish ambition or vain conceit.
Rather, in humility value others above yourselves,
not looking to your own interests
but each of you to the interests of the others.*

PHILIPPIANS 2:1–4

Dear Lord, you have given me encouragement, comfort, and love. You gave me life. You formed me in my mother's womb, protected my life, and brought me into this world, just as you did for every member of our human family. Help me to be your ambassador on this earth. Stir my soul, Lord, with your tenderness and compassion. Show me how you would have me look to the interests of others, born and unborn, even when I cannot imagine what difference I can make. Amen.

The Knight Shift

Shawn

I HAD NEVER SEEN AN ABORTION FACILITY IN MY LIFE. I HAD never met a woman who'd had an abortion—at least not that I knew of.

But there I was, in September 2001, standing outside a ten-foot-high, wrought-iron fence on "abortion day," which was every Tuesday at this Planned Parenthood abortion facility in College Station, Texas. I felt awkward and unsure of myself. I didn't even want to look at anyone going in or out of the place.

What am I doing here? I wondered. But then I looked at the adorable girl who'd invited me—Marilisa. Let's face it—a woman can have a lot of power over a man, especially when that man is an incoming college freshman captivated by the beauty and spirit of the girl he still can't believe is willing to date him. She was pretty and smart, and I was (and still am) intimidated by her beauty inside and out. I watched as Marilisa spoke gently through the fence to a frightened-looking girl about to enter the abortion center.

Maybe if I just stand here with my head down, I can get through this.

Never in my wildest imaginings could I have foreseen the future God had for me in the pro-life movement. I already had a direction; I was headed for pre-law at Texas A&M and then on to law school.

Marilisa first got involved in helping women in crisis pregnancies by volunteering at a maternity home. That led her to praying at abortion facilities. She'd invited me to come with her so I could see what it was all about. As for seeing—all I wanted to do was keep my gaze glued to the ground.

Then I noticed a movement, looked up, and saw a girl about my age, eighteen or so, step out of a car in the Planned Parenthood parking lot. Clearly confused, troubled, and uncertain, she scanned the group of pro-lifers on my side of the fence. I couldn't help but wonder what was going through her mind. I wondered whether most of us, if we were told that four or five hundred dollars and a "simple" fifteen-minute surgery could make our greatest fear, worry, or embarrassment go away, wouldn't jump at it. Maybe that's why 3,300 women choose abortion every day in the U.S.

Her boyfriend was with her, and they disappeared into the facility.

Two hours later, they came out of the building and hurriedly climbed into their car. She looked up and met my stare; her eyes were brimming with tears. Such a difference from two hours before. She was no longer considering an abortion—she'd had an abortion. A deadness in her eyes cried out to me, *There is nothing you can say to me now. It's too late for me.* As her boyfriend drove her away, tears flowed freely down her cheeks.

I have no idea what happened to her after that. But something certainly happened to me. Abortion was no longer a philosophical debate or political issue for me. It was personal.

As Marilisa and I drove away from the abortion center that day, I couldn't stop talking about what I'd seen. Marilisa talked as well. "I befriended a brand-new Planned Parenthood volunteer today," she said. "Her first day. She seemed sweet. Really naïve, though. They've snagged another one. Her name is Abby."

I was only half listening. My mind was still on the weeping girl. I had no idea that she had just met Abby Johnson, who would soon become my arch-nemesis on the other side of the fence. But that's a story for another day.

On Tuesday of the following week, Marilisa didn't even have to ask. I was going back to stand and pray outside that fence with or without her. We became dedicated volunteers for Coalition for Life.

In time, we also became husband and wife, and Marilisa started working for David Bereit at the Coalition.

One day when I went to their office to pick her up after work, David stepped out of his office and asked when I was planning on going to law school. I'd just returned from a visit to Notre Dame's law school, and I told him I expected to be heading there in a year.

"That's great, Shawn. Would you come work for the Coalition until then?"

This might be the only time in my life when I'd have the freedom to devote much time to the cause I had grown so passionate about. I said yes.

"One more question. After you graduate, would you consider doing this full time?" He asked it so casually.

"Yes, I'd consider that." The words seemed to have by-passed my brain and spilled out of my heart without thought or hesitation.

"Good," he said. "That's what I want."

I imagine that the Irish priests from my Catholic high school would have been surprised but proud. I grew up in the piney woods of east Texas, in Tyler, which is about 4 percent Catholic. I was one of those few Catholics and often joked that it seemed to me that 90 percent of my Catholic school classmates were Southern Baptist. Little did I know this experience would prepare me for the joy of working with my evangelical brethren in the pro-life movement. Two priests in particular, Fr. Michael Doyle and Fr. Anthony McLaughlin, had a huge, positive impact on my life, pointing me to Christ throughout high school and often preaching on the sanctity of human life. Exuding joy, they instilled in me a love of Scripture. I have no doubt that God used their influence to prepare my heart for that brief conversation in June of 2004 that altered the direction of my life.

Fast forward two months to August 2004. Two weeks had sped by since David, Marilisa, Emily, and I had prayed the momentous prayer around the wooden table and somehow, by the grace of God, we were ready for the first-ever 40 Days for Life Campaign. We had recruited as many volunteers for the vigil as we could, but we'd done our best to keep that number and the twenty-four-hour aspect of the vigil a secret from the press. We wanted to surprise Planned Parenthood, and we wanted to avoid giving abortion advocacy groups in the area an opportunity to plan a demonstration of some sort. After all, this was to be a peaceful prayer vigil, not a demonstration or protest.

We began with an opening event outside a local church—and the local media was out in force. David, Marilisa, and I spoke, sharing how God had answered our prayers with the plan for 40 Days for Life. We presented the three components of the campaign—prayer and fasting, forty days of peaceful vigil outside Planned Parenthood, and community outreach.

Then we announced that the vigil would begin that night—at midnight—and that we already had dozens of volunteers signed up to pray and knock on doors. We urged the attendees that night to sign up to participate, too—which they did enthusiastically.

A few hours later, as I walked toward Planned Parenthood for the midnight start of the vigil, I was just hoping people would actually show up. I knew the Knights of Columbus would be there from the start—and would stay until 7:00 the next morning when Marilisa would arrive for the next shift.

I'll never forget the first person I saw when I arrived—Dr. Haywood Robinson. As soon as I saw his big grin, I knew for sure that God was at work through this crazy 40 Days for Life idea.

Dr. Robinson operated a local medical practice. But before that, he and his wife had been abortionists. They had both experienced a conversion and shut down their abortion business. You'll read more about Haywood in chapter 12. I'd had no idea that he'd be the first one to arrive. Yet there he was, smiling at me.

"Hey, brother," Haywood teased, "what took you so long to get here?" I knew this night was going to be something special.

But not everyone was happy. Planned Parenthood called the police the first day. In fact, a police sergeant came to check us out—

not just on the first day, but for the first few weeks. At the vigil site we had coolers, supplies, and signs identifying our event as 40 Days for Life. We had a permit and everything was in order, but even so, the sergeant confiscated everything we were using at the vigil, and it took us several days to get all our supplies back.

The toughest shift to cover was 3:00 p.m. to 7:00 p.m.—no surprise, considering that September temperatures can hit 100 degrees with high humidity in College Station. On one of those hot afternoons, as volunteer Cody Sain was praying at the vigil, someone drove by and tossed a coat hanger at him. It bounced off his head. There was a note attached. "Why don't you adopt them?" Whoever lobbed the coat hanger obviously didn't know why Cody was participating in 40 Days for Life and why he had willingly chosen the hottest part of the day to stand and pray. Cody is adopted.

That wasn't the only time pro-abortion passersby tried their best to get us riled. On another day, I was at the vigil praying with a few other volunteers when someone drove by and launched a dozen eggs at us. The volunteers were mortified.

I said, "Don't they realize we're fasting? And don't eat those eggs. They're raw! Remember the movie *Rocky*? Only Sylvester Stallone can eat raw eggs and get away with it." The volunteers laughed, defusing what could have been a nasty moment.

The Knights of Columbus led the night shift, with men like David Arabie, George Voorhees, Jason Ferguson, and Charles Vreeland, all witnessing the deep silence of an abortion facility at night. I remember one of the Knights telling me that first week, "The bond that has developed between the guys on the night shift is unbelievable." In fact, they named themselves the Knight Shift.

For many volunteers, this was the first time they'd been involved in any pro-life event, ever. Many were deeply moved by the sense of participating in a sacred moment, praying for the unborn children just before their deaths. Others were touched with compassion for the women who came and went. We had trained many of the volunteers on ways to gently welcome the mothers into conversations, offering alternatives and friendship.

For many, fasting was an entirely new experience. One family gave up television for forty days, telling their children, "For the next forty days the time we used to devote to the tube is going to be put into pro-life work instead." The kids balked a bit, but they did it anyway. By experiencing the combination of prayer and fasting, people began to recognize the spiritual solution to the spiritual crisis of abortion.

On the flip side of all that good news—it was hot! And that wasn't the only distraction. There was a "love bug" infestation in College Station that year, which meant there were love bugs everywhere. If you don't live in an area infested by love bugs, just imagine an enormous swarm of half-inch-long black insects flying aimlessly around during mating season. If you're driving through them, it looks like it's raining love bugs. Turn on your wipers, and all you get is dead bugs smeared all over your windshield. I think poor Marilisa accidently ate about twenty of those pesky bugs one day.

The campaign's most dramatic event—which could only have been the work of the Holy Spirit—came on Day 39. Planned Parenthood had scheduled a fundraiser at a hotel just two miles away from the abortion facility on the night before the final day of the campaign. They had planned their fundraiser before we had even announced the campaign, so they were stuck with the date and location. We couldn't resist—what a great time for a march!

More than four hundred of us marched from the abortion center to the hotel where Planned Parenthood was holding the fundraiser. But we had no idea the fundraiser would be taking place *outside* with nothing but a gate separating us from the Planned Parenthood group so all their supporters could see the hundreds of community members who were opposed to their presence in College Station. There's no way this was a simple coincidence. You can't make this stuff up!

We could hear their party, and they could hear our prayers. Planned Parenthood was clearly nervous about security. There were police officers everywhere. In fact, we were told later that there were actually sniper rifles with their crosshairs on David Bereit's head during the event because Planned Parenthood had singled him out as a potential threat.

When the campaign was over, we realized God had done something incredible. Not only had the pro-life movement in College Station been revitalized, it had been empowered like never before. Community awareness of abortion had skyrocketed, which moved more people than ever to get involved to save lives and help women. People shared stories of spiritual breakthroughs, of conversations with mothers in crisis, of minds changed, hearts transformed, and lives saved.

We waited eagerly for the latest abortion numbers to be reported by Planned Parenthood.

Imagine our joy when, a few months later, the numbers were released and we saw that our local abortion numbers had dropped by 28 percent during that time. That meant that more than one hundred lives had been saved! We celebrated and gave thanks like never before.

Despite this huge decrease in abortion numbers, Planned Parenthood showed no signs of slowing down. In fact, they expanded. One of their consistent volunteers—the very one Marilisa had befriended on her first day as a new volunteer—was hired as a staff member. By then we at the Coalition knew and spoke to Abby Johnson frequently as we prayed outside the black wrought-iron fence.

Our forty-day campaign had come to an end—and we thought 40 Days for Life was over for good. We'd had an idea, we'd pulled it off, and now it was done.

God, of course, had some huge surprises in store for us.

"For my thoughts are not your thoughts,
neither are your ways my ways," declares the LORD.
"As the heavens are higher than the earth,
so are my ways higher than your ways and
my thoughts than your thoughts."

ISAIAH 55:8–9

Father, never let me doubt your power to accomplish your will. And remind me to not try to limit the breadth and grandeur of your vision. My dreams and aspirations may be modest, but yours are sweeping, majestic, and awe-inspiring. Give me the courage to dream big along with you. Amen.

Cloud of Witnesses

Shawn

HOW READY ARE YOU TO STEP OUT AND FOLLOW GOD, NO MATTER what he has in mind for you?

If you're like me, you'd feel a lot more comfortable answering that question once you've had a sneak preview of what he actually has in store. Am I right?

There's a verse in I Corinthians, 2:9, that pretty much describes how well David and I anticipated God's plans for us.

> *"What no eye has seen,*
> *what no ear has heard,*
> *and what no human mind has conceived"—*
> *the things God has prepared*
> *for those who love him.*

In other words, we were clueless!

It was during that first 40 Days for Life campaign that David received a call from Jim Sedlak, a leader at American Life League, a national pro-life group, offering him a full-time position in the Washington, D.C., area—which, somewhat to his surprise, he accepted. Suddenly, my boss, mentor, and dear friend was gone. I'd been so thrilled with how God had been using the two of us as a team in Coalition for Life and in the launch of our one-time 40 Days campaign. David's move had surprised me, but thankfully, we kept in close contact—almost daily. I became director of Coalition for Life in College Station, and soon he and I were comparing notes on how to end abortion on a local and national level.

Just a few months after our campaign, we got a call from some folks in Dallas. They wanted to do 40 Days for Life there with a campaign that would end around the January 22 *Roe v. Wade* anniversary date.

Marilisa and I were skeptical about whether the success of our first campaign could be duplicated elsewhere, but the group asked for our help. How could we say no? We drove to Dallas and spoke at their kickoff event, which got great media coverage. They had a hugely successful effort outside a notorious late-term abortion center. Lives were saved, and the pro-life effort in the Dallas/Fort Worth area received a huge jumpstart.

While there, I was interviewed by a reporter from the *Dallas Morning News*, who asked me how many other cities we wanted to take 40 Days for Life to. That caught me by surprise. Before the invitation from Dallas, the answer had been zero. I still had no clue of what was to come.

But it soon became clear that God had gotten so far ahead of us that David and I would have to play catch-up for quite a long time. Soon thereafter, a group in Kitsap County, Washington—just outside of Seattle—got in touch with us. They, too, wanted to do a 40 Days for Life Campaign. So we helped them coordinate their own local campaign.

Another 40 Days for Life Campaign followed in Houston, Texas—and then yet another in Green Bay, Wisconsin. I spoke at the Green Bay kickoff event, along with a Protestant minister, an evangelical pastor, and the local Catholic bishop. Afterward, the bishop pulled me aside and said, "I really hope this continues to spread throughout the country. May God give you courage!" I gulped.

On the plane home from Green Bay, it finally started to sink in that 40 Days for Life was no longer just a small, one-time campaign in College Station. Why was 40 Days for Life succeeding and spreading? We believe it's because it is based around our culture's most urgent need: prayer.

As soon as I returned home from Green Bay, I called David and told him, somewhat frantically, how excited I was by what I'd seen there. We discussed the national potential for 40 Days for Life—a daunting prospect, considering my responsibilities as director of Coalition for Life and as the father of a baby girl—with another on the way.

A second Wisconsin campaign sprang up in Madison.

Then I got the phone call you'll read about in chapter 8, from the woman with the beautiful North Carolina accent. The results Katherine Hearn and her group experienced in Charlotte were similar to those in every other city—lives were saved, pastors from many different churches embraced the campaign, and entire communities were getting involved on a large scale.

Charlotte was the sixth location that had done 40 Days for Life since our initial campaign in Texas. Katherine's phone call was my "that's it!" moment. I was finally convinced that God really was trying to get our attention. David and I talked, brainstormed, prayed —and got very nervous. What would happen if cities across the country—simultaneously—did what these other cities had done independently?

In April of 2007, David and I invited the leaders of the six cities that had done 40 Days for Life campaigns to join us on a teleconference. We had tons of questions about what had worked well and what not so well in their efforts, questions that we still ask local leaders after 40 Days for Life campaigns.

But our main question was this: Could—*and should*—40 Days for Life be rolled out across the country to meet the need to fight abortion locally?

The six campaign leaders all said yes, and their reason was simple. The campaign, they believed, was driven by the Holy Spirit.

We decided that the fall of 2007 would see the launch of the first nationally coordinated 40 Days for Life Campaign. David and I thought we could organize this on nights and weekends, by phone and by email, so it wouldn't interfere with our full-time jobs. (Right! What were we thinking?) The next step was a webcast to announce that first nationwide campaign.

We spread the word the best we could. We emailed everyone we knew both personally and professionally and asked all of them to share the invitation with everyone *they* could think of. We established an application period to follow the webcast, during which cities could sign up to join the fall campaign.

David and I set what we thought was an ambitious goal—twenty-five cities. From our experiences in College Station, we knew what a tremendous sacrifice was required to run a 40 Days for Life Campaign. We would be ecstatic if as many as twenty-five people were willing to accept the challenge and sign on for this first nationwide effort.

In July of 2007, we said a prayer, held our breath, and opened applications. The first city to sign up was Sacramento, California. For the next few days, it was a city here, a city there. We started to think we might actually hit double digits—and ten cities really wouldn't be all that bad.

On the final day for applications, we checked again—and were shocked. About eighteen hours before our deadline, the number of applications had hit forty! That would be pretty cool—forty days and forty cities. But then came the forty-first application, and they kept coming. By the end of the final day, we had received applications from eighty-nine cities in thirty-three states!

This just blew us away—and it was also quite humbling. We had indeed underestimated what God had planned for 40 Days for Life. So much so, that we were *still* thinking this nationwide 40 Days for Life Campaign would be a *one-time-only happening*. We *really* had no idea what God had planned for us!

There was so much to consider. For starters, there was the matter of money. We had none. Zero dollars. And as for our "workforce"—with eighty-nine cities, the "nights and weekends" plan David and I had been sticking to so far clearly wasn't going to cut it from this point on. This was going to have to be a full-time job for one of us. Either David or I would have to leave his current position.

Again we prayed, and it became clear that David should leave his paycheck behind and concentrate all his energy on 40 Days for Life. It wouldn't have been fair to the organization he was working for to devote so much time to 40 Days for Life. But without his total commitment to 40 Days for Life, the campaign might not happen. We would depend on God to show us how David could answer this call while continuing to support his family.

I knew there was one man I could call on to get us onto the right track—Emil Ogden, the generous World War II veteran and Knights of Columbus leader who had given David a check for $10,000 at the meeting where we had announced the initial 40 Days for Life Campaign in Texas three years earlier. When I brought Mr. Ogden up to speed on what had happened since the end of our original campaign, right up to the point where eighty-nine cities had signed up for the nationwide 40 Days for Life Campaign, he just said, "What do you need?"

"Seed money. About $15,000 should get us through the campaign." Looking back, I chuckle at my naïveté. I had no idea how big or how expensive this project would get.

He calmly said, "I'll come over to your office and write you a check."

I watched as he wrote the check. The first donation we received for this new mission again exceeded my hopes. It was for $20,000.

"It's a sacrifice for me right now because my business has been down," he said. "But I figure an extra $5,000 can go a long way with something like this." With a smile, he ended our meeting.

David took a leap of faith and resigned from his job on August 15—just over a month before the launch of the fall campaign. The first-ever nationwide 40 Days for Life hit the ground running as we prepared local leaders, sharing every aspect of local pro-life activism we knew.

David and I committed to visiting as many of the cities running campaigns as possible. The Bereits had recently decided to homeschool their children, which meant they could travel as a family and not be separated for days and weeks at a time. They drove their minivan from their home just outside of Washington, D.C., through Pennsylvania, Ohio, Illinois, Indiana, Wisconsin, and Michigan, and then made a brief stop at home before heading south. David put the entire campaign on his own shoulders and carried it through that first fall campaign. He averaged three hours of sleep a night, and some nights he would get to a hotel at 2:00 in the morning, answer emails until 4:00, sleep from 4:00 to 6:00, and then get up to drive to the next city. We didn't want to be seen as a top-down operation, sitting in our offices and just telling people in their local cities what they should do to end abortion. We wanted to be out on the sidewalks, standing and praying side-by-side with God's people in their communities.

Everywhere we went during the campaign, we heard reports that matched those from the six cities that had conducted individual campaigns as well as our own in College Station three years earlier. Lives were saved. Hearts were changed. Pro-life efforts that had grown dormant sprang back to life with great enthusiasm. God was doing marvelous things.

When the campaign ended, our reaction was pretty much the same as it had been in College Station in 2004. "*Whew!* Thank goodness that's over! Let's take a break, and then things will get back to normal."

But something happened. We began hearing from people who had missed out because they hadn't become aware of 40 Days for Life until after the campaign had started. Again and again, we heard, "If we'd only known, our city would have joined!"

You'd think by now we would have foreseen the follow-up question:

"When are you having the next one?"

Have you ever read the eleventh chapter of Hebrews, in which St. Paul addresses the role of faith in salvation history? You read name after name of the faithful through the ages, and then the first verse of the following chapter refers to these saints as "a great cloud of witnesses."

As I stand back and consider all the faithful pro-lifers who have worked in years past in this effort, as well as those working now on behalf of the unborn across our nation, this verse takes on a new meaning for me.

Fix your eyes on Jesus. And run the race set before you!

Therefore, since we are surrounded
by such a great cloud of witnesses,
let us throw off everything that hinders
and the sin that so easily entangles.
And let us run with perseverance
the race marked out for us,
fixing our eyes on Jesus,
the pioneer and perfecter of faith.

HEBREWS 12:1–2

Thank you, Lord, for the many ways you provide for me. For your daily provision of food, shelter, and other of life's necessities that, even if it doesn't come easily, does come when I need it. Thank you for the provision you make when I'm called to special challenges, such as 40 Days for Life. Continue to meet the needs of 40 Days for Life for financial support and for the energy and emotional resilience to stand and pray for long hours, often in the face of adversity. Help me to not take your provision for granted but rather to feel anew a humble and loving gratitude each time I experience it. Amen.

DAY 5

If My People

Shawn

WE POURED EVERY OUNCE OF ENERGY WE HAD INTO THAT FIRST
nationwide campaign in the fall of 2007.

We gave hundreds of media interviews. We traveled thousands
upon thousands of miles. We made hundreds of phone calls. We
answered thousands of emails. We sacrificed time with our families. We sacrificed sleep—boy, did we sacrifice sleep! And before
we'd even caught our breath, we were being asked when the next
campaign would be!

In my exhaustion, I didn't know whether to laugh or cry. Fortunately, I had learned by now that it was far more effective to simply
pray. Inside the verses at the end of the previous chapter in this
book, Hebrews 12:1–2, is the heavenly advice we need when we are
stretched to what we *think* are our limits—and beyond.

And let us run with perseverance the race marked out for us,
fixing our eyes on Jesus, the pioneer and perfecter of faith.

So we did just that—we fixed our eyes on Jesus. This was God's
movement, not ours, we reminded ourselves. We'd been given the
privilege of overseeing the launch of the 40 Days for Life approach,
and with that privilege came responsibility. We hadn't planned to
expand the reach of this initiative, but now that it was spreading,
we had to commit ourselves to that expansion. And above all, we
needed to fix our eyes on Jesus and run the race he was so clearly
marking for us—and to pray, because the busyness of our lives was
about to increase dramatically.

There was no mistaking where that path was marked. The clamor for a second nationwide campaign was loud and clear—and thrilling! We thought a campaign in the fall of the following year—at the soonest—would make the most sense. Once again, we'd underestimated God's plans.

We kept hearing the same schedule for the next nationwide campaign consistently suggested by people all over the country—people who hadn't consulted one another. The next campaign, they insisted, should coincide with the Lenten season—the *upcoming* Lenten season in 2008. Ash Wednesday, the first day of Lent, was February 6. That gave us a mere ten weeks!

But in what seemed like the blink of an eye, fifty-nine cities signed up to take part simultaneously in the second nationwide campaign, including some that had just wrapped up the first nationwide campaign. We were astonished.

Both David and I hit the road intensely during spring 2008, training local leaders for the upcoming campaign and helping the local campaigns organize and prepare. When we were finally able to take a breath, we realized we had spent so much time traveling that we had overlooked something fairly important.

We were broke. And I don't mean minor cash-flow issues. I mean *broke*!

Emil Ogden had generously given us seed money, and local leaders were always willing to pass the plate for us when we spoke at their campaigns. We bent over backward to be exceptional stewards of every contribution we'd received along the way. On the road, we stayed with family and friends and did whatever else we could to keep costs down. We always paid campaign costs before anything else—including salaries.

That approach had a downside. By March 2008, David, the only paid employee, had gone eleven weeks without a paycheck. The two of us had amassed a $14,000 debt. The 40 Days for Life bank account had been almost totally drained.

While we were excited about what was going on with 40 Days for Life and amazed at what God had done, we also had a serious concern. Were we finishing not just the second but perhaps also the *final* 40 Days for Life nationwide campaign?

The campaign ended, and David had still not been paid. We talked on the phone about the organization's—and our own—financial situation. For a man with a family, a mortgage, and no paycheck, he was unbelievably calm.

David had always been brave about leaps of faith: quitting his pharmaceutical job to serve as director of Coalition for Life, leaving Texas to take a position with a national pro-life group, and the biggest leap of all, leaving that job to run 40 Days for Life—a campaign whose only asset was its name.

We didn't feel we could impose on Mr. Ogden again; he had been generous enough already. So we prayed. And then we prayed even harder.

In the midst of all that, I got a phone call from my mom, who was in tears. My eighty-five-year-old grandmother was dying in the hospital. My pregnant wife and I loaded our two kids—a two-year-old and one-year-old—into the car for the unexpected three-hour drive from College Station to my hometown of Tyler, Texas. When we got to the hospital, I prayed with my granny and said my good-byes.

As I was walking out of the hospital room, David called my cell phone. He sounded serious. "I don't know where you are or what you're doing," he said, "but can you get on a conference call? Someone wants to give us a gift. He came across 40 Days for Life and wants to get on the phone with both of us in the next ten minutes."

I had never met the man we spoke to that day; David had met him only once. He was businesslike and direct. "I've been following 40 Days for Life," he said. "I've been very impressed with it. I like supporting pro-life efforts that are making a difference. What's your financial situation?"

Silence.

"Shawn?" David muttered.

I guessed that this first question was for me. I said, "Well, we're broke."

"What do you mean by broke?"

"We have $71 in our checking account, maybe less," I said.

Silence again.

Here we were just thirty seconds into the call, and I could think of nothing to add. I really expected him to say, "Well, good luck with that," and hang up.

Instead, he said, "I'm wiring you $50,000 right now."

A longer silence followed. First, I had to start breathing again. Then I figured I'd better say something. "Thank you!" I said. "That will be extremely helpful."

I'm sure there were more profound things I could have said, but I was so shocked, and to be honest, so humbled that this stranger had decided to give $50,000 based only on what he had seen and heard about 40 Days for Life from a distance, that I was speechless. Grateful! But speechless.

David and I wanted to make the most of that $50,000. We were used to running local organizations, not a national outreach run mostly online. So we decided to go back to the one thing we knew how to do fairly well. We would host a webcast event.

With our new donor's permission, we would use his $50,000 as a matching challenge. We would set a deadline to give our potential contributors an incentive to donate. It had to be simple, and it had to work. If the fundraiser wasn't successful, there would no longer be a 40 Days for Life.

We scheduled the webcast and set a seventy-two-hour time frame to meet the matching challenge. We had never asked our email list for donations before and had no idea what the response would be. In the first two days, we raised $14,000. Encouraging, yes, but we were still $36,000 short of hitting that $50,000 goal. And that was important because if we could match the $50,000 with an equal amount from the webcast, we would have enough to cover our debts and set everything up for a third nationwide 40 Days for Life Campaign in the fall, about which we were already receiving inquiries.

On the final day of that three-day challenge, we received an additional $88,000—raising a total of $145,000 in just seventy-two hours. Our 40 Days for Life organization had once again been provided for by God's miraculous intervention. It was now clear to us that, beginning with that one hour of prayer back in 2004, God had decided to use this effort—and he was going to see to it that it would continue to grow.

And in fact, 40 Days for Life continued to grow rapidly. For the fall 2008 campaign, we grew from eighty-nine cities in 2007 to 177, and then to an amazing 301 sites in 2011 and 316 in 2012. For the spring campaign, numbers increased from 59 communities in 2008 to 136 in 2009, and then to 261 cities in 2012.

God has used this campaign in ways we never expected.

From the hour of prayer at that little wooden table, this campaign has now been completed more than two thousand times in 481 cities in fifteen different countries. More than half a million people have participated in 40 Days for Life. Our post-campaign surveys consistently show that, for 30 percent of those participants —*over 150,000 people*—40 Days for Life is the first pro-life activity they have ever participated in.

God has heard and answered their prayers with thousands of babies saved, dozens of abortion workers changing their hearts and leaving their jobs—and more and more abortion facilities closing their doors forever following 40 Days for Life campaigns on the sidewalks outside their doors.

But one of the most amazing outcomes can never be measured. It's the impact on individual lives. Through 40 Days, God transforms.

More than 90 percent of the five hundred thousand participants in 40 Days for Life report experiencing spiritual growth and a renewed sense of hope after praying and taking part in a local 40 Days for Life Campaign. That's something we hear from young and old and from men and women. People from all walks of life and all religious traditions report they are transformed by God through this forty-day journey.

Without question, the key is prayer. Being busy is good, and activity can accomplish a lot. But without prayer, activity can distract us from *why* we do this—to serve our Lord, not to clutter our schedules.

A deeply felt but adrenaline-fueled campaign that motivates us to run out and change our culture might be laudable, but it wouldn't last very long. We'd get tired and frustrated and quit. But if our mission is rooted in prayer—if it's centered on God—then he will work miracles. And indeed he has with 40 Days for Life. He continues to do so to this day.

Yes, the measurable results are great. There are children alive today who would have been abortion statistics if 40 Days for Life volunteers hadn't cared enough to go out and witness to a mom or dad at the most critical moment of that child's life—the day they were scheduled to die.

There are women who, after having abortions, had given up on themselves, given up on healing, and given up on accepting God's bountiful mercy. But they have found God's healing, and he is now using them to save the lives of unborn children.

There's far too much despair in our culture. The abortion industry knows all about that despair—it's what abortion survives on. Women sometimes have abortions because they have lost hope. And people of faith are not immune to despair. All who work on the pro-life cause at times feel powerless in the face of the multimillion-dollar abortion industry and consider throwing in the towel. *This is just too overwhelming,* we think. *There's nothing I can do. Why bother even trying?*

But God has already answered that question, in 2 Chronicles 7:14:

> *If my people, who are called by my name, will humble themselves and pray and seek my face and turn from their wicked ways, then I will hear from heaven, and I will forgive their sin and will heal their land.*

We have spent the first five days of your forty-day adventure giving you a behind-the-scenes view of how God raised up 40 Days for

Life to intervene on behalf of the unborn—and all those affected by abortion. Now it's time for you to meet a few of the people God has deeply touched—and profoundly used—through 40 Days for Life.

May the true accounts you are about to read build your confidence and strengthen your faith as you continue on this forty-day journey, trusting God.

This is our time in history. We are the ones who have to take up the challenge and begin the journey. We have to look at the abortion crisis and know that responding to it is vital, it's local, it's hard—but it's worth it.

And it starts with you.

> *Therefore, I urge you, brothers and sisters,*
> *in view of God's mercy, to offer your bodies*
> *as a living sacrifice, holy and pleasing to God—*
> *this is your true and proper worship.*
> *Do not conform to the pattern of this world,*
> *but be transformed by the renewing of your mind.*
> *Then you will be able to test and approve what God's will is—*
> *his good, pleasing and perfect will.*
> ROMANS 12:1-2

Dear Lord, give me the strength to set aside my own fears, desires, aspirations, and plans and conform to your perfect will. Help me with priorities—when it's a choice between some new comfort or diversion for myself and the possibility of saving a life, help me see that choice in clear terms. And remind me to be grateful for all you're already doing, not only for me and my loved ones but for the unborn and the desperate families searching for answers. Help them to find the right ones. Amen.

The Downpour

David

SPLAT. ONE BIG RAINDROP HIT THE WINDSHIELD. WITHIN moments, the fine mist Mark had been driving through gave way to a hard, steady rain.

By the time he pulled up to park just outside the abortion center property, it was pouring. Though he felt a little guilty about it, his first thought was, *Whew. Now I can just stay in the car. I can pray just as well here as I could standing on the sidewalk in front of the facility.* God would hear his prayers just the same, he assured himself. And he could stay warm, dry, and comfortable. Besides, this way, he wouldn't have to worry about who might see him.

This was an important day for Mark—he was stepping out in a big way. Stirred by a recent presentation inviting volunteers to help save lives by publicly standing and praying outside an abortion center, Mark had signed up to participate in his very first 40 Days for Life prayer vigil. As he penned his name on the volunteer list, he felt the excitement of personally taking action on behalf of the unborn. Until that moment, even though he was pro-life, he had been hesitant to get personally involved. Now he was making an important commitment, and he felt good about it.

But as the day of his shift in the forty-day vigil approached, he was surprised by the apprehension he began to feel. What if a coworker drove by the center and recognized him? Or what about the guys he hung out with on weekends? If they found out, would they think he had joined a group of pro-life "radicals"? Would they give him a hard time? Was he ready and willing to talk about protecting the unborn if a friend, or even a stranger, challenged him? He didn't feel ready. In fact, if he had followed his feelings this morning, he wouldn't have come at all.

But he had made a commitment. So this morning he'd swallowed his misgivings, climbed into his car, and headed to the Planned Parenthood abortion facility in Kalamazoo, Michigan.

And then the rain had started.

Now he sat in the car with the engine running, arguing with himself. *No other prayer volunteers are here*, he thought, scanning the abortion center, its parking lot, and the public sidewalk in front of it. *The place looks quiet. I'll just pray here in the car.*

But a few minutes later, another vigil participant arrived. Mark watched as the man parked his car, got out, opened his umbrella, chose a spot on the sidewalk right in front of the abortion center, and stood in the rain, head bowed.

The longer Mark watched the man, the more uncomfortable he became. After a few moments, he rolled down his window and called the second man over. "Hey, how you doin'?" Mark said, as the man crouched outside his window. "I'm Mark—I'm with 40 Days for Life too. Jump in—we can pray in here where it's warm and dry."

The man smiled and shook his head. "No thanks, man," he said politely. His dripping umbrella splattered rain on both of them. "I signed up to stand in peaceful vigil in the public right-of-way in front of the abortion facility, and I feel that's what I'm supposed to do. But thanks anyway."

Mark didn't argue with the inner voice that told him his job was to do just what the other man was doing. Overcoming his initial reluctance, he got out of his car, opened his umbrella, and joined the other prayer volunteer on the sidewalk.

Side by side, the two men stood praying in the rain as cars zipped by, splashing water on them.

"We must be an odd sight!" Mark laughed nervously. "I wonder what those people driving by think. I hate to admit it, but I'm wondering what good could possibly come from the two of us standing in the rain out here."

The other man looked at him and smiled, then bowed his head in prayer again.

Mark followed his example and began to pray. He prayed for the women inside. He prayed for the babies those women carried, that God would save their lives. He even found himself praying for the workers inside, just as the 40 Days for Life speakers he'd heard had encouraged them all to do.

Meanwhile, the rain pelted him. His pant legs stuck to his skin. He could feel the water squishing between his toes, thanks to a big splash from the last car that sped by, soaking his shoes.

The rain came even harder as a car carrying a young couple pulled into the abortion center driveway. To his surprise, Mark saw they had a baby in a car seat. He made eye contact with the woman, and with unexpected certainty he knew she was there for an abortion. The gravity of the moment washed over him; he was witnessing the final events in a life-and-death story—the story of her unborn child. Clearly uncomfortable, the young woman tore away her gaze, then hung her head as her husband parked and got their child out of the car. The three of them dashed through the rain and into the building.

Mark and his prayer partner continued to pray. Now he had a face he could pray for, even though he didn't know the woman's name. His prayers took on a whole new intensity.

Ten minutes passed. The rain smacked his umbrella loudly. Another car drove by and showered their already drenched pant legs.

Suddenly the door of the facility opened. There she stood, the same young woman. Without hesitation, she stepped out into the pouring rain and briskly walked directly toward them on the side-walk. Both men rushed to shield her with their umbrellas.

With desperation showing clearly on her face, her words poured out in a voice high with emotional stress. She was pregnant, she told them. The child was not her husband's. It was he who had insisted on an abortion, he who had driven her and their baby here today.

"I'm a fallen-away Christian," she said, her voice broken, "but I just returned to God."

"God never left you," Mark's prayer buddy told her. "He's always with you." The two men took turns speaking truth to her. The words tumbled out of them, rushed and urgent. Both men sensed they were part of a real-life drama, unfolding before their eyes.

"God is with you right now, and he loves you," Mark heard himself say, barely able to believe that this was him speaking to her, boldly and publicly. He sensed God's presence in a way he'd never known before.

As the three of them huddled under the two umbrellas, she told them that inside the center she'd felt pressure from her husband and the abortion staff. "That's when I asked to come outside. I wanted to see you."

What she said next sent shivers through Mark.

In a voice choked with emotion, she explained that she had made an appointment with her pastor that very morning to seek his advice. If he advised against abortion, she had decided, she would not go through with it. But at the last minute, her pastor called her back and canceled the appointment. Something had come up, he said. He didn't have time to meet with her.

"So I kept my appointment for the abortion, thinking maybe God hadn't heard my prayer. But as my husband was driving me here to the abortion center"—she took a trembling breath, then continued hoarsely—"I cried out to God. I was desperate! I asked him for a sign if he didn't want me to have this abortion. And just as we were turning into the lot, I saw you!"

Mark could hardly breathe.

"Two guys standing outside *in the pouring rain, soaking wet— praying*! I just knew you were praying. I couldn't believe it! God answered my prayer after all! He sent two strangers to stand out in the rain and wait for me and pray for me!"

The men assured her that she was not alone. God could carry her through this painful, difficult time. Then Mark's prayer companion took their hands and led them in the Lord's Prayer. She squeezed their hands, smiled through her tears, then turned and went back inside the building. Two minutes later, she and her husband, carrying their child, came out, climbed into their car, and drove away. She waved to Mark and his companion as they left, resolute in her decision to spare the life of her baby.

"God made his love and presence known to all three of us that morning," Mark told me later. "And a baby's life was actually saved!" I could hear his amazement. "What a powerful God we have!" His newfound confidence in God flooded over both of us.

I've met a lot of Marks while crisscrossing this planet, inviting people to just show up and pray—and trust God to answer. I've seen men and women rise to the challenge and take their stand to pray, despite their misgivings and fears. They have stood in blistering heat, frigid cold, rainstorms, snowstorms, windstorms, and even in personal life-storms. Mark's discomfort and his misgivings are common to about 90 percent of our first-time volunteers. His experience perfectly demonstrates the natural timidity that causes us to shrink from the abortion issue—even if we're pro-life. Mark was hesitant to get involved, before *and after* he signed up, and the rain gave him another chance to try to slip back into his comfort zone. And I can relate. Like Mark, I was nervous the first time I went to pray outside an abortion facility, and even today there are times when I wish I could stay in the security of my comfort zone.

Mark couldn't have known what would come out of just one rainy hour on a sidewalk. None of us know that when we stand and pray—not you, not me. But God knows. He always knows who will be driving by—and when. He knows the work he is doing in their hearts. And, unlike Mark, you, or me, he knows the part of his bigger plan that we are to play.

I love how God used Mark in Kalamazoo to answer the question our friends, co-workers, family, churchgoers, and passersby so often ask: "Does it really do any good to stand out there praying, especially when it's difficult?"

The miracle of this one life saved wasn't about Mark doing something extraordinary. It was about him doing something simple, despite his hesitation. It was about God using that small act of love, the simple act of getting out of his car in the rain. That's all God is asking of us. God can use us, apprehension and cold feet and all, just as he used Mark in his reluctance, timidity, and nervousness. He can, and does, use us to save lives when we are willing to hand those weaknesses over to him, take a small step, and trust him to do the rest.

For me, God used Mark's story to demonstrate that when his people gather to stand and pray, no matter the weather, there is always a downpour—the pouring out of God's Holy Spirit on his praying people. So step out of the car and into the downpour!

"Again, truly I tell you that if two of you
on earth agree about anything they ask for,
it will be done for them by my Father in heaven.
For where two or three gather in my name,
there am I with them."
MATTHEW 18:19–20

Dear Lord, you know what holds me back. It's easy to tell myself that I am too insignificant to make a difference, especially when you call me out of my comfort zone. I confess, Lord, that all too often I have trouble seeing past the rain on my windshield and forget—or even worse, don't even believe—that you have a grand, eternal plan and that you call me to play my part in it. Today I pray for your strength in the simple obedience to step out no matter what the world thinks of me. And I ask you to give me the boldness to play my part in your work of saving lives. Amen.

DAY 7

Voices

Shawn

"WHERE WERE YOU TWENTY YEARS AGO WHEN I HAD MY ABORTION here?"

Pam's tone was serious but her look was warm, so I understood that this was not an accusation. Still, her eyes searched my face for an answer. It was a cold fall day in 2008 and the two of us, having met just that day, were standing side by side in vigil outside an abortion facility in Connecticut during a 40 Days for Life Campaign.

"Well ... I was in second grade," I answered with a grin. We laughed together at the obvious age difference between us. But this was a sobering thought for me: She was still looking for some way to bring peace and closure to a wound inflicted twenty years earlier, still open, still hurting.

Every day since, I've carried with me Pam's question and my memory of the pain in her eyes. They drive me to invite volunteers to do for women what no one did for Pam—offer a loving alternative to abortion as well as healing and restoration when they have had an abortion.

My introduction to the devastating impact abortion has on women took place in early 2004 during my junior year at Texas A&M University. David, then the director of Coalition for Life, had just hired my new bride, Marilisa, to help lead the pro-life group. Eager to support Marilisa in her new role, I attended a gathering put on by Coalition for Life that included both opponents and supporters of abortion. Five post-abortive women gave their testimonies that day. I will never forget the hush that fell over the room as they spoke.

The five were from vastly different backgrounds. One was married. One was a victim of rape. Another was in the military, another was an immigrant, and the final one was a young teenager who simply wanted to go to college. At the time of the gathering, I was already heavily involved in the pro-life movement, but hearing their raw experiences in their own voices took my conviction to a whole new level. For the very first time, I truly saw the pain of abortion—pain I would never know personally, but that in the intervening years I have witnessed time and time again. Their stories left me shaken and heartbroken, wanting to do something more to help them and the millions of others like them.

On that New England fall day in 2008, when Pam asked me, personally, "Where were you?" I realized I had to find a way to make that question not only personal but *urgent* to as many people as possible. Pam's question, made universal, has the power to expand the reach and impact of 40 Days for Life in its mission to bring hope and healing to those who bear the psychological scars of aborting their children.

So I ask you: Where are you as women in your own town are walking into abortion facilities—unaware, unsuspecting, feeling alone in a crisis, and deceived into believing that abortion is the only answer for them?

You may already be a part of the pro-life movement or on the threshold of getting involved. Or perhaps you've wanted to help bring abortion to an end or help women in crisis pregnancies or suffering the aftermath of abortion, but you have felt unsure how to personally make a difference. Maybe you know the devastation of abortion personally, through your own experience or that of a loved one. Or maybe you've been disillusioned by the anger, the controversy, even the hostility and hatred that have swirled around the battleground of abortion, and you've wanted no part of it. Whatever your situation, today we invite you to keep reading and to pray that God will show you the next step.

I've heard many impassioned pleas over the years to get involved in saving the unborn, but none as compelling as the voices of those who've lost so much—post-abortive women. Often, in the immediate aftermath of abortion, they bury their feelings as they try to re-enter life and move on. But for many of these women, at some point the pain resurfaces. Most, I have learned, carry this pain in secret.

One compassionate organization, Priests for Life, reaches out to such women through its Silent No More Awareness Campaign. As you listen to the voices of these post-abortive women, each paragraph a different woman's voice, you'll hear that the relief abortion promises is the last thing a woman feels when the surgical procedure is over.[2]

I'm always wondering what my child would've been or done in life. A part of me is missing. A piece of the puzzle is lost. I just hope that I can help other women who have had abortions or are contemplating abortion.

—

The abortion was painful. The doctor and nurse were cold. It was horrible. When I left the clinic I felt hollow. Something died inside of me that day. I truly believe every girl and woman who has an abortion, whether they admit it or not, feels that same empty feeling that I felt. I immediately cut off all contact with my former crowd and friends and made a complete new group of friends. I got into drugs and alcohol. Sometimes the memories and guilt would surface and I would cry and cry, but nothing ever helped.

—

I went to Planned Parenthood thinking they would help me plan to be a parent. However, they just gave me a list of doctors who performed abortions and sent me on my way. Most of it is a blur. I remember going from room to room with a group of about ten women. We talked about contraception and I can't really remember whatever was said about the abortion. I got there about 1:00 and left about 6:00 or 7:00 that night. I remember holding the nurse's hand so tight during the abortion I was afraid it might break. It was painful. I was relieved at first, but then I started drinking alcohol more and more often. I wouldn't talk about the abortion. About a year later I wanted to commit suicide. To this day, my parents don't know. I came to regret it and accept the forgiveness and healing power of Christ.

———

I'll never see or hold my baby, at least not on earth. It was traumatic. I hated myself and I didn't want to live. It negatively affected my relationships with children and men. I became very hard of heart, not helping other people. Until Jesus came into my life I had a hard time accepting love.

———

Not only was this precious life within me being destroyed, but also my own sense of worth, my spirit of love and goodness and dignity given to me when I was being formed in my own mother's womb. It was being replaced by a deep inner self-hatred that no one but I myself could ever know. The torment that wrenched my inner being was probably as close to hell as I could ever get.

———

The abortion was painful and a miserable surprise. I was crying in the waiting room before the abortion so they put me in a separate room to wait because they said that I was scaring the other girls. Terrible emotional pains and shame followed, and I had no idea where they came from. My boyfriend told me that intelligent people make these laws and they wouldn't make the laws if they weren't right. Thank you for stopping people from having abortions. There was no opposition whatsoever when I had mine. All I had was the guilt that I had been bad and the feeling that this abortion would make it right. No one points out that, either way a person goes, it is a decision that stays with them all their life. I think I could live with myself a lot easier having given the child up for adoption. Abortion doesn't make the baby go away. It just makes a dead baby.

From these stories, we see why Satan is called not only the tempter but the accuser as well. First he encourages the sin. Then he turns into the accusing prosecutor. He wants us to think about

God's mercy before we sin and God's judgment after we sin instead of the other way around. He mixes lies with truth to maneuver us into thinking that abortion is actually a good thing—in some cases, even a responsible thing. But the moment the abortion is over, he accuses, embitters, and shames. He is, after all, a "roaring lion looking for someone to devour" (1 Peter 5:8). Abortion, like all sin, gives incentive to rationalize. But, like all sin, forgiveness, healing, and a new beginning can be found in the mercy of Jesus Christ.

When Pam asked me, "Where were you when I had my abortion twenty years ago?" she was really asking, Where was love that day? Where was hope? Where was the way out? Pam's heart cry is echoed every day, at every abortion facility. And while we cannot do everything for everybody, we *can* stand and pray and offer to the women who show up any particular day the opportunity to choose an alternative to abortion. If they choose abortion, we can show Christ's love for their soul afterward.

You are about to meet two women who understand that better than most. But before you turn to the next story, turn to God in prayer, for he is the one who will lead us in the right way—his way, the way of love.

If I speak in the tongues of men or of angels, but do not have love, I am only a resounding gong or a clanging cymbal. If I have the gift of prophecy and can fathom all mysteries and all knowledge, and if I have a faith that can move mountains, but do not have love, I am nothing. If I give all I possess to the poor and give over my body to hardship that I may boast, but do not have love, I gain nothing. Love is patient, love is kind. It does not envy, it does not boast, it is not proud. It does not dishonor others, it is not self-seeking, it is not easily angered, it keeps no record of wrongs. Love does not delight in evil but rejoices with the truth. It always protects, always trusts, always hopes, always perseveres. Love never fails.

1 CORINTHIANS 13:1–8

Dear Lord, your love is so far above my own, I confess that I am not sure how to love people I've never met. But your Word says we love because you first loved us (1 John 4: 19). You love each woman entering and leaving every abortion facility. As I read the voices of some of those women today, I could sense their loss and pain. Today, I pray for the women in my town who have gone through the painful experience of abortion. I thank you for the people you have called to the front lines to stand and pray and be a witness that you love us all. Increase my love for those women today, Lord, and give me the boldness to take the next step in showing your love to them in concrete ways. Amen.

Hope on the Sidewalk

Shawn

WHEN I WAS THE DIRECTOR OF COALITION FOR LIFE IN BRYAN, Texas, the phone rang while I was sitting in my office one mild spring day in 2006.

A beautiful North Carolina accent swept me into a conversation with a woman introducing herself as Katherine Hearn. I found myself wanting barbeque and sweet tea. Katherine told me she had discovered online a report that Marilisa had prepared on our first-ever local 40 Days for Life Campaign back in 2004. In my characteristic zeal—and with perhaps a touch of Irish impatience—I cut her off immediately and said, "You should consider bringing that to Charlotte."

In her charming southern way, she said, "Well, we already did that, Shawn. Yesterday was Day 40."

My eyebrows shot up. This wasn't the first time we had heard from someone who, after reading about our campaign, was inspired to duplicate the effort in their own city, completely on their own. But I still find myself awed each time I hear it, another reminder that the 40 Days for Life model was inspired by the Holy Spirit and not by our human efforts.

That conversation was the beginning of an exciting journey for pro-lifers in Charlotte, North Carolina, and the beginning of a friendship David and I still cherish with Katherine Hearn and her friend and co-laborer, Andrea Hines. Katherine is an evangelical and Andrea a Catholic. Both women had experienced the personal devastation that followed abortion. Both had found healing in Jesus

Christ. And both were determined to reach out to other women in crisis to help them avoid making the same mistake.

Katherine and Andrea started by visiting as many churches as they could to talk about their own abortion experiences and build up a team of volunteers. Besides that initial effort in the spring of 2006, since the fall of 2007, every fall and spring Katherine and Andrea—through the organization they started called Charlotte Coalition for Life—have led 40 Days for Life Campaigns. Over fifty-two churches and organizations throughout the Charlotte area participate with them. Emboldened by their compassion for women and the unborn, they've mastered the art of leading campaigns within Charlotte, covering multiple abortion facilities in prayer at once.

In one spring alone, their campaigns saved a total of fifty-three babies from abortion!

Both Katherine and Andrea could easily have written one of the testimonies you read in yesterday's chapter. They each have a story of trauma, pain, guilt, emptiness, and shame. What I love about both of these women is how they have put their pain and healing to work, offering hope to women who now stand in the same shoes Katherine and Andrea were in years ago. They reach out to those whose pain is still raw to bring healing and forgiveness through Jesus Christ. And they offer comfort, help, and alternatives to women on the brink of making the same destructive choice they made in ending their own pregnancies.

It's crucial that, during a 40 Days for Life Campaign, our teams of volunteers are constantly praying *and* visible—before, during, and after an abortion. Our presence on the sidewalks is powerful in two critical ways—we are the last sign of hope for the mother and baby when they arrive, but also the first sign of mercy to the women as they leave. We can't prevent all women from having abortions, but we can do these two things: present the opportunity to turn around at that last moment, and just as importantly, for those women who do go through with their abortion, offer the opportunity to find the mercy of God at a time when they feel they're beyond mercy.

Time and again we have heard from those we have helped that when women leave abortion facilities, they expect judgment from the volunteers standing out on the sidewalk. They assume we are self-righteous Christians who can't wait to tell them they're going to hell. Instead, they receive hope and love. In the moments after an abortion, just when the women feel there is no hope, when they're feeling most alienated and vulnerable, that's when our volunteers express to them the mercy of Jesus. The love and acceptance expressed by our volunteers—expressed by you, expressed by me—could be the only sign that woman will ever encounter in her life that there is, in fact, healing after abortion. We don't, after all, know anything about the world those women are going home to. Katherine and Andrea and the millions of women who, like them, have had abortions know that women don't need judgment after an abortion. They feel that for themselves, without being prompted. We need not judge, and it is not our place to judge. Instead, we show mercy because mercy is what penetrates the hearts of broken people. And, as with Katherine and Andrea, once that mercy invades a broken life, God can move in miraculous ways beyond our wildest imaginations.

The inspiration Andrea and Katherine have given to their volunteers cannot be measured, but we *can* count the hundreds of babies who are alive today because of the faithfulness and courage of these two women.

Katherine and Andrea didn't find out about one of those saved lives until after the fact, via a text message to one of their volunteers.

"Hi! How are you?" the woman wrote. "I'm happy I didn't do it. I want you and the people that you are with to know that it meant the whole world to me that all of you care about me while not even knowing me. Thanks, and I hope to hear from you soon."

The volunteer who got the message instantly texted back to schedule more time to talk.

The woman replied, "I would've done a really bad thing if you were not out there that day. I hope this is as encouraging to all of y'all as it was to me, and that you continue to save lives."

She has no idea how encouraging her words are to us. When we stand and pray day after day for forty days and nights, when we watch women walk in and out of an abortion facility, we seldom know whether we're making any difference at all. We simply trust God and do our part, knowing that he will do his part, whatever that might be. When we hear back from one of those women that our presence made a difference, we excitedly share the news and celebrate with one another.

Five years after I received that first phone call from Katherine, I saw for myself that she and Andrea truly understand the importance of celebrating and sharing the news of lives saved. They invited me to attend a Charlotte 40 Days for Life event. When I arrived, they showered me with their warm southern hospitality and had me speak to a group of their volunteers. Afterward, eyes gleaming with anticipation, Katherine placed in my hands two copies of a book—one for me and one for David.

Not sure what to expect, I opened it—and there, some smiling up at me, were photos of dozens of beautiful babies. Some had their eyes wide open, while others had their eyes scrunched tightly shut; some were peacefully sleeping, others laughing, crawling, even reaching out toward me with tiny fingers. Page after page, the entire book was a collage of pictures of just some of the babies who had been saved from all of the 40 Days for Life Campaigns in Charlotte, North Carolina, since the day I first received that phone call from Katherine five years earlier!

I was seeing for myself the faces of children who are alive today because these two women had the courage and made the choice to trust our Lord in his infinite mercy and to help women who were in the same position Katherine and Andrea had once been in. Overcome with emotion as I carefully turned each page, seeing the faces of these precious children, all I could think was, "*I am making everything new*" (Revelation 21:5).

And he does. He is in the business of taking brokenness and reshaping it into wholeness. For each of the babies on the pages of that book, he turned a desperate last resort into a life with a new beginning. In the cases of Katherine and Andrea and so many other women buried in the shame and grief that follow abortion, he has filled them with the mercy and healing power of Christ.

Who knows which of the women you are praying for could be another Andrea Hines or Katherine Hearn?

As we stand and pray on the sidewalk, that is the hope to which our faith clings.

The desert and the parched land will be glad; the wilderness will rejoice and blossom. Like the crocus, it will burst into bloom; it will rejoice greatly and shout for joy.

The glory of Lebanon will be given to it, the splendor of Carmel and Sharon; they will see the glory of the LORD, the splendor of our God. Strengthen the feeble hands, steady the knees that give way; say to those with fearful hearts, "Be strong, do not fear; your God will come, he will come with vengeance; with divine retribution he will come to save you." Then will the eyes of the blind be opened and the ears of the deaf unstopped. Then will the lame leap like a deer, and the mute tongue shout for joy. Water will gush forth in the wilderness and streams in the desert. The burning sand will become a pool, the thirsty ground bubbling springs.

ISAIAH 35:1–7

Dear Lord, I pray these verses from Isaiah for women who have suffered an abortion. They know the desert. Their souls are parched, their knees give way, their hearts are fearful. Do for them, Lord, what you have done for Katherine, Andrea, and so many other thousands of women. Open their eyes and ears, quench their thirst, fill them until they are bursting with your life and shouting for joy. Use me, Lord, in whatever way you will, to invite them to your streams in the desert. Amen.

Invisible Answers

David

PRAYER IS THE FOUNDATION OF 40 DAYS FOR LIFE.

It was one hour of prayer around a wooden table in Texas that led to the birth of 40 Days for Life. It is prayer that moves hearts and minds. Prayer is what speaks to the thousands of women who have turned around at the very last moment before their abortion. It is prayer that opens the hearts of abortion workers and prayer that offers hope and healing to women as they leave a facility after they've had an abortion. Prayer sustains discouraged volunteers and motivates hopeful leaders to bring this campaign to their community.

Prayer is our strongest weapon. It takes the focus off ourselves and places our hope in God and his holy will.

And prayer humbles us when God answers on his schedule and not ours.

Ouch. That one's tough, isn't it?

We all nod our heads that, in theory, it makes perfect sense for God to answer prayer in his own way, in his own time. After all, God knows everything. But it isn't easy when we pray, and pray, and pray, and don't see that God is answering.

I think the apostle Paul knew that feeling too. When he wrote his letter to the Corinthians, he said, "For now we see only a reflection as in a mirror; then we shall see face to face. Now I know in part; then I shall know fully, even as I am fully known" (I Corinthians 13:12).

On this earth, through our human eyes, we see only "in part."

The challenge is to keep on praying, trusting that God hears, listens, loves, and acts even if we cannot see the evidence. My years with 40 Days for Life have taught me lessons in the importance of persistent prayer in the face of God's mysterious silence.

During the first nationwide 40 Days for Life Campaign in the fall of 2007, God took me to Providence, Rhode Island, to learn just such a lesson.

When Shawn and I realized God was exponentially growing 40 Days for Life into a nationwide movement, we agreed that we should both try to travel to as many of the vigils as we could to personally thank and encourage the leaders and volunteers. My wife, Margaret, and I made it a family affair, so beginning in the fall of 2007 we took to the road nearly nonstop. We homeschooled our children, Claire and Patrick, while traveling in our minivan (which had well over one hundred thousand miles on the odometer) to campaign sites all across America. On many days, we would visit campaigns in three or four different cities before collapsing into bed in a cheap hotel.

Our travels that fall took us across the United States, including visits throughout New England. One of the 40 Days for Life locations we visited was Providence, Rhode Island.

When we pulled up and parked in front of the Providence Planned Parenthood abortion facility, we met the two women who were praying there—a mother and her daughter. The mother was Joanne, the local 40 Days for Life Campaign director. Her daughter, Eleanor, was also very involved in their campaign.

Joanne told us that, as excited as she was about 40 Days for Life when she first heard about it, she had not been actively involved in pro-life efforts before and was unsure if she could successfully conduct a local campaign. So she asked Eleanor if she would be willing to help, and Eleanor readily agreed.

Joanne's next step was to meet with local believers about 40 Days for Life. She shared her excitement with them and asked who would be willing to get involved, but met with little success. Her pastor allowed her to invite parishioners to participate, but that yielded just thirteen volunteers from a church of over two thousand people. Most of the faithful, it seemed, were wary of anything as "radical" as praying outside an abortion facility. Many churches were cautious about what might be seen as a political protest.

Discouraged, Joanne decided to reach out to a local political group instead. When she met with one of the group's leaders, she shared her hopes for what 40 Days for Life could accomplish in Providence and asked if the group would participate, since they shared a common cause. But the political group was unable to help—their bylaws excluded praying outside clinics—or anything that might be considered religious.

Bewildered and frustrated, Joanne reached out to friends, family members, church friends, and others in the community. Again and again, Joanne was told no. In fact, Joanne told us, throughout their entire 40 Days for Life Campaign, only a handful of people had participated. Most hours of their vigil were covered by the same few people, often one at a time.

Besides the rejection, the faithful handful also endured per-secution while praying peacefully outside the clinic. Workers at the Planned Parenthood center ridiculed them as they walked by. Sometimes the volunteers' signs were grabbed and thrown. Drivers yelled vulgarities and gestured obscenely. Even some of the police officers bullied them. And the many hours praying on the sidewalk alone left them feeling weary and discouraged—not to mention what they spent feeding parking meters!

Always the optimist, I told them, "But I'm sure you've seen some positive signs that your efforts are making a difference, right?"

No, they replied, they hadn't seen a shred of evidence that their efforts had made the slightest difference in the number of abortions in Providence. But they quoted Mother Teresa: "God has not called us to be successful; He has called us to be faithful."

Margaret, Claire, Patrick, and I prayed with Joanne and Eleanor for an hour, and then we had to leave. As I hugged them both, I assured them of our prayers, and they committed to press on until the end of the campaign. But I left Providence with a heavy heart. I had witnessed the dedication and sacrifice that Joanne and Eleanor had invested in their effort, and I prayed that somehow God would show them a sign that their efforts were making an impact.

At the end of that fall campaign, I called Joanne, hoping to hear how my prayer had been answered. Joanne thanked me for calling but explained that nothing had changed for the rest of their campaign. They had not seen any indication that 40 Days for Life had made a difference. She did insist that, despite the challenges, their participation in 40 Days for Life had been worthwhile because of the spiritual growth their little group had experienced. And they were heartened by the occasional pedestrian who joined them in prayer when the opposition was especially hostile. But beyond those blessings, there was no marked drop in abortions. No saved babies to report. They thought they had failed.

I hung up the phone, tears welling in my eyes. I had so hoped they would see evidence that their efforts had been worthwhile. I felt that my prayers on their behalf had not been heard. Oh, how little I knew!

Several months later, I heard from an exuberant Joanne.

"David, I've got the most exciting news! A local pastor in Providence, Fr. John Codega, contacted me. A couple has asked him to baptize their baby when he's born, and they have the most incredible story."

Faced with an unexpected pregnancy, and feeling tremendous stress, the couple had scheduled an abortion. As they headed into the Providence Planned Parenthood abortion center, they walked past people in prayer on the sidewalk.

"The couple sat in a room with about a dozen other young women, mostly with their moms. The baby's father was the only man there. The baby's mother was handed a clipboard. He was ignored.

"She completed the paperwork, and then they sat without speaking for several minutes. As he looked around the room, no one spoke. All he could think about were the people outside on the sidewalk. He turned to her, and at the same time she looked at him."

I hung on Joanne's every word, tears rolling down my cheeks.

"Without speaking, they both got up and walked out. As they walked to their car, they passed the people on the sidewalk, who were still praying. The couple didn't say a word to them—just got in their car and drove away."

The baby had been spared! But there was more: This great blessing occurred during the seemingly barren Providence 40 Days for Life campaign!

"I wanted you to know," Fr. Codega told her, "that a little boy, whose life was saved by your prayers, is about to be born. His name is Robbie. If it had not been for you, he would not be alive." The couple had given the pastor a picture of the 4-D ultrasound of Robbie in his mother's womb, and he offered to email it to Joanne. When we got off the phone, Joanne emailed me the ultrasound picture of Robbie, and I shared it with Margaret, Claire, and Patrick. Together we celebrated the faithfulness of Joanne and Eleanor, and we thanked God for hearing and answering our prayers and theirs.

———

Several months later, the 40 Days for Life volunteers in West Palm Beach, Florida, had a similar celebration. Toward the end of the fall 2008 campaign, my family visited the West Palm Beach vigil during a whirlwind tour of Florida sites. The volunteers told us that a car had recently pulled up to the volunteers praying in front of the local abortion center and stopped. A mother popped her head out of the window and called out, "I don't know if you remember me, but a year ago you stopped me from going in there. Now look in the backseat of my car—he's *perfect!*"

They looked through the back window and saw a beautiful sleeping baby named Shamus. Just a year earlier, during the fall 2007 campaign—at the same time that Joanne and Eleanor were introducing 40 Days for Life to Rhode Island about 1,400 miles north—Shamus's mom brought him to be aborted in West Palm Beach. As she pulled into the facility for her abortion appointment, she saw the volunteers and spoke to them. She changed her mind, gave birth to Shamus, and months later brought her baby boy to show off at the same prayer vigil that helped save his life. Those volunteers, too, had to wait before seeing God's answer to their prayer.

During our visit, the 40 Days for Life prayer volunteers showed us the photo they took that day of the mother's broad smile and of baby Shamus in front of the center where he had been scheduled to be aborted.

Shamus and Robbie are two of the hundreds of babies *that we know of* who were spared from abortion during that first nationally coordinated 40 Days for Life Campaign in the fall of 2007. Only God knows how many more were saved, and he knows each of them by name.

Lesson learned: Just because we don't *see* the answers to our prayers, that does not mean God is not already at work answering our prayers.

This is one of the reasons Shawn and I knew we had to write this book. Joanne, Eleanor, the West Palm Beach volunteers, and I are among the hundreds of thousands of believers who sometimes get discouraged when we pray for lives to be saved yet don't see results. The work God is doing in the heavenly realms, inside the hearts and spirits of people, is often invisible. Over the years, whenever Shawn and I have heard of a life saved, a woman healed of pain and regret, an abortion worker leaving her job, or an abortion facility closing its doors forever, we would rush to tell one another and then rush to share the good news with our leaders and volunteers *because we all long for the encouragement of seeing answers to our prayers.*

So don't lose hope! Invisible answers are still answers. Answers that unfold over a period of weeks or months or years or decades are still answers. Even when we have forgotten the prayers we prayed, God is still at work answering those prayers.

God is still answering the prayers that Joanne and Eleanor prayed in 2007. Today, the Providence, Rhode Island, 40 Days for Life Campaign has grown enormously. Over eight hundred people and dozens of local churches participate, and many more lives have been saved over the years since that first fledgling effort. Recently,

Joanne was given a Human Life Guild Award by Bishop Thomas Tobin of the Catholic Diocese of Providence, which now directs 40 Days for Life in Rhode Island.

And as for the prayers in West Palm Beach ... personally, I think one day Shamus will make a fine 40 Days for Life Campaign coordinator. What a story he will have to share.

> *Let us not become weary in doing good,*
> *for at the proper time we will reap a harvest*
> *if we do not give up.*
> GALATIANS 6:9

Dear Lord, help me to accept your timetable rather than insisting on my own and to not be discouraged when the two don't coincide. When I face frustrations, roadblocks, disappointments, and persecution in my attempts to do your work, as I surely will, help me to not simply bear them but to rejoice in them, because they are what strengthen me and help me to grow to be more like your Son. It is no small privilege to participate with him in his sufferings—even in this small way. Amen.

53 Days for Life

David

In June 2007, Eric Scheidler, executive director of the Pro-Life Action League, got a call from his dad, Joe, founder and national director of the League—and the man I wrote about on Day 2 whose speech at our Coalition for Life banquet stirred me to consider doing full-time pro-life work.

"I'm hearing a rumor," Joe said, "that Planned Parenthood is opening an abortion facility near a high school in Aurora." This wasn't just close to home for Eric—it *was* home. At the time, he was living in Aurora, which is close to Chicago.

"You're kidding," Eric said. "Where did you hear this?"

"A contractor who had been approached about doing some work on the building thought the blueprints were a little fishy. He'd been told it was going to be a regular medical building. But it had way too many recovery rooms and surgical rooms for that, so he thought it might be an abortion center. He talked to his pastor about it, and then it came to me through the grapevine."

So Eric checked it out. At the site there was a sign for Gemini Office Development. Through the Freedom of Information Act, Eric was able to find out that a representative of Gemini had indeed claimed this building was going to be a multi-use medical facility and that Gemini didn't yet know who their tenant would be.

Eric stood outside the construction site and watched. "The funny thing was, for a multi-use facility, it had a very small entrance—just one door. It didn't look like a multi-use facility at all. So we asked the city, 'What's really being built here?' And we found out that, in fact, this nearly completed building was scheduled to open on September 18, 2007, as the largest Planned Parenthood abortion facility in the United States at 22,000 square feet. I realized that we needed to not just pray but to pray on a biblical scale."

Although we were just then gearing up for our first nationwide 40 Days for Life Campaign, Eric was familiar with what we'd done locally and the good results we'd had. He liked our approach. "We needed forty days of prayer," he said. "But that meant we had only four or five days to mobilize."

So Eric and his mom, Ann Scheidler, called me, and I walked them through the procedures for organizing a vigil. Eric and his team had a great motivating factor working for them: the urgency of their situation. This was a crisis for those in their community who opposed abortion. The largest facility in the country was about to open in their own backyard! And it was happening because of the deceptiveness of Planned Parenthood. Those things would motivate people to come out even on short notice and spend long hours at this vigil. They would be alarmed and upset. If anything called for emergency action, this did.

Eric announced that there would be a Monday morning meeting in the basement of his church. Despite a serious rainstorm—"It was the classic raining cats and dogs thing," Eric laughs—the church basement was packed to capacity, with more than eighty people, all of them soaking wet. "When I suggested that we could maybe have a forty-day, around-the-clock prayer vigil, people *jumped* at the chance. In no time at all, we had volunteers for the entire forty days.

"That was Monday the third. Thursday the sixth we started our vigil. That gave us exactly forty days before the facility's scheduled opening."

Things had gone fairly smoothly so far. But as soon as the vigil began, the police showed up. "Not just the police—the *chief* of police came out." And thus began a long and exhausting series of obstacles thrown at the volunteers by the police, the city, and Planned Parenthood. "We were told we had to keep moving—which isn't true. You can stand and pray, or hold a sign—you don't have to move. They told us we couldn't stand on the sidewalk, we had to stand on the parkway. Then the next officer would come and say we couldn't stand on the parkway, we had to stand on the grass."

Eric and many pro-lifers went to the next city council meeting. "We kept those twelve city council members up until 1:30 in the morning at that first meeting—they got a great crash course in the pro-life movement. After that, we attended the city council every two weeks for seven meetings in a row.

"Planned Parenthood ignored us at first. They thought we would go away. Then we started to demand that the city council of Aurora investigate exactly *how* Planned Parenthood had come to town. How could it be true, for instance, that Gemini Office Development didn't, as they claimed, know when they applied to build who their tenant would be—considering that Gemini is a wholly owned subsidiary of Planned Parenthood? There's no way they didn't know! That's a lie. We outed them on those and many other lies, and then the press got them to admit they had lied.

"They must have realized, at that point, that they were starting to lose the battle of public opinion. So apparently they thought, 'We've got to do yard signs.' So we did yard signs of our own—and for every one of their yard signs, we had hundreds of yard signs throughout the community. You couldn't drive down a block in Aurora without seeing a yard sign every couple of houses."

Next came the Jericho march.

One of Eric's volunteers, John Thorne, proposed having a Jericho march. Supporters would be invited to prayerfully march around the block where the new Planned Parenthood facility was being built, staying on public property the whole way. The block was about a mile and a quarter in circumference. Eric gave John the go-ahead to organize it to take place every night for a week, thinking they'd be lucky to have twenty people come.

The first march was on a Sunday evening at dusk. They had four hundred people come out, including about two hundred Hispanics who prayed the rosary in Spanish as they walked around the block.

At least two hundred people showed up every single night that week —people of all faiths, all races, all walks of life.

The big finale of the Jericho march was to take place on Saturday morning, the seventh day, when they were planning to march seven times around the block, echoing the biblical story.

The city decided to try to stop it.

After lengthy arguments, during which Eric and his attorney pointed out to the city how bad they would look arresting grandmothers and children for praying, the city finally agreed to let them walk *one* time, not seven. Eric agreed. "Getting people arrested really wasn't our purpose, nor was it our purpose to fight with the police. Our fight was with Planned Parenthood."

Saturday morning dawned. A thousand people arrived to pray. Since they were able to walk around the block only once, most were already done marching by the time the news cameras showed up. Instead, they were milling around a huge vacant lot across from Planned Parenthood, many of them holding signs saying, "Planned Parenthood: Bad for Aurora" and "Stop Abortion Now" and "Keep Abortion Out of Aurora." The cameras rolled.

"All the publicity because of the effort of the city to stop the march," Eric says, "meant that we got our message out in a way we never could have otherwise. That was one more way God showed us what we could do when we first turn to him in prayer, then listen to how he wants us to act on the grace that comes from that prayer. And then simply trust him."

As the end of the forty-day vigil approached, that also meant the date was fast approaching on which Planned Parenthood was expecting to open their facility. But the city, despite all the resistance it had offered to Eric and his team and volunteers, had opened an investigation into the deceptive practices used by Planned Parenthood in their dealings with local officials. I came to town to speak at an event on the final day of the vigil, and that's how I happened to be there to accompany Eric to the federal courthouse in downtown Chicago to observe what happened when Planned Parenthood sued the city, arguing that they should be allowed to open on their scheduled date regardless of the investigation.

We went to the courtroom of Judge Charles Norvell, who heard arguments from the city attorneys and from Planned Parenthood and then announced that he would rule two days later—September 17, the day before Planned Parenthood was expecting to open their center and the day of the rally at which I was scheduled to speak.

On the seventeenth, Judge Norvell ruled that the city did indeed have a right to first complete its investigation. He refused to force the city to give Planned Parenthood their occupancy permit so they could open their doors.

So the rally on the eighteenth, which had been intended to be a pep talk and a regrouping on the eve of Planned Parenthood's opening, instead became a massive celebration of Planned Parenthood's *not* opening, at least not on the day they had intended. "This was one of the things we had prayed for," Eric says, "and God made it happen."

"Instead of Planned Parenthood opening on September 18, the pro-life community of Aurora was celebrating another day free of abortion in our community."

Why did I call this chapter "53 Days for Life"? Because Eric and his team decided, "What we're doing seems to be working—let's keep praying twenty-four hours a day!" So they began to add days, keeping the vigil going, praying around the clock, in the hope that the Planned Parenthood facility would never open.

It was the fall of 2007—the weeks leading up to the start of our first nationwide 40 Days for Life Campaign. Because of the national attention the 40 Days for Life vigil in Aurora had received, the excitement across the country for what this kind of prayer effort can do exploded. We had originally thought we'd have fifteen or, if all went well, maybe twenty or twenty-five cities join in our fall campaign. But—I'm convinced—because of the attention that vigil in Aurora, Illinois, received, that first nationwide 40 Days for Life Campaign kicked off with *eighty-nine cities in thirty-three states.*

The prayers in Aurora helped seed the prayers around the country just weeks later.

The city of Aurora completed their investigation—and the results were a grave disappointment. Planned Parenthood was given permission to open their doors—though nearly two weeks later than they'd expected to.

"David," Eric asked, "what do you think we should do now? People are going to need some encouragement and guidance on how to respond to having an abortion facility opening in their community."

"You do what you've been doing," I answered. "All around this country, right now, people are holding vigils like the one you just completed, and they're doing it in front of operational abortion centers. They offer alternatives. They stand and pray. And sometimes, God honors those prayers by saving lives and closing those facilities. That should be the goal now."

During their fight to keep the Planned Parenthood facility from opening, thousands of people came out to pray. Those people spoke out, they came to city council and other meetings, and they talked to the press. As sad as it is for an abortion center to open, God provided a tremendous work of grace in Aurora that year. The bridges he built in Aurora—between Protestant and Catholic, between Hispanic, black, and white, all uniting to fight for a common cause—were truly miraculous. That strong framework is something the pro-life community there will be able to build on for many years to come.

"What I appreciate about the 40 Days for Life movement," Eric says now, "is that it focuses us on prayer. It makes prayer the beginning of all that we do.

"Prayer is something anyone can do. You don't have to hold a sign. You're not asked to talk to the press. You're just asked to stand and pray outside the abortion facility for an hour. Anyone can do that."

And God heard them,
for their prayer reached heaven,
his holy dwelling place.
2 CHRONICLES 30:27

Lord, the psalms are full of stories of times when David's enemies came against him, but you interceded on his behalf and confounded the efforts of those enemies so that the things they thought would defeat David defeated them instead. I pray today that you would confound the efforts of those who destroy innocent human life and those who try to thwart the volunteers who stand and pray for the unborn. Let their efforts to defeat us work against them instead. And when they fail, open their eyes to see that they failed not because they opposed us but because they opposed you. Amen.

72 Ransom Avenue

David

I HAVE TO BE HONEST. IN THE EARLIEST DAYS OF MY PRO-LIFE work, I gave God lip service.

Oh, I believed faith was important to pro-life efforts, but I focused my energy on human techniques: the practical, the strategic, the political. In other words, the same plan of attack any secular organization would have used. I'd think, "Sure, we've got to pray. But I've got to concentrate on getting the right people elected to office first. Let's get the right laws passed first. Let's develop a focus-group-tested marketing plan first."

I hate to admit it, but it wasn't until the first-ever 40 Days for Life Campaign in College Station, Texas, that I realized how wrong-headed I'd been. And during that campaign, as I was praying and fasting about the protection of human life, I had an experience that completely rocked my world.

During our first campaign in 2004, everyone on the team was not just busy but stretched to the breaking point, with hardly a minute to come up for air let alone sleep or eat. And on top of that, I had another commitment: Before the hour of prayer that birthed 40 Days for Life (the one described in chapter 1), I had committed to go out of town to speak for another pro-life organization—a wonderful pregnancy resource center in Grand Rapids, Michigan—and I had to keep that commitment.

Pregnancy resource centers have been at the center of pro-life efforts from the very beginning. Over and over, in city after city, we have seen the work that is being done tirelessly to help women by providing free medical care, help with housing allowances, food, job training, child care, parenting classes, and continuing education. The funding for these services comes entirely from the generosity of local friends and neighbors whose gifts say "you matter" to the thousands of women, men, and children who are assisted each day. We leap at every opportunity to partner with these fellow advocates in the cause of life.

Leaving the 40 Days for Life Campaign in capable hands, I caught an early morning flight into the Gerald R. Ford International Airport in Grand Rapids. The director of the resource center, a dynamic young man named Jim Sprague, was waiting for me. As we got into Jim's car, he said, "David, I know you're tired, but we have two options. I can either take you to your hotel where you can rest up and get ready for tonight ... or I can show you something that could change your life."

I laughed. "Jim, that's not fair. How can I turn down a life-changing experience?"

He smiled, and we drove to downtown Grand Rapids. Zigzagging our way through the city's one-way streets, we finally pulled up in front of 72 Ransom Avenue, a large building that looked like an old church. Jim turned off the car's engine. "Now, David," he said, "you're going to meet the new owners of this building inside. I just want to warn you—this is going to be very intense."

I had no idea what I was in for.

We walked up the stone steps and through the large wooden doors into the entryway, where we met the new owners Jim had mentioned. And they shared with me the history of the building.

This building at 72 Ransom Avenue was erected in the late nineteenth century as Congregation Emanuel—a Jewish synagogue. After many years of gathering there to worship God and celebrate life, that congregation outgrew 72 Ransom and moved into a bigger facility in 1949, selling the building to the Holy Trinity Greek Orthodox Church. That congregation, too, gathered there to worship God and celebrate life. But over time they also outgrew the building and they too moved. So they decided to sell 72 Ransom.

An investor's group bought the building with the intention of making a profit. They turned it into a commercial property, and in 1994 leased it to the highest bidder—a notorious abortionist.

That building, which for a hundred years had served as a church, honoring God, the author of life, was turned into a place of death. This site became the Heritage Clinic for Women—the largest abortion center in Western Michigan. (Over the next eight years, twenty thousand children would be aborted inside the walls of that former church building.)

Many Christians in Grand Rapids were deeply disturbed by this, and over the next few years, a group of ministry leaders began to meet together regularly to pray. Their specific intention was to reclaim that building for God.

They thought their prayers had been answered on February 25, 1999, when they learned that the owners had put 72 Ransom Avenue up for sale. They prayed, they waited, and they looked for an opportunity to acquire the building but ran into obstacle after obstacle. For four long years, their prayers never ceased and their faith never wavered—even as every effort to reclaim the building failed.

During this time, they decided to form a ministry called LIFE International, which has a goal of opening pregnancy resource centers in every nation of the world where abortions are performed. Part of their plan was the acquisition of 72 Ransom Avenue.

Finally, at the end of 2003, with the help of numerous donors and local business owners, they made a strong offer for the building, one the building's owners were willing to accept, and the group was able to negotiate the purchase of 72 Ransom Avenue.

In 2004, the new owners shut down the abortion business and kicked the abortionist out of the building. Five days after the last abortions were performed in the building, LIFE International took possession and began turning it into their world headquarters. And shortly thereafter, I was standing in the entryway, meeting the leaders of LIFE International, who had just taken ownership of the building.

They gave me a tour of the building, which was virtually unchanged from the way it had looked just days earlier when the abortionist left.

In the entryway was a stairwell going up as well as down. I was told that when a woman would come in for an abortion, frequently she would have a boyfriend, family member, or someone else along with her. They would send her downstairs and the support person upstairs. They didn't want to take the risk that the support person might persuade the pregnant woman to not go through with the abortion, which would cost them several hundred dollars of lost revenue.

At the bottom of the steep stairs, the pregnant woman was directed into a waiting room filled with beautiful, padded couches. After filling out her paperwork, she would sit with other women on a couch to quietly wait for her abortion appointment.

What she didn't know was what was in the very next room.

When the door into that next room was opened, I was stunned. Years earlier, parts of the ceiling had collapsed from water damage, and since nothing had ever been repaired, there was a strong smell of rot and mildew. Cockroaches scattered across the floor as we stepped in. This was literally a foot away, through the wall, from where women sat while they waited for their abortions. I recoiled at the thought of such conditions in a facility providing surgical procedures.

We walked into the next room down the hall—the main "procedure" room, where the majority of the abortions were performed. Most of the surgical equipment had been removed, but since abortions had been performed there until shortly before my arrival, there was still a large rectangle of dried blood and rust marking where the surgical table had been attached to the worn linoleum floor.

The abortion suction machine had been removed from the wall, but I could see mold where it had been attached. There were a few surgical tools on the counter that had been left exactly as they were on the last day of abortions, mere days before—unsterilized and showing signs of rust.

I asked, "What is that indention on the floor—that arc worn into the linoleum?"

My guide said, "That's where the abortionist stood, at the foot of the surgical table, moving back and forth extracting, often in pieces, the thousands of children who died in this room."

Chills ran up and down my spine.

Then they took me to the final room in that downstairs hallway—the recovery room where the women were sent to recuperate after the abortions. As I took in the dismal room, I couldn't help but think that by the time the women arrived here, the abortion business had already gotten everything it wanted from these "clients"—the procedure was over, and they'd paid their money. What must they have felt as they stepped into that last miserable room to sit on these old, rotted chairs with their stained seats? My host explained that here the abortion staff would give each woman a little cup of juice and a cookie, then just leave her to fend for herself. When she felt ready, she would stand and walk out—possibly without any companion at all.

That walk through 72 Ransom Avenue changed me forever. Shortly before my arrival, children were dying there and women were being wounded there. This was a wake-up call. No longer was abortion just "an issue" to me. No longer was this just one of many good things we could be doing. On that day, I faced the reality that we are engaged in an epic struggle between good and evil, between light and darkness, between heaven and hell. This is a spiritual battle.

But the building's new owners weren't through with me yet. They had another story for me—of what happened when they first took possession, five days after the last abortions had been performed there. And when I heard their story, I realized the vital importance of putting our trust—first and foremost—not in political strategies, fundraising, nor the media, but in God Almighty.

On that first day, they called one hundred twenty-five friends, pastors, and leaders of many other ministries to come and pray over the building. They prayed in every room and filled the building with voices lifted in worship and prayers of dedication and cleansing.

The following Sunday night, a group of nine LIFE International board members gathered in the entryway to pray over this former church that had become an abortion center—to reclaim it for God.

Someone suggested, "Why don't we start our prayers wherever the abortionist would start his day every morning?" So they went downstairs, past all the rooms, all the way to the back hall, where a large metal door opened out into the alley where the abortionist would park his car. They decided to start their prayers in that hall near the large, closed door.

They gathered in a circle. They held hands. And they prayed fervently for God to reclaim this building. When they were finished, the new director of LIFE International, Kurt Dillinger, closed their prayer by saying, "Amen."

At that moment, the empty building's silence was shattered as the big steel door—which had been closed and latched—burst open, swinging wildly outward to slam against the bricks of the building's alley wall. All who stood there felt a rush of air go out the door. A few seconds later, they felt a gentle breeze come back in. They were stunned. A board member asked, "What just happened?" Shaken, another board member pulled the door closed and said, "I think something just left in a hurry."

One of the workers in the building pulled me aside during the end of my tour to share a personal experience that happened shortly thereafter. A woman walked through the front door of 72 Ransom and asked him, "What happened to the strong man?"

In confusion, he said, "I'm sorry—but what strong man? What are you talking about?"

"You know," she said. "The statue of the muscular, demonic figure that used to be perched on the roof. I walk by here all the time, and I always see it. It's not there today. What happened to it?"

"There never was any such statue," the man told me. But the

woman who came to the door was completely serious. He could tell she had seen *something*—something that was no longer there.

The LIFE International staff went on to explain that they believe they experienced a spiritual transfer of ownership of that building. And having been there right after those events occurred, I believe them.

And after hearing about that experience, I believe that what we need in our communities, in our states, and in our nation is a spiritual transfer of ownership.

Yes, we need to be engaged in human solutions to the crisis too. Abortion has earthly consequences. Children die. Women are wounded. But we cannot put all our trust in human solutions. It's not just about who wins the next election. It's not just about who's got the best messaging or marketing plan. We must understand that, while abortion has earthly consequences, at its root it is a spiritual crisis that demands—first and foremost—a spiritual solution.

Our land is in desperate need of healing. Fortunately, God has given us the spiritual antidote to remedy this crisis:

If my people, who are called by name,
will humble themselves and pray
and seek my face and turn from their wicked ways,
then will I hear from heaven,
and I will forgive their sin and will heal their land.
2 CHRONICLES 7:14

Dear Lord, as you lead me into the spiritual struggle this verse calls your people to, remind me that the battle is truly yours. Thank you for equipping me with your armor. Lead me daily to put it on! Thank you for allowing me to serve under your command and for hearing my requests for direction and protection. Amen.

Haywood

Shawn

I ARRIVED A FEW MINUTES EARLY AT OUR WELL-WORN LOCAL diner. I had been hired by our local pro-life group, Coalition for Life, only three days earlier, and my new boss, David Bereit, had invited me to join him for his weekly breakfast meeting with his friend and confidant, Dr. Haywood Robinson.

Though I'd never met Haywood in person, his reputation in our town of College Station, Texas, and beyond was larger than life. He ran a large medical practice and was on the board of admissions at Texas A&M College of Medicine. He was plugged in to the medical community and the medical academic community nationwide, so I felt excited and eager, my palms a little sweaty.

When Haywood walked in, arms outstretched for a warm, back-slapping greeting, my nervousness evaporated. Clearly, Haywood had never met a stranger.

"Shawn, welcome to the team, brother! And watch out for this guy," he boomed, motioning toward David. "I've heard so much about you and Marilisa. So great to finally meet you." His deep voice resonated with energy and warmth, and I suspected I'd just met a lifelong friend.

Haywood's physical presence held a certain power and magnetism. My first thought was that he was a younger version of Morgan Freeman—and who doesn't love Morgan Freeman?

Soon we were laughing and sharing our stories of how we had gotten involved in this work. I could see why David considered his weekly breakfast with Haywood almost sacred. Something about

Haywood's presence bolstered my faith, my confidence, my joy. I didn't know it at the time, but before long David would move to the Washington, D.C., area, and Haywood and I would continue our breakfast tradition—with him having coffee and me eating enough for two. He never believed that I could eat chips and salsa at 6:00 a.m., but to me that was my birthright as a Texan.

Haywood and his wife, Noreen, both black, had excelled academically in their youth. They went to medical school, got married, and opened a medical practice together. Their practice provided a healthy income. But they saw an easy way to bring in more money —performing abortions.

During his med-school residency, he'd learned procedure after procedure. Then came a day he'd not been looking forward to—his turn to be trained in abortion. His wife-to-be, Noreen, was one of his instructors. Although he accepted abortion as part of medicine and as something he had to learn, he was uncomfortable with it. So he watched one. It bothered him. Then he did one. It bothered him again. Then he did another, then three, and four. Eventually, he admits, the procedure became routine—his conscience had been deadened.

When they opened their husband-and-wife medical practice a few years later, he and Noreen started moonlighting as abortionists on weekends. They made thousands of extra dollars at it every year. As Haywood explains it, they used that money simply to "have a good time. It was blood money."

Then Noreen got pregnant. Overjoyed at the new life growing inside of her, they celebrated each phase of the development of their unborn child. And as they did, that old discomfort Haywood had first felt over abortion resurfaced—and grew. Finally, they realized they couldn't have it both ways. They could not, on one hand, celebrate as a miracle the continuing development of their own unborn child, and, on the other hand, abort the babies of other mothers at that same stage of development. They couldn't continue to provide prenatal treatment for a young pregnant mother and then offer to kill her unborn child. Noreen and Haywood experienced a dramatic conversion. They never performed another abortion.

Once they broke with the abortion business and experienced the miracle and privilege of birth and parenthood for themselves, they threw themselves into the pro-life movement with a passion. And this led to their support of 40 Days for Life, their friendship with David, this breakfast, and now, Haywood's friendship with me.

Haywood participated in a number of 40 Days for Life events, including the very first vigil in the fall of 2004, at which he was the first person to show up at midnight for the very first hour. I will never forget arriving at the fence outside of Planned Parenthood that historic night and seeing Haywood's smiling face—a man who had worked as an abortion provider standing and praying at midnight for an end to abortion. What a great moment! In the years after, he would become a much-sought-after speaker at pro-life events; he and I sometimes shared the podium.

In fact, our most powerful shared experience unfolded a few years later, when Haywood and I traveled together to speak in Madison, Wisconsin.

The University of Wisconsin Hospital and Clinics at Madison was voting on whether to perform late-term abortions, up to twenty-two weeks of gestation. Steve Karlen, a dynamic, twenty-five-year-old 40 Days for Life leader in Madison, called me, his voice intense and filled with anxiety.

Steve's work on a 40 Days for Life Campaign the previous fall had created so much momentum that soon he was working with groups across the state of Wisconsin and beyond, organizing opposition to late-term abortions at the University of Wisconsin at Madison. Unfortunately, he wasn't finding much optimism among his colleagues. And many of the medical school board members had said they were inclined to support the motion to perform late-term abortions. But none of that stopped Steve from throwing all his energy into his efforts.

"Shawn," Steve said, "you have to come out. We have a rally planned for just a few days from now, and we need you—and Dr.

Robinson." Although Steve had never met Haywood, he knew that as a physician, teacher, and part of the Texas A&M School of Medicine, Haywood was the perfect person to speak at the Madison hospital rally.

The next day, a Friday, Haywood and I boarded a plane in sunny, 75-degree Austin, Texas, and flew to bitterly cold Madison, Wisconsin.

Steve greeted us exuberantly. We were both a bit mystified that Steve was so ecstatic to announce that the temperature was 4 degrees above zero—until he explained that this was the first day in weeks above zero degrees. Even so, Haywood and I weren't exactly ready to pull out the Hawaiian shirts and flip-flops.

"Well, guys, the event is outside," Steve said—not exactly welcomed news. At the site, we found three thousand shivering pro-life people gathered, along with the media and some curious staff and students from the medical school. Despite the distracting cold, you could sense the tension. The media had been covering this story for weeks. Everyone, pro-life and abortion advocate, realized how critically influential the decision of this university medical school could be on the future of late-term abortions at medical schools across the United States.

Haywood and I handled the tension in our usual way—humor—agreeing that this was the coldest we had ever been in our lives and that we were both removing Madison from our list of potential retirement locations. But as the rally unfolded, the enthusiasm and courage of this overwhelming crowd was enough to warm our hearts no matter what the weather conditions.

Haywood was to speak for ten minutes, and I would follow.

He stepped to the microphone. "As I stand before you," he began, "I stand a sinner saved by grace. Don't be impressed by the credentials or the outward appearance. See as God sees. God looks at the heart. When I was a young man I came from a modest home. I wanted to help people. I made good grades. I was a nice guy. Everybody liked me. But I did not know the Lord."

Haywood went on to tell people of Madison to stand up and fight for the children of their state. He spoke of the miracle of life, of the privilege of healing and guarding precious human lives, and how his own eyes had been opened to the incongruity of taking life when one has dedicated one's life to medicine as a healer.

His powerful words were met with cheers from the pro-lifers and raised eyebrows from many of the medical professionals and students.

More than a year after the rally—and after *more* rallies, and *more* vigils in Madison—I received an ecstatic phone call from Steve. The University of Wisconsin at Madison had informed the attorney general that their plan to begin offering late-term abortions had been scrapped.

"I have no doubt that it was you, Shawn, and Dr. Robinson who provided the tipping point." We were heroes, Steve said.

But I knew the truth. God was the hero. God had rescued Haywood and Noreen from a practice that had been eroding their souls, then handed them 40 Days for Life as a platform to spread the word. God had touched a young Steve Karlen in Madison, Wisconsin, filling him with the courage first to lead a 40 Days for Life Campaign, then to bring together the opposition to late-term abortions and plan the rally that helped dissuade that medical school from carrying out late-term abortions. And, of course, God had inspired three thousand people, some of them new to pro-life activities, to take a stand for the value of the lives of the unborn, a value they held so dear that a few hours in the bitter cold was but a small price.

Yes, God is the hero in this drama of death versus life. And as only an omnipotent God can do, he calls together all the players he needs and casts them to play their parts. Steve, Haywood, three thousand others, and I played a part in preventing late-term abortions at the medical school in Madison, Wisconsin. But that event, magnificent as it was, was only one scene in the much larger drama unfolding in our lifetime—the struggle to protect the lives of unborn children.

That struggle continues. What part are you playing now? What did God orchestrate in your life to bring you to this point? How might he use you in the future if you take another step forward on behalf of the unborn and the men and women whose lives are being scarred by the violent act of abortion?

David and I have had balcony seats for the pro-life debuts of many thousands of people, and almost all of them have one thing in common—they never imagined that their personal involvement could save a human life or make a difference in this extraordinary movement. In fact, nearly one-third of the participants in 40 Days for Life campaigns are newcomers to the pro-life movement. Once they discover their individual contribution makes such a huge difference, they return again and again and invite others to join them.

As for Haywood, his story continues, and he serves in many capacities in the pro-life movement. He is now chairman of the board of LEARN, an organization headed by the Reverend Dr. Johnny Hunter that reaches out to African-Americans, spreading the pro-life message. Abortion has devastated the black community, a fact that hit me hard when Haywood took me to the LEARN national conference during the fall 40 Days for Life Campaign in 2007. The African-American community makes up 12 percent of the U.S. population, and yet they make up 30 percent of all abortions. Nearly half a million black babies are aborted every single year, and Haywood is dedicated to saving his community from this genocide.

Haywood and I could not be more different. I'm white and he's black. I'm Catholic; he's evangelical. He's a doctor; I barely made it out of high school biology. He's from Los Angeles, California, and I'm from Tyler, Texas. But these differences have no effect on the bond that unites us and so many others in this culture war. Our two paths crossed years ago in an old diner. Your path crossed ours this very day as you read our story.

Seek the truth. Seek your place in it. For truth leads to one source: Jesus Christ. Haywood and I invite you to discover your path, by turning to the Source in prayer—today and every day.

You did not choose me,
but I chose you and appointed you
so that you might go and bear fruit—
fruit that will last.

JOHN 15:16

Lord, thank you for the many heroes of the pro-life movement —those who have taken brave, principled stands and, in many cases, have paid a high price for it. Thank you for the inspiring leaders who have roused, empowered, and motivated the movement. But help me to also recognize the unsung and often hidden heroes who labor anonymously on the sidewalks, in pregnancy resource centers and pro-life organizations, through one-on-one advocacy—those whose names I don't know and whose faces I may never see but who make up an indispensable part of the pro-life movement. Remind me to celebrate and affirm both types of heroes whenever I come across them. Amen.

The Last Moment

Shawn

THE DOORS OF THE ABORTION CENTER FLEW OPEN AND A FRIGHT-ened young woman ran out as fast as she could—barefoot!

Yes, this is a true story.

Drama often accompanies major turning points, especially in those final seconds. We love this in our society, whether it's the field goal at the end of a football game or a bride walking out on her groom at the altar. Every decision that has huge, lasting implications and a final this-is-it turning point has the potential for drama.

The "I do" at the altar. The "I hereby resign" on the resignation letter. The "I accept this nomination." The final signature on the mortgage agreement or the legal papers. They are all huge. They matter. They have long-lasting consequences that affect our lives and the lives of those around us in big ways—good or bad. But I believe that when the decision is as grave as abortion, changing one's mind at the last moment is even more critical. From the moment abortion is considered as an option, a life hangs in the balance, right up until the surgical procedure that ends that life.

A 40 Days for Life vigil presents many opportunities for women to change their minds. These moments leading up to an abortion —whether the mother is driving in for an ultrasound, or scheduling her appointment, or arriving on the actual day of her abortion— provide opportunities for volunteers to play a role in saving the life of a child. These opportunities are what motivate many volunteers to go out for the first time to peacefully pray outside the abortion facility.

I always encourage volunteers by telling them that, as I said earlier, they are the last sign of hope for the baby and the mother as she goes inside the facility to have the abortion. And they are also the first sign of mercy to the woman after the abortion. We are there before, during, and after the abortion. By simply peacefully praying outside, we are witnessing to the hope that the woman might change her mind and not go through with the abortion. Our presence tells such women that they are not alone in this decision.

Once a woman enters a center for an abortion, there is little the volunteer at a vigil can do besides simply pray that, as she sits in the lobby and fills out her paperwork, she might change her mind. But let's be honest—at that point, the chances of a woman walking back out without having an abortion are slim. Planned Parenthood, according to their own annual report, did 329,445 abortions in 2010, compared to a mere 841 adoption referrals, which in fact they just pass on to another organization.[3] Those numbers are staggering. This is "choice"? Their own statistics confirm the obvious: Planned Parenthood has a product to sell—abortion—and a profit to make from the sale. I know that their literature suggests otherwise, but their results speak for themselves. Among our 40 Days for Life volunteers are former Planned Parenthood workers, even managers, who have confirmed that they were encouraged to increase abortion numbers at their facilities. These directives have been widely reported in the news media.[4]

You can understand, then, that maintaining hope as the door closes behind a mother who has gone inside a facility for an abortion is extremely difficult for many volunteers.

What is the absolute last moment for a woman to change her mind before having an abortion? It's not after the family or boyfriend suggests abortion is the right choice or offers to pay for an abortion. It's not after a phone call to Planned Parenthood or another abortion provider to make an appointment. It's not after they drive to the facility and go inside. It's not after they fill out paperwork in the lobby, wondering how it came to this. It's not even after their name is called and they're walking down the hall to have the abortion.

No, the very last moment is the moment that many post-abortive women say was the moment they knew they were about to lose part of themselves forever. It's the moment when they lie down on the table and brace themselves for the actual abortion. At that last moment, according to women who've been there, abortion seems inevitable. It also seems unimaginable to change your mind after all you have been through up to that moment. Everything seems so final, so irreversible. It seems unimaginable to get up and leave at that moment …

But that is exactly what one young mom did in Orange, California, during a 40 Days for Life Campaign in spring of 2011!

Prayer volunteers at the 40 Days for Life vigil in Orange County were caught by surprise as the doors of the abortion center flew open and a frightened, barefoot young woman ran out. A young man who appeared to be her boyfriend or husband came out right after her, apparently looking for her.

The 40 Days of Life volunteers welcomed her to approach them. After she spoke to them for a few moments, they offered to buy her lunch at a local restaurant and listen to her story. Over lunch, the volunteers were wise not to lecture or instruct her. They just listened.

The barefoot woman, let's call her Lea, was six months pregnant and had come for an abortion, driven by her boyfriend. While she was lying on the table inside the abortion facility, with the IV in place as she was being sedated, she was still alert enough to realize that what she was doing was wrong and that she did not want her six-months-along baby to die. She couldn't go through with it. She found the strength to sit up and climb off the table, remove the needle from her own arm, get dressed in the operating room—except for her shoes!—and run out to safety.

That barefoot run saved her baby's life. With every step, she displayed her love for her baby and found the courage to overcome all the despair, hopelessness, and fear that had put her on that table in the first place. All the decisions that led Lea to that table on that day could not override her last-minute love and inspiration to choose life and sprint her baby to safety.

One 40 Days for Life volunteer who was there that day said, "Our prayers from the outside helped give her the courage to leave that table and run away. I now realize how important our role is out here on the sidewalks."

One day that child will grow up and hear about what those volunteers saw that day, how her mother, half sedated and barefoot, had the courage to run from that operating room to a few strangers who were standing outside simply praying. That child will learn that her mother was able to tune out the voices of the world just long enough, at the most critical moment, to listen to the voice mothers know naturally in their hearts—the voice that tells them that children are not choices. They are gifts from God, and they deserve to be protected by their mothers.

Never underestimate what God can do when we just do the basics. We can show up in spite of the busyness of our lives. We can take an hour or a few hours once or twice a week during a 40 Days for Life Campaign to go out and pray. We could easily list a hundred other things we *could* be doing due to our many other important obligations or to any of the other responsibilities that constrain us every single day. But we choose to stand for life for a few precious hours.

That's not an act that requires heroics. The hundreds of thousands who have taken the step to volunteer discover that it really takes only a small effort to do a huge thing—to stand and pray as a witness to someone whose whole world is crashing down on them to the extent that they feel abortion is their only option.

And though our part is small, we must never downplay God's

huge part—that he uses our presence to demonstrate his love. God *can* get inside these abortion facilities. He *can* speak to the hearts and minds of those who have come for abortions, as well as of those who work there. We don't know their backgrounds—but he does. We don't know the situations surrounding their pregnancies—but he does!

Today, pray that more people will step forward to represent God on the sidewalk at what is, for so many women, an otherwise hopeless moment on a hopeless day. And pray for more women to escape the table and to run as fast as they can for the lives of their children.

For he says, "In the time of my favor I heard you,
and in the day of salvation I helped you."
I tell you, now is the time of God's favor,
now is the day of salvation.
2 CORINTHIANS 6:2

Lord, today I pray for a sense of urgency to defend your unborn children. Every abortion ends the unrepeatable life of an innocent human being made in your image and likeness. Protect me against indifference and renew in me the hope that at any moment your grace and witness can work to save a life so close to being lost. Today is the day of salvation, and in you I place my hope! Amen.

Unplanned

Shawn

"YOU'RE NOT GOING TO CONVERT ME!" ABBY JOHNSON SHOUTED at me as she marched back into the Planned Parenthood abortion facility where she served as director.

I watched her through the black wrought-iron fence that separated her world from mine, and I confess that I was smiling. I wasn't going to give up hope for her. Abby's journey and mine in the world of abortion had begun on the very same day, just a few years earlier. On the first day I went to pray at an abortion facility at the invitation of my then girlfriend now wife, Marilisa, Abby also responded, for the first time, to an invitation she'd received to volunteer for Planned Parenthood at the same facility. Marilisa had even chatted with her on that long-ago day. And neither of us would discover that we'd shared that experience until we stood side by side on the *same* side of that fence!

Who could have guessed on that "first day" that later she would become director of that Planned Parenthood facility and I'd become director of Coalition for Life? Yet there we were, frequently eyeball to eyeball through that ten-foot-tall fence for eight years.

Over those years, we'd sometimes appeared in media interviews together, each of us speaking against the activities of the other. I had given countless speeches in front of her abortion facility at 40 Days for Life kickoff events (Abby was there for our first six campaigns), at different *Roe v. Wade* events, and at prayer rallies. I suspect Abby has heard me speak more than any other person! Over time, I began to see Abby as different from her colleagues. While Abby at times had a sharp edge, she would on occasion speak kindly to volunteers and treat me with respect. Many Planned Parenthood workers ignored us, and I was actually afraid of a few of them because of their coldness and glares through the fence, but not Abby. I came to admire this in her; it gave me hope. I could see that her conscience was not dead. Abby and I were the same age, and I often wondered about the path that had led her to this work, though I figured I would never know the answer.

But all that changed in the fall of 2009.

I was rushing around town on a busy Monday morning, and when I got back to my office, less than fifty yards from Abby's Planned Parenthood center, a staff member came into my office trembling and said, "Abby's here. She's in the counseling room."

I groaned. What was up this time? Was she accusing one of our volunteers of trespassing? Had someone on staff ticked her off? She'd never been inside our office before, so it had to be serious.

I walked into the counseling room, and there sat Abby on a couch where we had counseled hundreds of women, many of whom had been in and out of Abby's Planned Parenthood facility. I couldn't believe my eyes. The 2008 Planned Parenthood regional employee of the year sat in her scrubs, her Planned Parenthood security tag dangling from her neck, weeping like a baby.

"Tough Monday?" I asked, to lighten the mood.

She half-smiled between tears and said, "You could say that." Then she told me what she has now told the whole world in her best-selling book *UnPlanned*.[5] Just a week earlier, she'd been asked for the first time to assist with an ultrasound-guided abortion. Here's Abby's account of it:

> "Thirteen weeks," I heard the nurse say after taking measurements to determine the fetus's age.
>
> "Okay," the doctor said looking at me, "just hold the probe in place during the procedure so I can see what I'm doing."
>
> . . . At first, the baby didn't seem aware of the cannula. It gently

probed the baby's side, and for a quick second I felt relief. Of course, I thought. The fetus doesn't feel pain. I had reassured countless women of this as I'd been taught by Planned Parenthood. The fetal tissue feels nothing as it is removed. Get a grip, Abby. This is a simple, quick medical procedure. My head was working hard to control my responses, but I couldn't shake an inner disquiet that was quickly mounting to horror as I watched the screen.

The next movement was the sudden jerk of a tiny foot as the baby started kicking, as if trying to move away from the probing invader. As the cannula pressed in, the baby began struggling to turn and twist away. It seemed clear to me that the fetus could feel the cannula and did not like the feeling. And then the doctor's voice broke through, startling me.

"Beam me up, Scotty," he said lightheartedly to the nurse. He was telling her to turn on the suction. In an abortion the suction isn't turned on until the doctor feels he has the cannula in exactly the right place.

I had a sudden urge to yell, "Stop!" To shake the woman and to say, "Look at what is happening to your baby! Wake up! Hurry! Stop them!"

But even as I thought those words, I looked at my own hand holding the probe. I was one of "them" performing this act. My eyes shot back to the screen again. The cannula was already being rotated by the doctor, and now I could see the tiny body violently twisting with it. For the briefest moment it looked as if the baby were being wrung like a dishcloth, twirled and squeezed. And then the little body crumpled and began disappearing into the cannula before my eyes. The last thing I saw was the tiny, perfectly formed backbone sucked into the tube, and then everything was gone. And the uterus was empty. Totally empty ...

My eyes traveled back to my hands. I looked at them as if they weren't even my own.

How much damage have these hands done over the past eight years? How many lives have been taken because of them? Not

just because of my hands, but because of my words. What if I'd
known the truth, and what if I'd told all those women?

What if?

I had believed a lie!

Abby told me that story sitting in my office. Let me rephrase that.
Abby *sobbed* that story to me—runny nose, rivers of mascara, piles
of tissue. It was not a pretty sight—but then again, it was. It was one
of the most beautiful sights I'd ever seen.

My instant feeling toward her was mercy. I was shocked and
humbled that she had come right next door, to us, to *me*, to tell
what had happened. I was awed by how God had changed her heart.

She tried to quiet her rattled breathing, then with a look that was
both serious and desperate, said, "I want out. I want out of Planned
Parenthood. Please—help me find the way out."

She'd been right that day at the fence. I didn't convert her. But
God did.

Twenty-four hours after that conversation in our office, Abby
resigned from her job of eight years. She wanted to move on quietly with her life. She wanted a new job and a new life for her and
her family. I began putting out phone calls in search of a job for
her. And she began praying at the fence alongside those who had
been praying for her for eight years. I also put her in touch with Dr.
Haywood Robinson, the former abortionist who was now a loving
advocate of the unborn. I knew he could help set Abby on the road
to healing.

All of us in the Coalition were ecstatic. The joy I felt at seeing
Abby, someone I'd known for eight years, have a change of heart
cannot be put into words. But I felt a check deep in my soul. The
Irish are gifted at finding the worst in every situation, and despite
my joy, I knew that not everyone would be joyful. Abby would
need protection. I was waiting for the other shoe to drop. Planned
Parenthood directors do not have conversions and resign from
their jobs. And they certainly do not join "the other side" and start
praying outside their own clinics! It had never happened before.

Planned Parenthood, I suspected, would want to make sure it never happened again.

A few weeks after Abby's resignation, after she had turned down an offer for more money to return to Planned Parenthood, the other shoe dropped. Planned Parenthood filed a lawsuit against Abby and me, seeking an injunction to silence us. And the funny thing is, we hadn't even gone public! Abby had wanted to quietly heal, not run to the papers or the media. But irony of ironies, Planned Parenthood put out a press release announcing their lawsuit. Go figure.

Their goal was to shut her up, and instead they handed her a megaphone!

Our phones lit up. Abby's phone lit up. The media swarmed, the speaking invitations poured in, and the pro-life movement, globally, heard all about Abby Johnson.

The day of the hearing, I met two people I'd always been curious about. First, as I approached the courtroom, I saw Abby's mom walking toward me. I was nervous—had Abby gone home at Christmas and Thanksgiving for the past eight years and bashed this evil Shawn Carney person? Imagine my surprise when her mom, with her big Texas smile and even bigger Texas hair, joyfully kissed me on the cheek as if she had known me for years and said, "Thank you for getting her out of there." The second was Doug, Abby's husband, and he was so warm I felt we were old friends within minutes. I'd had no idea that, behind the scenes, these two people had disagreed with Abby on abortion, had not approved of her working at Planned Parenthood, and had been praying for her.

As we entered the courtroom, Abby and I knew that we had done nothing wrong and that this was a scare tactic, an attempt by Planned Parenthood to punish us as an example to other employees who might leave in the future. Other Planned Parenthood employees who, behind the scenes, had confided in Abby and sought my help to get them, too, out of Planned Parenthood were now going to take the stand and throw Abby under the bus. I knew that Abby's whole world was being flipped upside down because of her decision. But true to form, she remained courageous and strong through the hearing.

And praise God, it took the judge only an hour to throw out all of Planned Parenthood's claims! The media ate it up. Abby was on *The O'Reilly Factor* and a parade of national media programs telling her story *because* of this injunction. Today Abby is one of the most powerful voices for the unborn.

I never imagined on all those afternoons in the hot Texas sun that a chapter like this would exist in a book like this. But we don't write the stories. God does. As Mother Teresa says, we are just the pencils. We simply fulfill our small roles and pray for the courage to trust the words that, in today's cynical world, are the most difficult ones to grasp: With God, all things are possible.

> *Jesus looked at them and said,*
> *"With man this is impossible,*
> *but with God all things are possible."*
> MATTHEW 19:26

Dear Lord, I pray your holy word today. Now to you who are able to do immeasurably more than all we ask or imagine, according to your power that is at work within us, to you, O Lord, be glory in the church and in Christ Jesus throughout all generations, forever and ever![6] Amen.

From Boys to Men

Shawn

EVERY ABORTED CHILD HAS A FATHER.

That father might be old. He might be young. He might be single, married to the mother, or married to another woman. Poor. Middle class. Wealthy. Though they come from many different backgrounds, socioeconomic groups, ethnicities, and levels of maturity, they have one major commonality: Each fathered a child whose life was ended by abortion.

Many have something else in common. The father of the child to be aborted is often driving that day and paying for the abortion for his girlfriend or wife.

I've been watching fathers driving in and out of abortion facilities for over ten years now, and my observation is that the body language of those fathers as they drive onto the abortion facility grounds is almost always that of defeat. They do not feel like men on that day.

No matter what their demeanor or attitude—stubborn, angry, determined, resigned, desperate, scared, controlling, sad—my encounters with these men over the years tell me they will eventually comprehend the gravity of what happened in that facility on that day. They will realize they fathered a child who was lost and that the role they played in the abortion leads to pain and regret for them as well as for their wives or girlfriends. Conventional wisdom tells us that abortion is just a women's issue, something for the mother alone to deal with. I don't believe that. I know from experience that the conscience of a father will, over time, bear the weight as well.

Women seldom initiate first contact with prayer volunteers at a 40 Days for Life vigil—their boyfriends or husbands do. Some are quick to defend what they are doing, even before the volunteers have asked them a question. Justification and rationalization are verbalized far more often by the men driving than by the pregnant women, especially when they see other men standing and praying. And when one of those fathers has locked eyes with me, I have often sensed his aggressive defensiveness.

I confess, I've had to wrestle with my own attitudes toward these men. Sometimes, especially in my first few years on these vigils, seeing a boyfriend casually walk his girlfriend into an abortion facility often sparked anger in me. Other men praying on the front lines have confessed the same feeling. Abortion can be devastating for women, yet so often the fathers try to downplay it, acting as if it's no big deal. But one thing became clear to me during my college years, even though many young men seem to not yet be aware of it: Abortion hurts men as well as women.

I've had three unforgettable encounters with fathers of the unborn that have drastically reshaped my understanding of how abortion deeply impacts men by stripping away everything real manhood is about. Those encounters have been invaluable to me, because it wasn't until I finally understood the depth of the damage that I became able to see them through the compassionate eyes of our Lord.

The first of those encounters was with a peer. Like me, this guy was about nineteen or twenty years old. I was praying outside the Planned Parenthood abortion facility in College Station, Texas. In those days, we always held a sign displaying the number of abortions that had taken place in the community. It read, "Please pray! (Number) of babies have died here." We updated the number every week.

One day, as I stood on the grass holding the sign, a young man was driving his girlfriend out of the facility after their abortion. She was weeping, her head in her hands. Smirking, he called out through his open car window in a smart-aleck tone, "Hey, dude— why don't you go ahead and add one more number to that sign!"

He looked at me for what seemed like an eternity. I met his gaze. I couldn't deny that a part of me was angry with him, but that anger quickly melted into grief. I inclined my head toward his girlfriend in the passenger seat next to him, her body heaving as she sobbed. He turned, looked at her for a long moment, and then slowly turned back to me. But the smirk was gone. His expression now was one of shame. I could see the gravity of what they had done hit him in that instant, and my heart went out to him. His attempt at bravado to gloss over what he had helped his girlfriend do had failed. He had wanted to show everyone, including himself, that this abortion was no big deal. Clearly, that wasn't true. Could it be that, at that moment, he saw the deep anguish abortion had left in the devastated woman by his side—and perhaps in himself? Did he wonder what today's decision would do to their relationship?

Did I feel superior to him at that moment? Victorious, as if I'd just stared him down and put him in his place? No, because the Holy Spirit used the experience to open my eyes. I was struck with the realization that I, being roughly the same age as the driver of the car, was looking at a mirror image of my own spiritual immaturity. The truth is that we are all lost at some point in our lives, clueless to the consequences of our sin and the effects of that sin on others. How often do we—perhaps especially men—underestimate those consequences, or try to downplay them, or mask them with a swagger because we are afraid to face them? Men often hide fear and pain with anger or bravado.

Armed with that realization, I wanted more than ever to connect with him and to place in his hands the information we had available on post-abortion healing for women *and* men. But in the blink of an eye the traffic cleared, and the young couple sped away. That encounter did its work in my own heart, though. I never looked at the fathers of the unborn with anger again.

The second incident happened less than two years later. I was praying in front of an abortion facility on a sweltering summer day. A minivan pulled up, carrying a young Korean couple with two children who appeared to be about three and six years old. As soon as they parked, the wife immediately got out of the car and, leaving the rest behind, rushed into the abortion facility. The man stayed in the car with the two children. He watched me through his windshield. I just sat there, my head bowed in prayer. But whenever I looked up, he was still watching me.

At first I thought he might be angry that we were there praying. And it appeared that my supposition was correct a few minutes later when he leapt out of his minivan, jumped on the black wrought-iron fence that divided us, and, clinging to those bars, started screaming at me. At first, I couldn't understand his words because of his heavy Korean accent. I assumed the worst.

Then I began to recognize the words he was yelling over and over: "I love children! I love children! Please go get her!"

I moved closer to the fence, and he explained to me that he didn't want the abortion. "Please, go get her!" he screamed. "Can't you do something? I love children!" He pointed desperately to his other two kids in the minivan. "I don't want her abortion. Can't you go in and do something?"

His grief was gut-wrenching, and I wanted to spring into action. But what could I do? Behind him was the building where his wife was aborting his child against his will. He thrust his arms through the fence toward me. Then, all of his options exhausted, he began to weep.

As he quieted, I gently said, "There's nothing I can do. I can't go in there and get your wife. But you can."

Oh, how I wanted him to. I wanted to see a dramatic rescue by a heroic father.

But in a voice broken by weeping gasps, he said, "She won't listen to me. I've tried and tried to talk her out of it." His voice gradually rose until, once more, he was screaming, pleading with me to get his wife and baby out of that abortion facility. His grip on the bars of the fence loosened; he slid to the ground, his shoulders slumped and heaving.

I was just a college kid with no children of my own yet, but his grief pierced me. Tears came to my eyes, and soon I was weeping with this dad who obviously loved his family. He had done everything he could think of to save the life of his unborn child, yet here he sat in the hot parking lot of a Texas abortion facility, helpless—appealing to me, a kid myself, to intervene when we both knew I could do nothing.

Time passed, the two of us just sitting in the heat. Though we were divided by the black wrought-iron fence, I felt bound to him by this shared grief. Eventually, his wife came out of the abortion facility looking dazed, emotionless, numb. Without another word, he stood and slumped back to the van to take his seat behind the wheel. I watched as they drove away. He looked like a broken man.

Abortion, I realized, puts men in the position of being helpless to protect their own flesh and blood. It strikes at the very heart of their manhood. And men hate being helpless.

It would be another four years before the third encounter that further shaped my understanding of abortion's effect on fathers of aborted children—an encounter I'll share in the next chapter. God must have known I needed time for these first two encounters to do their work in my heart. I needed to see these men as he did, through eyes of mercy, compassion, and forgiveness. Only then would I be equipped to effectively train other men to stand and pray in compassion and full understanding—rather than in judgment and condemnation.

It's so easy to judge others, isn't it? We all hate to admit it, but the truth is that finger-pointing and looking down on the sins of others comes all too naturally to us. Jesus identified this weakness we all share:

> Why do you look at the speck of sawdust in your brother's eye and pay no attention to the plank in your own eye? How can you say to your brother, 'Let me take the speck out of your eye,' when all the time there is a plank in your own eye? You hypocrite, first take the plank out of your own eye, and then you will see clearly to remove the speck from your brother's eye.
>
> MATTHEW 7:3–5

Are these verses speaking to you as they speak to me? When you talk to your coworkers who support abortion, when you hear of doctors and abortion workers taking innocent human life right in your community, when you see men acting like boys by shrugging off their responsibilities or minimizing the trauma of an abortion, are you tempted to judge them?

Then join me, along with the apostle Paul, in praying these words from Romans 7:24–25:

> *What a wretched man I am! Who will rescue me*
> *from this body that is subject to death? Thanks be to God,*
> *who delivers me through Jesus Christ our Lord!*

Yes, thanks be to God! He does rescue us. And he invites us to be his partners in bringing the good news to others—the good news that forgiveness and healing are available through the sacrifice and mercy of Jesus Christ. In tomorrow's chapter, you will see just how patiently God can wait for us to get the message.

> *Whoever does not carry their cross*
> *and follow me cannot be my disciple.*
> LUKE 14:27

Lord, help me to make my attitude toward the mothers and fathers of the unborn who are desperate enough to contemplate abortion one of humility, empathy, and love rather than of judgment. Help me to understand that those who work in the abortion industry often began that work with the best of intentions and may be personally dismayed by abortion itself. Remind me of my own sins you have graciously forgiven so that I remember that forgiveness is possible for all who are willing to repent of their sins and truly believe. Amen.

The Thirty-Seven-Year Secret

Shawn

IT WAS MARCH 2009.

I had just spoken at the night shift of a 40 Days for Life vigil in front of the largest Planned Parenthood center in Iowa and then prayed with the volunteers. The night was frigid, and I was shivering when an older man approached me and introduced himself.

Charlie appeared to be in his seventies. "I've never done anything in the pro-life movement before this 40 Days for Life Campaign," he said quietly. "It's been a long journey to bring me to this point." He paused, and I had the feeling I was about to hear a story.

It was not my first trip to Iowa for a 40 Days for Life Campaign. The previous fall's 40 Days for Life Campaign in Texas had captured national attention, and in response I'd traveled to eight Midwestern cities in Illinois, Nebraska, and Iowa, speaking about the devastation of abortion and encouraging volunteers to stand and pray for every family—every man, woman, and child—affected by abortion. I drew on the two encounters I'd had with fathers of aborted children, described in yesterday's chapter, as I interacted with abortive fathers and encouraged volunteers.

Now, just a year after that first trip to the Midwest, God had brought Charlie across my path.

His eyes grew intense as he said, "In 1972 I drove my girlfriend, in the dead of night, to a doctor to have an illegal abortion. We broke up afterward. In time, I turned my life around, got married, and now I've been married to a wonderful woman for nearly forty years. I have children and grandchildren now, but I've never escaped the guilt of that abortion in 1972. I kept it a secret even from my wife—until just a few months ago."

We stood in the cold on the barely lit sidewalk, our backdrop the eerie silhouette of the Iowa abortion facility. Charlie's voice became gradually more emotional as he explained to me that, through his church, he heard about Rachel's Vineyard, a national effort that holds retreats across the country for women and men who have been through an abortion. He saw it as a sign from the Holy Spirit that he should finally seek healing. He went on a men's retreat for those who had participated in an abortion. His eyes misted as he told me that his wife decided to go on a retreat herself as a member of a family who had been impacted by abortion. She wanted to discover how to help her husband through his healing.

Rachel's Vineyard has chapters all across the country. They have my deepest respect; I know of no other organization that has done more to lead both men and women to healing after abortion.

After attending the retreat, Charlie sought some way to play a positive part in the tragedy of abortion. His church encouraged him to participate in 40 Days for Life. And that brought him here to his first vigil. He eagerly went straight to the front lines to pray with and talk with the younger men taking women in to have abortions, sharing with them about the mistake he still regretted nearly forty years later.

He smiled broadly. "And now, standing here praying and sharing my story with these younger men, God is healing me. I have never felt such peace—and such joy."

He wiped the tears brimming in his eyes and thanked me for coming. As I watched him walk away on that frigid Iowa night, it occurred to me that abortion does not go away as women and men drive out of the parking lot of an abortion facility.

A famous prayer by St. Augustine says, "My heart is restless, O God, until it rests in Thee."

These three encounters with fathers of aborted children had

taught me much about the insidious, little-understood impact of abortion on men.

Men react in a variety of ways to the unwanted pregnancy of a girlfriend or wife. Some, frightened by the thought of what having a baby might mean for them, think that a fifteen-minute surgery can eliminate all their problems—no baby, no responsibility, no guilt. Some try to swagger or bully their way past the consequences of their actions. Some feel the weight of their guilt for having chosen to end the life of their baby, but they try to ignore, bury, or deny that guilt. Others give in to the brokenness; they surrender the wholeness they could have had, too proud or stubborn to confess, repent, and seek forgiveness—or perhaps they're unaware of the healing God offers to those who confess. Some convince themselves that abortion is a "women's issue," or a political issue, and doesn't involve them personally.

But here's the good news. Boys can grow up and become men! It may take days, months, years, or decades, but we can stand before God, repent, and accept the responsibility to grow into real men. Real men know how really weak man is.

Bravado won't get us there. Cowering in shame won't get us there. Silence and surrender won't get us there, and neither will blame-shifting, finger-pointing, or burying our heads in the sand.

Real men are willing to pursue the will of God at all costs. Real men own up to the consequences of their actions. Real men admit their mistakes and flaws; they face their challenges rather than running from them. They confess. They lay their pride on the altar. In fact, real men lay down their lives for those they love. Real men seek to love their wives "just as Christ loved the church" (Ephesians 5:25).

After my conversation with Charlie, I walked back to my rental car in the deserted shopping center next to the Planned Parenthood building. Even though it was late, I wanted to call my wife, Marilisa. All I could think about was how long this man had carried the guilt of that abortion—thirty-seven years! Decades! Decades of busyness. Decades of raising kids, building a career, watching sports, and filling his life with all the distractions men love. But none of that could relieve his guilt. Now, in his seventies, with the support of his wife, he had found the path to healing. He was on his way to peace of heart.

Charlie had shown me that it's never too late to face our sins, accept our responsibility, ask for forgiveness, and experience the compassion of our heavenly Father.

> *The LORD is compassionate and gracious,*
> *slow to anger, abounding in love.*
> *He will not always accuse,*
> *nor will he harbor his anger forever;*
> *he does not treat us as our sins deserve*
> *or repay us according to our iniquities.*
> *For as high as the heavens are above the earth,*
> *so great is his love for those who fear him;*
> *as far as the east is from the west,*
> *so far has he removed our transgressions from us.*
> PSALM 103:8–12

Lord, I thank you for the Charlies of the world—people who have acknowledged their wrongdoing, have sought forgiveness for it, and now model for the rest of us the life of the sinner saved by grace, living in humble thanks for that forgiveness. Help all of us in the pro-life movement to see a potential Charlie in each of the young mothers and fathers who approach abortion centers as we stand and pray on the sidewalks. And help me to become more like Charlie myself. Amen.

What Child Is This?

David

ONE DAY IN THE SUMMER OF 2008 IN FRONT OF ONE OF THE BUSI-est abortion facilities in Dallas, Texas, Don Ancelin, a sidewalk counselor, noticed one of the security guards of the facility known as the Aaron Center approaching, apparently ready to start his shift.

But then the guard changed direction and came toward Don. He stopped a few feet away and said, "I've got some news for you."

Don felt a slight surge of adrenaline. Was the guard about to tell him he had to leave? "Uh, good news or bad news?"

The guard smiled ruefully and said, "Good news for you. Bad news for me."

Unsure what was coming next but with his curiosity definitely piqued, Don said, "What do you mean?"

The guard sighed. "We're closing."

"You mean—closing early?"

"No, I mean closing for good. That's bad news for all of us who work here—they told us we would have to find new jobs in the next few weeks." The guard offered a desultory wave and headed inside.

Elated but hardly believing what he'd heard, Don went home and told his wife, who celebrated the news of the closing with a prayer of thanksgiving at church the next day. A 40 Days for Life vigil coordinator was at church that day and heard the prayer. Excited by the news, she sent out an email to inform her pro-life network, and a copy of that email went to Karen Garnett, executive director of the Catholic Pro-Life Committee, the group that had organized 40 Days for Life in Dallas. *Could this possibly be true?* Karen wondered.

"So we had our communications assistant, Milissa Kukla, who had previously led a 40 Days for Life Campaign herself in Ann Arbor, Michigan, call this abortion center and see if they were taking appointments for the week of June 30."

"I'm sorry," Milissa was told by the woman who answered the phone. "We aren't taking appointments. We're closing this facility."

"Oh—you're moving?" Milissa asked. "Can appointments be scheduled maybe a couple of weeks from now at the new facility?"

"No, we're not moving," the woman answered. "We're closing down. Completely. June 28 is the last day we're accepting appointments."

"We lost no time in spreading the news!" Karen said. "We had radio stations ready to go on the air with it. This was the best news all week. Some people said it was the best news we'd had in seven years, when another abortion facility in Dallas closed!"

There's a history behind the overwhelming joy of the pro-life community in response to this news. To understand it, you have to go back to a law passed by the Texas legislature in 2003 that mandated that, to perform abortions past sixteen weeks' gestation, an abortion facility had to qualify as an ambulatory surgical center. At the time that law went into effect in January 2004, no facilities qualified. That meant that, at least for a window of time, there were no late-term abortions being performed in Texas. But every pro-life activist in Texas knew that situation couldn't last forever. In fact, construction of new facilities and remodeling of existing facilities began immediately.

Then in 2004, we held our first 40 Days for Life Campaign in College Station, Texas. One of the participants in that first vigil, a Texas A&M Aggie student named Ben Seward, is the son of Carol Seward, who had been a sidewalk counselor in Dallas since 2000. In 2004, the year Carol began to direct the sidewalk counseling ministry in Dallas, Ben told her about the 40 Days vigil he had just helped with in College Station. That was about the same time Carol and Karen got word that the Dallas Aaron Center abortion facility was about to begin remodeling to become an ambulatory surgical center. Something had to be done.

Carol and a couple of other members of the pro-life team in Dallas drove down to College Station to meet with Shawn and Marilisa Carney and me to find out how they could bring 40 Days for Life to Dallas.

Their request was an absolute shock to Shawn and me. When we'd finished that first 40 Days for Life Campaign in fall 2004 in College Station, we never expected it would happen again *anywhere,* not even in College Station. So when we heard that people in Dallas were thinking of doing this, certainly we were flabbergasted. It had, after all, been the most difficult and challenging pro-life effort we had ever undertaken. Who else would be crazy enough to do this?

And frankly, had that second 40 Days for Life vigil not happened in Dallas, there may never have been another 40 Days for Life anywhere—and there are more campaign locations every season! I'm so thankful the people in Dallas had the willingness to say yes to the Holy Spirit and take on such an ambitious project.

Of course, we offered whatever help we could. The Dallas leaders strategically chose December 12, 2004, to January 22, 2005, for a 40 Days for Life vigil in front of the Aaron Center. That would coincide with the remodeling and reconstruction of this facility. Also, Catholics recognize December 12 as the feast of Our Lady of Guadalupe—patroness of the unborn. And January 22, of course, is the anniversary of the *Roe v. Wade* U.S. Supreme Court decision that imposed the legalization of abortion on America in 1973.

"Shawn and Marilisa came up from College Station and participated in the kickoff for our 40 Days for Life on December 12," Karen explains, "and that was great—because we needed all the help we could get! We were no strangers to sidewalk counseling and providing a prayerful presence; we'd been doing that since 1997 at all the abortion centers in Dallas, but just during their operating hours. To decide to go for forty straight days, twenty-four hours a day, seven days a week—through the holidays, on Christmas, on New Year's—honestly, it had to have been an act of the Holy Spirit that we were able to make a decision to do something like that.

"I'm not going to pretend it wasn't difficult. Especially the night shift. Our team members Carol Seward, her husband, Lew, and Diane Sutton and her husband, Morris, ended up actually renting an apartment near the vigil site. They lived way down in a suburb south of Dallas, and it would have been a long commute to get to the site. They took most of the midnight-to-7:00-a.m. shifts themselves.

"The turnout was phenomenal. We had eighty-nine churches participating through the forty days—eight hundred people! Many of them had never prayed in front of an abortion facility before."

To grasp just how difficult it was to build and maintain a team twenty-four hours a day for this vigil, understand that it wasn't just that it took place over the Christmas and New Year holidays. That, in fact, brought one of the unexpected blessings of the vigil: standing there in front of the facility and singing Christmas carols with the other volunteers, with people from many different denominations joining in.

"I was out there myself on Christmas Day," Karen recalls. "I remember being there with a Lutheran family and a Messianic Jew —all at the same time. We sang hymns together and prayed together on the day of our Lord's birth, even though the abortion center wasn't open that day."

It was also a challenge that the vigil took place in a difficult location—not just *near* a major freeway, but right on the sidewalk of the service road, at 6546 LBJ Freeway in Dallas. There were safety issues. How do you safely manage children and families standing and praying with cars whizzing by mere feet away? Even during the hours the facility was open, it was hard for the volunteers to be able to reach out and speak to the mothers going in. No, it wasn't just hard—it was formidable.

"But of course," Karen reminds us, "there's always a flip side. Because there was so much traffic going by on the freeway service road, our public witness during the 40 Days for Life Campaign was that much more public! We would hear from people who got a haircut from someone down the road that the barber or stylist would say, 'What's up with that crowd on LBJ?' It was the first time many people had heard that was an abortion center, let alone one remodeling for late-term abortions. Community awareness was definitely raised! And since that time we've had more people involved in pro-life activities in Dallas than ever before."

Now fast-forward three-and-a-half years. A sidewalk counselor talks to a security guard in front of that very abortion facility and gets the news that it's closing ...for good.

To understand why the pro-life movement in Dallas was particularly elated by this news, you have to know more than just that they'd had a 40 Days for Life Campaign in front of it a few years earlier. You also have to understand that the facility had been providing late-term abortions not only for pregnant women in Dallas but had also been seeing women who'd been driving in from other cities and from Louisiana, Oklahoma, and other nearby states.

The 40 Days for Life vigils are always organized and led at a local level. But as with that facility in Dallas that closed, the implications of many abortion facilities go far beyond the local level—and our ultimate goals go beyond local as well. As Karen says, "The ultimate goal, obviously, for all of us is to have abortion-free communities. No more abortion. And yet the perseverance that's required, day in and day out, faithfully praying—we call the campaigns '40 Days,' but I confess, sometimes it feels like it's forty years, forty years in the desert, forty years of journey. We wonder at times, *Is it ever going to end*?

"Legal abortion in this country *will* end when Roe is overturned. Until then, we just have to keep hanging in there, persevering. And pressing for the closings of the facilities, as we did with this one in Dallas—one facility at a time."

The Aaron Center shut its doors for good on August 27, 2008. The empty building was subsequently bulldozed.

Away from me, all you who do evil,
for the LORD has heard my weeping.
The LORD has heard my cry for mercy;
the LORD accepts my prayer.
All my enemies will be overwhelmed with shame and anguish;
they will turn back and suddenly be put to shame.

PSALM 6:8–10

Lord, sometimes I say, like Karen in this story, "It feels like forty years, not forty days. Is it ever going to end?" Remind me then that you haven't forsaken me or our common struggle to save lives from abortion, and that in the end your will will be done. The enemies of that struggle will be ashamed and dismayed, forced to turn back in disgrace. But better yet, you have given us, through your power, Lord, the possibility of turning enemies into allies and friends. Give me that opportunity today. Amen.

DAY 18

The Text Message

Shawn

As we've mentioned before, David Bereit and I were deter-mined to visit as many local campaigns as possible during the first years of 40 Days for Life. We felt that we, as national leaders, needed to show support—and what better way to do that than to visit each site, even if only for a few hours?

We had to be good stewards of our limited funds, so we put together travel itineraries that relied on long hours on the road and in the air and staying with family or friends or at inexpensive hotels whenever possible. We did things that no one in their right mind should ever try—too many cities in too little time!

On one of those whirlwind trips, I went to twelve cities—stretch-ing from Bellingham, Washington, to Bakersfield, California—in three days. Eight plane flights in all. It was absolutely insane!

One of the stops on that trip was Reno, Nevada. I had never been to Reno before. I was dead tired and figured I could catch up on my sleep on the plane. That shows what a rookie traveler I was at the time. The plane was filled with chatty people heading for a weekend in the casinos.

I met Carol Marie, the local 40 Days for Life coordinator, at the airport. We headed straight to the abortion center, where more than a hundred people were standing in vigil at 9:30 in the evening!

It was a diverse gathering. There were Catholics, Protestants, evangelicals, young people, old people, and a variety of ethnic groups.

I met two young guys who had just started volunteering and

120

loved 40 Days for Life. They were both snowboard instructors at nearby Lake Tahoe. As a guy from Texas, that was the first time I'd ever met a snowboard instructor—and it happened in front of an abortion facility at a 40 Days for Life Campaign. You never know!

A few years later, in the fall of 2010, I was back in Reno for the 40 Days for Life kickoff. On this trip, my father-in-law, an OB/GYN, decided to come along. He had often said he wanted to come on one of these 40 Days for Life trips with me, but I'd never thought he was serious.

He lived in College Station, Texas—the birthplace of the 40 Days for Life Campaign—and he had never seen a campaign outside his town. I suspect that part of him wondered if I was just making up all these stories about how 40 Days for Life had spread throughout the country and around the world! He wanted to see for himself.

I hadn't seen much on my first visit to Reno; it had been a short trip, and it was dark the whole time. The abortion facility had been closed. This time, it was daylight—and quite different.

I had already heard the history of this notorious abortion facility. It was run by one of the most hostile, confrontational, and vulgar abortionists in the country. This man had done everything he could to try to disrupt the peaceful vigils. His goal was to discourage vigil participants, and he threw everything he had at it.

He hired people to harass the small group of volunteers praying in front of his facility. He even had professionally made signs that would point toward those who were praying. One of the signs was pretty basic: "No trespassing." Another said, "God is pro-choice" in huge black letters. Another read, "These protestors are terrorists" —again in big black letters.

This was an abortionist with an agenda and a hatred for pro-lifers like no other abortionist we'd ever encountered. He even made a sign that said, "Please go pray that priests stop molesting children." He installed a sprinkler system. Now, understand that he had no grass to be watered—he was in the middle of the Nevada desert. His sprinkler system pointed directly at the prayer volunteers on the public sidewalk. And the sprinkler heads would spray all day long to discourage those volunteers. He had professional-grade loudspeakers installed outside so he could play aggressive, offensive chants and music to try to disrupt the prayers of those outside his facility.

In short, he hated 40 Days for Life.

My father-in-law was shocked. He couldn't believe that somebody like this abortionist really existed—and it was especially stunning to my father-in-law, a physician himself, that something like this could come from a doctor.

It was a beautiful day but very hot as we walked up to the vigil site and met a small group that included Carol Marie, the local 40 Days for Life coordinator, as well as Kent, the other local leader. We also met a young volunteer named Laura, new to 40 Days for Life. She had been taking her turn standing and praying for the past few weeks.

Laura pulled me aside, saying she just had to share something with me. "You know," she said, "despite all the ridiculous antics of this abortionist, despite the loud music and the signs and his nonstop verbal abuse—despite all that, it's worth it."

I agreed, but wanting to hear what she would say, I asked, "What do you mean?"

She told me a story. A few weeks before, she'd been praying near the exit of the abortion facility. A woman who had gone in for an abortion appointment drove out of the parking lot.

"She rolled down her window and asked for my cell phone number," Laura said. "I don't give my number to strangers, but when you're out here praying, everything changes. I gave it to her. And just a few moments later, I got a long text."

Laura pulled out her cell phone and showed me this text message:

I just wanted to send you guys a text to let you know that what you do out there does make a difference. When I went to that abortion clinic last week to drop off my money to terminate my pregnancy, I saw people standing out there with signs. I didn't expect to see that and part of me felt ashamed. I drove through the gates anyway and

*went inside, gave them my money and made an appointment for
2:30 p.m. today. As I was driving away I couldn't help but think
that maybe there was another way. All this week I thought and
prayed about it and I realized in my heart what the right thing
to do was. I can't help but think that had you guys not been there
that day to remind me that I had another choice, that maybe one
more baby would have died today. Don't stop what you're doing.
It matters. It did to me. From the blonde lady in the white SUV
who picked up her money instead of aborting her baby today.*

Laura had tears of joy in her eyes as I read the text message.

"This text proves your point," I said. "It's all worth it, no matter what the abortionist throws at us. We never know what God is going to do when we answer his call to be here."

I looked back up at the abortion facility. The insulting signs were still there. I thought about the persecution endured by Christians through the ages as they stood for what they believed, starting with Jesus himself and proceeding through the martyrs, right up to the 40 Days for Life volunteers here in Reno and in New York and everywhere else our volunteers have stood peacefully and prayed while they've been insulted and harassed.

Human society is immersed in spiritual warfare—every day, in every state and every country. The fight against abortion is just one of the fronts on which Christians are called to wage spiritual warfare. We are reminded of that frequently on the sidewalks, praying peacefully during our 40 Days for Life vigils. In Reno, our volunteers prayed in front of an abortion center run by an abortionist who hated pro-life people not because they were pro-life but because they believed in and were faithful to a God he despised. His signs may have been directed toward the volunteers, but they actually insulted our Lord.

We are fighting abortion, yes. But we are also fighting godlessness —the idea that nothing has meaning, that nothing has purpose, and that we are taking part in a game in which we can treat other human beings any way we want, as if we are in charge rather than God.

Carol Marie, Kent, and Laura ignored this abortionist's rhetoric, his intimidation, his antics, and his godlessness. And they prayed themselves through this test.

Jesus didn't just suggest that we would face persecution. He promised it. And although prayer is our greatest weapon in the spiritual battles we face, it is perhaps also our most underused weapon. But these prayer volunteers used it, because it is the most powerful and effective tool in the face of evil.

That young woman who sent her text to Laura saw two vastly different worlds when she came to the abortion center that day. When she drove past the sidewalk where our volunteers stood and prayed, she saw the love and mercy of our Lord. But on the other side of the fence, when she went in for her abortion appointment, she saw the world's hatred for that love and mercy. She knew she had to choose. She ended up choosing love and mercy—because even in the face of the greatest evil and the greatest persecution, love and mercy can overcome evil.

That young woman had the chance to choose life because Carol Marie, Kent, Laura, and the rest of the volunteers in Reno were willing to step forward courageously, ignoring and enduring persecution to persevere in prayer.

"I believe that when we go to the sidewalk and pray to end abortion we each are given a special grace," Carol Marie said. "Because we are each called to play our own particular role in this effort, that grace varies from person to person, and thus the experience also differs. How is God calling you to help? What role are you meant to play?"

The world says that prayer doesn't matter. God says otherwise. He sent his Son to teach us to pray. Prayer matters.

It certainly mattered to that mom and her baby!

Blessed are you when people insult you,
persecute you and falsely
say all kinds of evil against you because of me.
Rejoice and be glad,
because great is your reward in heaven.

MATTHEW 5:11–12

Almighty Father, you allowed your Son to face persecution and ultimately death, and I know that no slave is above his master. Help me be a light in a culture that is trying so hard to forget about your love and sacrifice. I pray for all Christians around the world who are facing persecution for your sake today, no matter what the reason. May your name be glorified through their temporary humiliation. I ask this through Christ our Lord. Amen.

A Sweet Ending
to a Bitter Story

Shawn

MINNEAPOLIS/ST. PAUL IS THE COLDEST METROPOLITAN AREA IN the United States.

Brian Gibson leads a pro-life ministry there called Pro-Life Action Ministries. For years, Brian has done everything from helping set up pregnancy resource centers to providing sidewalk counseling to presenting free and loving alternatives to women entering facilities for abortions throughout the Twin Cities.

His decades of service for women and the unborn have received local, statewide, and national media attention. In fact, in 2003, during the thirtieth anniversary of *Roe v. Wade*, ABC's *Nightline* did a feature on Minneapolis/St. Paul, describing it as one of two places shaping the abortion debate in America.

The second place featured on that episode of *Nightline* was a little town called College Station, Texas, which Planned Parenthood had just named the most anti-choice place in America, due in part to their ever-growing dislike for the local pro-life leader there, David Bereit.

Those two communities would unite once again when 40 Days for Life, which started in College Station, went nationwide in the fall of 2007.

Brian didn't participate in that first nationwide 40 Days for Life Campaign, but after he saw the effects in the eighty-nine cities in thirty-three states that participated that fall, he wanted to run one too. In fact, he couldn't wait. After the fall campaign, Brian urged us to launch a spring 40 Days for Life Campaign.

A spring campaign too? David and I had been thinking of the campaign as a one-time activity, which at most might become an annual event—once a year, in the fall. Doing *two* nationally coordinated 40 Days for Life campaigns a year seemed daunting, especially since we were still trying to recover from having eighty-nine cities participate in the fall campaign—when we'd been expecting twenty or twenty-five.

But Brian was persistent. So, bolstered by Brian's nudges, we decided there was enough momentum from the fall to announce plans for a spring campaign, scheduled for the same time when many denominations are observing Lent in preparation for Easter. That meant we would have to scramble to process applications and train leaders, many of whom would be new to pro-life activism, before the end of the year.

Ash Wednesday was early that spring—February 6. That hardly counts as spring anywhere in the country, especially in Minneapolis/ St. Paul.

But Brian was undaunted. In fact, he wanted to go whole hog, including a twenty-four-hour vigil throughout that 40 Days for Life Campaign. Before the campaign, Brian had sought a permit from the city to have an ice-fishing tent for volunteers at night so that those who stood and prayed between sundown and sunrise could have the warmth of the tent when they needed a break from the bitter cold. "A *what* tent?" I asked. But the request was turned down; there would be no tent. The volunteers would just have to brave the elements.

As the spring campaign began, David and I found it humorous, given that I'm from Texas and David, although originally from Pittsburgh, had lived in Texas for seventeen years, that on one of our training calls Brian asked, "What do you guys recommend for fighting the cold during the overnight vigils?" Other than relocating his vigil to the Florida Keys, we really had no sound advice to offer, so we invited Brian to answer that question for all our leaders, especially those in Midwestern and northern cities where cold weather would be a major issue.

During a training webcast dedicated to weather, Brian came up with a prophetic philosophy that 40 Days for Life leaders have come to cherish: "You aren't too cold—you just aren't wearing enough layers." One needs a sense of humor when leading others in standing and praying outdoors at 40 degrees below zero.

For that first Minneapolis/St. Paul 40 Days for Life Campaign in spring of 2008, Brian chose a site in St. Paul right outside Regions Hospital. And as he'd anticipated, that spring wasn't really spring. Day One was February 6, twenty-four-hour vigil and all. Despite his optimism about battling the weather, Brian left a message for David a few days into the campaign: "Man, it's cold!"

Jokingly, David replied with Brian's own advice: "You aren't wearing enough layers!"

Brian's immediate response: "No, it's just really cold!"

But the cold didn't shake Brian's or his volunteers' faith or dedication. In fact, it helped both. That's because women were choosing life! *A lot* of women were choosing life!

Brian attributes the success of their campaign to the very thing that was so bothersome and so painful—the cold weather. He believes the cold weather spoke to the hearts of people driving by as well as women entering the facility. Minnesotans take winter very seriously. They respect the cold, and they certainly respect volunteers more when they see them out there in February because they know exactly what they're enduring. They wouldn't be doing it unless they were absolutely committed.

Regions Hospital is a massive hospital that provided many of the abortions in Minneapolis and St. Paul. After that first spring 2008 campaign, Brian made Regions the site for all his 40 Days for Life Campaigns. He had been targeting Regions Hospital for years with efforts such as petition drives to try to get them to stop performing abortions. Finally, by bringing 40 Days for Life to that community, he drew 3,500 Christians to pray outside of that hospital. "Coming out and praying makes the difference," Brian said.

During the fall of 2011 that prayer added up in a big way—Regions Hospital announced that they were no longer going to offer abortions!

After seven 40 Days for Life Campaigns, the hospital had decided to stop performing abortions. Brian heard from pro-life workers inside the hospital that it was the vigils that had made the difference. More importantly, he learned that the pro-abortion director of the OB/GYN department was extremely angry with Brian and the volunteers for their pro-life presence over the past three-and-a-half years and blamed *them* that he'd had to stop offering abortions.

As the media covered this huge story, officials from the hospital admitted that abortions had dropped 40 percent over those three-and-a-half years! Forty percent—an appropriate number for Brian, who so faithfully led those cold 40 Days for Life Campaigns.

Seven 40 Days for Life Campaigns. Brian could write a book on all the challenges: the cold, the rain, the sleet, the ice, the snow, the physical pain they endured. But all that inconvenience melts away when you hear that the hospital no longer carries out abortions. The cold didn't deter Brian, nor did it deter the 3,500 volunteers who stood with him from going where abortions happen and standing there twenty-four hours a day, no matter how cold it got.

Brian summed it up this way: "We had done many things to try to stop abortions at Regions. But when we focused on prayer, that's when we saw the change, and that's when this hospital closed its abortion practice. It was 40 Days for Life. It was coming out and peacefully praying. And God answered those prayers."

On that day there will be neither sunlight nor cold,
frosty darkness. It will be a unique day—a day known only
to the LORD—with no distinction between day and night.
When evening comes, there will be light.

ZECHARIAH 14:6–7

Lord God, help me to see you working in the midst of my earthly discomforts. Give me strength as I grow weary, because I know that persistent prayer can overcome any cold, heat, or persecution. And may I trust you with all results, for you alone have the power to end abortion.

Medical Waste

Shawn

ABORTION IS GRAPHIC.

Abortion is so graphic that, despite decades of legalization, we can hardly talk about it without stirring passion like no other issue of our time. Abortion is the most common surgical procedure in the United States, and yet the mere mention of it polarizes an office party or a Thanksgiving dinner with extended family. And there's a good reason our culture likes to keep abortion in the shadows. Outside of the context of a political debate, a judicial nomination, or even a sermon, when you're not talking about strategy or some abstract notion of morality, when you're simply considering the unadorned nature of abortion itself, then that nature is very simple: It's a practice that violently ends the life of a unique human being— a death followed by the nonchalant disposal of the body of a baby.

You don't often hear that reality discussed in the media or the backrooms where political strategies are formed. Even so, it's the elephant in the room. And it's why, despite four decades of legalization, abortion is one of the most controversial issues of our time.

When forced to acknowledge and confront the graphic nature of that death and the disposal of the body, many people have found their lives changed. Here are the stories of two of those lives.

More than half a million people have taken part in 40 Days for Life. Like about a third of them, John, a college student, was participating in his first pro-life activity when he signed up to stand and pray during a 40 Days for Life Campaign in College Station, Texas.

My office at the time was next door to the Planned Parenthood abortion facility where the vigil was taking place. Whenever possible, I liked to go out and meet new volunteers, thank them, and spend the first twenty minutes or so with them. I knew that, for many, that first step was difficult, especially for first-timers like John.

John is a big man, and tough. His first hour came on a beautiful Monday morning—it was sunny and 70 degrees when I introduced myself. First we exchanged small talk, and when John indicated that he was ready to begin praying, I stepped a few yards away so that my presence wouldn't distract him.

From the corner of my eye, I saw a truck pull in and park beside the facility. My stomach knotted when I realized what truck it was. I knew what it was doing there. I had watched these trucks coming and going regularly. But would John notice and ask me about it? And if he did, would I find the right words?

Sure enough, after a few minutes, John stepped closer and asked, "What's that truck for? I don't think I've seen one quite like that before."

I took a deep breath. "John, I'm sorry this truck came during your first hour of prayer. It's the medical waste truck."

"Medical waste?" John asked.

I thought carefully about my next words. "Planned Parenthood typically has a medical waste pickup after days on which they perform abortions. Last Saturday, they did twenty-four abortions. That's why the truck is here first thing Monday morning—to pick up the remains of those babies."

John fell silent. He appeared stunned at first, and then his expression slowly changed to deep sadness. The atmosphere on that beautiful, sunny Texas morning turned extremely dark very quickly. This young, powerful, six-foot-three-inch man bowed his head and began to weep. Through his tears, he said quietly, "I can't believe this goes on in America."

A few minutes later, we watched the driver of the truck exit the building carrying two silver, cylindrical canisters that held the bodies of twenty-four babies—human beings who had now become no more than statistics in the eyes of the world. Or a disposal problem. But to the brawny, big-hearted college kid by my side, they were lost brothers and sisters.

The truck soon drove off, but John had been forever changed. The darkness of abortion had hit him that day, and it hit him hard. He gave the only appropriate response he knew, at least for that morning—tears and prayer.

I watched him pray, reminded of the words of our Lord when he was covered in dirt, sweat, and blood on the day of his crucifixion. He looked at mankind and simply said, "Do not weep for me. Weep for yourselves and for your children" (Luke 23:28).

John was changed that day but not discouraged. What I considered a difficult circumstance for a first-time volunteer God used to inspire this young man to come out and pray more often during the campaign. And he didn't come alone; he encouraged his friends to join him.

To John, those had been babies—not medical waste. And he felt compelled to do something about it.

John's story is powerful but not unique. The cold dehumanization of the unborn has the power to get our attention, sometimes in unexpected places.

I spoke at a pregnancy resource center banquet in Moses Lake, a quaint little town in eastern Washington, during the first nationally coordinated 40 Days for Life Campaign in the fall of 2007. I met some great people who formed the heart of that beautiful state.

A young man named Kevin volunteered to drive me back to the airport after that dinner. Making conversation as he drove, I asked him what I thought was a simple question. I asked how he got involved in the pro-life movement. I thought I would get a simple answer.

For a few moments, Kevin just looked ahead at the road. I glanced at him—thinking he was taking a surprisingly long time to answer the question—and noticed the tears on his face. I wasn't going to get the simple answer I was expecting. Instead, I heard a story I'll never forget.

Kevin had worked in a medical lab at a Catholic hospital, examining organs removed during surgery. He looked for particular things, depending on where the organ had come from and what its intended use would be now.

One day, due to a mix-up, the Catholic hospital received a package intended for another hospital. Kevin opened the package, expecting to find an organ of some type, and instead found a Ziploc bag containing the remains of a baby girl who had been in her mother's womb for twelve weeks when she was killed by a saline abortion.

It was a horrific experience; his hands began to shake so badly that he almost dropped the bag. But even worse than seeing the body of that poor girl, Kevin said—and he wept even harder as he said it—was how the bag was labeled. Stunned at seeing the body, he turned the bag to see what the official label said. Bags containing human medical waste or by-products all have to be labeled in precise medical terms. His heart fell when, on the side of the bag, he read, "Product of conception (POC)."

Kevin had grown up Catholic, but had fallen away and had been away for a number of years at the time of this experience. But afterward, shaken by that painful experience into a re-evaluation of his whole life, he returned to his faith and vowed to see everyone as a child of God—not as a "product of conception."

After Kevin dropped me off at the airport, I couldn't stop thinking about his story. I thought about him driving to work on the day of that experience. I was sure the last thing on his mind had been renewing his faith, much less doing so because he found the body of a baby girl in a Ziploc bag.

Kevin's life had changed. Not because of an argument about abortion or a political debate on TV. That would have been easier and cleaner and probably less painful. Instead, he had seen the result of abortion right before his eyes—a dehumanized and discarded "product."

Every abortion ends with that same "product."

Our lives were not made for Ziploc bags. They have eternal worth and are destined for heaven.

I once went on a spiritual retreat where a humble and wise Franciscan priest reminded me that there is no better, happier, more freeing yet more difficult way of living than the Christian life. The cross of Christ was messy. Ugly. Graphic. Yet it led to salvation. Evil often looks clean, attractive, and even responsible. But at its core, evil is so graphic, so destructive, and so cold that it can make us rethink what is good, who made us, why we were made, and even what living is all about.

That reality hit both John and Kevin—and they responded.

John responded to seeing the remains of twenty-four babies in a silver canister by prayerfully fulfilling his modest role. He returned to the sidewalk; he didn't allow the graphic reality of abortion to shake his faith in the power of Christ to overcome death—no matter how inhumane and ugly it may seem.

Kevin responded to the ugly and graphic nature of abortion by returning to his faith in Christ, from whom all good things come.

The stories of these two faithful men reveal a side of our culture that is anything but faithful—in fact, it is evil. We don't have to dwell on the graphic nature of abortion to make a difference, but we do have to know about it. And we cannot ignore it.

Ultimately, those of us who oppose abortion need to respond to its violence as John and Kevin did—with hope and life-giving action. For it is when death and evil show their true colors that we must hold fast to our faith in the risen Christ and his promise of life everlasting.

Rescue those being led away to death;
hold back those staggering toward slaughter.
PROVERBS 24:11

For our struggle is not against flesh and blood,
but against the rulers, against the authorities,
against the powers of this dark world
and against the spiritual forces of evil in the heavenly realms.
EPHESIANS 6:12

Lord, make me a vessel of hope to all around me so that as I engage in the difficult work ahead and endure the painful realities of our culture's rejection of the sanctity of human life, I may experience the peace and joy that come only from you and that no one can take from me. Amen.

DAY 21

Abortion Row

Shawn

NEW YORK CITY IS THE ABORTION CAPITAL OF THE UNITED States.[7]

According to the *New York Times*, the city averages ninety thousand abortions a year. That's 246 abortions per day. Forty percent of all pregnancies in New York end in abortion. That's twice the national rate. For African-American women in New York, a stunning 60 percent of all pregnancies end in abortion.

These numbers are staggering—even to New Yorkers. A recent poll found that 64 percent of those questioned think there are too many abortions in New York. Surprisingly, 57 percent of the women who call themselves "pro-choice" agreed that there are too many abortions. With abortion so incredibly common in one city, New York presents a tremendous challenge for 40 Days for Life. Light always shines brightest, however, in the darkest of places.

Despite the overwhelming number of abortions done, more children have been saved from abortion during 40 Days for Life Campaigns in New York City than in any other participating community.

Under the leadership of Chris Slattery, 40 Days for Life has blossomed in New York City. Chris is a New Yorker to the core. He opened his first pregnancy resource center in 1985, left a successful advertising career in 1990 to go full time with pro-life work, and has grown his Expectant Mother Care centers to twelve sites to confront the overwhelming abortion problem in the city he loves.

Chris's passion, toughness, accent, and thousands-of-words-per-minute delivery stand out even in the Big Apple.

Chris has led multiple 40 Days for Life Campaigns in the South Bronx outside Dr. Emily Women's Health Center. Despite the name, there's no Dr. Emily there. The abortion provider is actually a man. This facility performs five thousand abortions a year. Because of that, Chris has regularly held his 40 Days for Life Campaign vigil outside their doors, and his young team, many of them student interns, continues their vigils and counseling efforts year-round outside Dr. Emily's, saving more than five hundred babies annually.

As Chris will tell you, the Bronx can be pretty tough on pro-lifers. The 40 Days for Life prayer vigils in front of Dr. Emily's are often joined by the Sisters of Life—a group of nuns that includes a number of young women. Their religious community provides housing in mid-Manhattan and counseling support for young pregnant mothers who have no place to go. It's not uncommon for abortion advocates to heckle the sisters and Chris's other female staff and interns. They will yell anything and everything, including insults that focus on the nuns' vows of chastity. I'll spare you the details, but it's horribly degrading. In one episode caught on video and posted on YouTube, the pro-abortion screams and chants were overwhelming, but the nuns kept their focus on their quiet prayer—and lives continued to be saved at Dr. Emily's.

The first time I visited Chris's efforts in front of Dr. Emily's was in the fall of 2008. The trip got off to a rocky start at the airport in Houston. I was nearly late for a flight to JFK; I was the last passenger to board a plane filled with New Yorkers headed for home. As I made my way to the back rows of the plane, a woman noticed my 40 Days for Life jacket. She gave me a look loaded with attitude and demanded in a thick New York accent, "What is 40 Days for Life?"

Did I say demanded? She *yelled* the question, and everyone within about ten rows suddenly laser-focused on me. I've answered that question often enough to do it in my sleep, so even though I was a bit rattled by her attitude, I explained the 40 days of prayer and fasting, peaceful vigil, and community outreach. I added that it had all started in Texas but I was on my way to visit a team in New

York—although somehow, I'm pretty sure most of them knew the moment I opened my mouth that I was no New Yorker.

When I finished my brief explanation, you could've heard a pin drop. Dead silence. Everybody in that section of the plane was looking right at me. But as the woman processed what I was saying, everything about her body language changed. She let out an extremely loud, "That's awesome!" Then she stood and gave me a high five. Everyone else just shrugged and went back to ignoring me.

When I landed in New York, I headed to the South Bronx and my meeting with Chris Slattery. The first thing out of his mouth was, "Are you stupid or something?" I was clueless. "That backpack— with the laptop computer in it," he said. "Around this place, I promise you it'll be gone in five minutes." He hid the backpack in his car trunk, explaining that walking around with a valuable computer sticking out for all to see was like advertising myself as a target for getting mugged.

Welcome to the South Bronx, I thought.

Chris took me to Dr. Emily's and introduced me to some of the sidewalk counselors in the right-of-way outside. Directly in front of the 40 Days for Life vigil, he had stationed a mobile ultrasound unit and the staff to run it in a van just large enough to hold the machine, a counselor, and the mother. Watching his volunteers in action, I began to understand how this team could save five hundred babies every year. I could see their compassion toward the steady stream of women who came and went, and their efficiency was impressive.

But New York, being America's abortion capital, has far more abortion facilities than just Dr. Emily's. On a follow-up trip to New York a year later, Chris took me to a section of Queens and showed me something I'd never seen before—two side-by-side abortion facilities, their entrances separated only by a donut shop. As I stood there dumbfounded that there was so much business that two abortion businesses could survive side by side, Chris informed me that there were *ten* abortion providers on a two-mile strip along and just off Roosevelt Avenue—he called it "Abortion Row." It was so bad that there were people on the sidewalk, handing out brochures soliciting women to come in and take a pregnancy test—an attempt to identify potential customers. It was as if they were promoting something as innocent as a coffee shop, inviting people in to sample the flavor of the month.

But the street hawking of their services wasn't the only disturbing thing about this section of Queens. Its reputation for danger and violence was frightening. When Chris first considered a 40 Days for Life vigil here, he went to check out the neighborhood and found crosses and candles with "in memory of" cards—little shrines—scattered around the sidewalks. One of the local business owners asked him what he was doing. When Chris told him he was planning a forty-day prayer vigil outside the twin abortion centers, the man looked at him and said, "Are you nuts?" He pointed toward the temporary outdoor "shrine" of crosses and candles, then toward a mobile police command center on the hunt for the murderers. "This was a drug deal that went wrong. This is a drug neighborhood. There was a murder twenty-four hours ago in this very spot."

Chris wasn't shaken.

But standing in front of those twin facilities and looking around, I couldn't believe how clearly dangerous the environment was. I considered the tremendous courage it took to reach out to women as they went into one of those competing abortion facilities. I found it a challenging experience to stand and pray there for *two hours*—I could barely imagine being here for forty days. Watching Chris and his faithful volunteers, I was reminded that, while 40 Days is carried out by ordinary people, it was God's idea and it's conducted through his inspiration and calling. And although Queens was, I must admit, a bit frightening to me, I could see that God Almighty was moving on the streets.

I filmed a short video of Chris on the spot. That impromptu video is still one of our most-watched online presentations—and no wonder. It demonstrates so clearly that God can overcome the most difficult circumstances in any city.

Chris Slattery went on to lead multiple 40 Days for Life Campaigns outside of those side-by-side abortion facilities in Queens. Then after one campaign, Chris telephoned. "Shawn!" he said. "Remember those two side-by-side abortion facilities in Queens, with just a donut shop between them? Well, now there's only one! One of them closed up and relocated. We don't know where they went, but we'll find out. Their business is a third of what it was. We've crippled them.

"I'm so proud of everyone here! I'm proud of the interns, the people running the ultrasound units, and the sidewalk counselors! Remember, they averaged five saved babies a day at one location. I'm in awe of the courage it took for them to stand there day and night, rejected, persecuted, heckled ..."

Chris spoke glowingly of his co-coordinator, Ray Mooney, and how often Ray was out there praying—often alone.

Despite the overwhelming task, Chris Slattery chose to take action. He did this despite the recent murder, despite the drug deals going on around him. He went out and did it in faith.

That first trip to New York started with a "That's awesome!" and a high five from a loud woman on an airplane. My second trip ended with a different sort of reaction from a random New Yorker.

I was on the subway heading to the airport for the flight home. A man in his sixties sat next to me, and we began chatting about weather, sports, family—the usual small talk. He asked what I did for a living. I said I worked for a nonprofit organization in Texas.

"What does the nonprofit do?" he asked.

I said, "It's a local pro-life organization that helps young mothers. I'm also part of a national campaign called 40 Days for Life."

He stood up and said, "You people make me sick. People like you are what's wrong with our country."

I just looked at him in silence, seeing that he needed to rant.

"You're lucky my wife's not here," he growled. "She would spit in your face. The moment women don't have control over their own bodies is the moment this country really goes down the tubes."

He stormed off to sit somewhere else.

Combine that with the high five I got from the woman on the plane on my previous New York trip, and I had just gotten a taste of the diversity of reactions that Chris Slattery and his team deal with daily. New Yorkers have a reputation for being outspoken, but these opposite responses aren't unique to New Yorkers. Rather, they are a good demonstration of attitudes held around the United States —and the globe.

Our culture wants to normalize abortion, but it can't. Abortion is one of the most common surgical procedures in the United States, carried out nearly 3,300 times every single day. And despite how frequently it happens, we still can't talk about it. Like no other issue, abortion bothers people on all sides of the argument.

Abortion bothered Chris Slattery too. It bothered him that there were so many abortion centers along a two-mile strip in Queens, New York, that he dubbed it Abortion Row. It bothered him that Dr. Emily's carried out five thousand abortions every year. But Chris didn't just accept it; he took it to the streets. He took prayer and mercy and hope into a very dark place, undaunted by those who said his efforts were a waste of time and by others who would get downright nasty. He did it because he saw 40 Days for Life as a way to save lives.

By helping make that happen, Chris Slattery and his team have saved thousands of lives. It may not be easy, but it's always worth it.

For I am convinced that neither death nor life,
neither angels nor demons, neither the present nor the future,
nor any powers, neither height nor depth,
nor anything else in all creation, will be able to separate us
from the love of God that is in Christ Jesus our Lord.

ROMANS 8:38–39

God, I pray today for the strength to react against the overwhelming circumstances the world presents. I am on earth to serve eternity, and I must keep heaven at the front of my mind in the midst of the many distractions and comforts the world offers that can separate me from you, Lord. Help me to place my confidence in your love, for your love overcomes all things and reunites this broken world with you. Amen.

A Gold Medal

Shawn

THE WOMAN'S EYES HAD BEEN FIXED ON ME FROM THE MOMENT I spotted her.

I was speaking to a group of about thirty gathered outside an abortion facility in Attleboro, Massachusetts, at a 40 Days for Life Campaign. This woman's face stood out for one reason—it had pain written all over it. I see it often, that look that tells me there is an abortion-related story hidden behind the eyes.

When I finished speaking, my voice was already strained from the exertion of talking over the sound of traffic passing nearby. But when I was approached by several people, I began my usual practice of one-on-one conversations, praying with people, listening to their stories, encouraging them in their commitment to the unborn. Every few minutes I scanned the crowd for the troubled woman, and every time I found her I saw that her eyes were still fixed on me. Clearly, she was not going to let me out of her sight.

Eventually, I made my way over to her and shook her hand, fully expecting her to launch into her story. Perhaps she'd had an abortion at this facility and that was why this was such a difficult time for her. She smiled and was very pleasant as we exchanged greetings and a little small talk, but then, to my surprise, she looked down and turned away. I stood waiting for a moment, but soon it became clear that our brief conversation had ended. A bit mystified, I moved on to someone else.

An hour and a half later, when my time at the vigil ended, I headed toward my car. Suddenly I heard a voice screaming at me—

"Stop! Stop!" I turned my head and there, sprinting toward me, was the same woman. I confess that I felt a surge of adrenaline, wondering if her rush was caused by anger.

She stopped in front of me, and as our eyes met, hers began to fill with tears. It seemed likely that she had been struggling with a decision, and now she had made it. Her face softened, her tears began to flow, and she told me her story—one I will remember until the day I die.

"When I was pregnant some years ago, the doctors told me that my unborn son would be born with severe handicaps. I was heartbroken. My doctor recommended that I have an abortion, and everyone I turned to agreed with him. I felt pressured to abort. I hate to admit it, but at the time, aborting my son began to make sense to me." Her voice shook.

I braced myself for the rest of the story. How many times had I heard the same heartbreaking scenario told through tears of regret and guilt? The stories of aborting children with disabilities always struck a particularly painful blow to my heart because of my own stepbrother, Jason.

When I was in the third grade, my mom married my stepdad, Ronnie, who had two children, Joshua and Jason. Jason had cerebral palsy, which made him unable to use the right side of his body. Jason walked by stepping forward with his left leg and then dragging his right. His right arm was so stiff that he couldn't use it at all. And though Jason was two years older than me, he had the mentality of someone about two or three years younger than me. When my mom first got engaged to Ronnie, I remember wondering what it would be like to have a brother who had such handicaps.

It turned out that growing up with Jason was a blast! He loved sports. Although he only had the use of one leg and one arm, he was able to play ball with the rest of us, and he loved it. He could throw a football. He could throw a baseball. And, using his one good hand, Jason could dominate us all in any video game known to man—or boy. And after he beat us, he would trash-talk about it, recounting his victories and enjoying every second of it. He also memorized the statistics for every sport. As a kid, I was sure Jason's sports knowledge rivaled that of top ESPN writers.

As I got older, Mom and Ronnie told me of the surgeries Jason had endured—dozens of operations throughout his life. Ronnie, who worked long, hard hours in the oilfields, sat by Jason's hospital bed every single time, sometimes all night, never complaining. He saw taking care of Jason as a privilege.

Jason is thirty-two years old as of this writing. Unfortunately, the joy that people like Jason could bring to many other families is being lost. And it's being lost because of abortion.

When I first got involved in the pro-life cause, I was stunned to learn that as many as 90 percent of the unborn children who test positive for Down syndrome and other chromosomal conditions are aborted. Anyone who knows people with Down syndrome knows they are among the happiest people in the world and can live long, productive, meaningful lives.

I was introduced to the abortion industry's impact on children with disabilities through a good friend, Dwight Baker, and his mom, Mike. Dwight, who is in his late forties today, has spina bifida. Anyone who meets Dwight can see he is disabled; he needs crutches to walk. I got to know Dwight when he was the president of the spina bifida club in College Station, Texas.

One time, to raise awareness of spina bifida, Dwight walked from College Station to Houston on his crutches. That's ninety miles! He and his mother prayed regularly in front of their local Planned Parenthood abortion center, and he has played such an important part in 40 Days for Life that he has been honored as pro-life volunteer of the year in his hometown.

At a prayer vigil in front of Planned Parenthood, Dwight's mom, Mike, shared their story, as well as her sadness over how many children are aborted when the parents find out the unborn child has spina bifida. Mike didn't know about Dwight's condition before his birth because the tests weren't available at the time of her pregnancy.

She would have never chosen abortion anyway. Some in her family encouraged her to abort Dwight's little sister, given the chance that the second baby might have spina bifida as well.

Mike refused. Today, both Mike and Dwight are living proof of the good that comes from honoring God's will. Dwight embraces life as a vibrant human being. He is a powerful advocate for others with spina bifida and for the unborn. Dwight's life is not defined by his disabilities; it is defined by his position as a child of God.

Once at a medical meeting, Mike and Dwight met a particularly condescending doctor who argued that it was no longer necessary to do any research on preventing spina bifida because, with modern testing, any baby who shows signs of this condition can simply be aborted. Put yourself in Mike and Dwight's places. Imagine being in a room filled with people with diabetes, heart conditions, cancer— and hearing a doctor announce that the world could be spared their existence if only we could have aborted them all for their conditions before they were born!

So there I stood in Attleboro, in front of an abortion facility, face to face with a weeping woman telling me her story of being pressured by her doctor to abort her son, confessing that to her it had begun to make sense. My mind was instantly flooded with thoughts of my stepbrother, Jason, of Mike and Dwight, and of hundreds of others whose lives have been touched by the love of someone disabled. I readied myself to share her grief and to speak compassion and healing into her life for aborting her son.

Instead, I heard her say, "I decided to keep my son. I refused to abort him." Her chin lifted. Her eyes shone. Waves of relief washed over me, and I could almost hear Jason and Dwight and Mike cheering.

"If it weren't for organizations like 40 Days for Life," she said, eyes locked on mine, "my son would be dead. I want to give you something in return for helping give me my son's life. I want to give you a reminder of what this is about."

She pressed something into my hand. I looked down. A gold medal.

"My son won this in the Special Olympics," she said, "and I want to give it to 40 Days for Life."

From the look in her eyes, I could see that this medal represented all the sacrifice and struggle she had gone through over the years raising her son. But most importantly, it represented her joy, a joy she wanted to share with 40 Days for Life. She gave me an intense hug, looked at me one last time, and walked away.

I don't know her name. I hope she reads this book so that she'll know what her gift meant to me and what it now means to so many others. I hope that her gift will give you the courage to speak up for the value of every human life.

Children are a gift from God.

Children bring great joy into our world. They teach us the miracle and simplicity of God's love; they remind us to not take ourselves so seriously and to enjoy the simple things in life. They demonstrate over and over the resilient power of love—both the receiving of love and the giving of it. They show us how much God is present in every life.

When Aldous Huxley released his classic book *Brave New World* in 1932, it was seen as provocative and outrageous. Reading it today, it is frighteningly reflective of actions, attitudes, and arguments taking place in doctors' offices, political hallways, living rooms, and yes, in abortion facilities all over the globe. No longer considered an alarmist, Huxley is now viewed by many as a prophetic genius. Those who consider themselves "enlightened" about such things rationalize, saying that being aborted is better than being handicapped. My friend Dwight, my stepbrother Jason, a certain Special Olympics gold-medal winner, and their parents would all beg to differ. Their lives totally dispel that condescending assumption.

Targeting children with disabilities for abortion shows the worst of our society. This eugenic mentality is extremely dangerous. It insists that, through abortion, we can rid our society of disabilities. Nothing is more degrading or dehumanizing than that. We live in a culture that claims to be tolerant and inclusive, but those values are crushed when selective abortion is proposed in cases of weakness or disability. Abortion is not a "solution" to disabilities. When stripped to its basics, this "compassionate" mentality is completely evil. It is neither compassionate nor merciful nor responsible to abort a child with disabilities. It is merely one step closer to living in a Brave New World.

According to the census bureau, there are 2.8 million children with disabilities in the United States. Though every one of them is different, each came from God. And that is the only requirement necessary to prove their worth: Each one is a unique, distinctive human life given from God.

Children with disabilities—and their parents—are daily examples of hope. They demonstrate the resilience of the human heart to press on, to fight for life, to overcome obstacles, and to display courage in the face of seemingly impossible obstacles. They run the race of life with endurance. I hereby award each and every one of them a gold medal.

The last will be first,
and the first will be last.
MATTHEW 20:16

O Father, fill me anew with your Spirit. Renew my mind, strengthen me in righteousness, help me and all those who join in this battle for the unborn to be people of salt and light. May every human being, from conception to natural death, be treated with the respect due those made in your image. Amen.

No Ordinary Heroes

David

WHAT MAKES A HERO?

Heroic efforts aren't made when things are easy or when the going is smooth. Heroic efforts are made when things get challenging, when there are obstacles to be overcome. In fact, the greatest heroes in history succeeded despite seemingly insurmountable obstacles. Those are the people we admire, respect, and applaud.

And the story of 40 Days for Life has been filled with people like that. They are my heroes.

One of those people is Anita Usher of Phoenix, Arizona. Anita and her husband have eight children, seven boys and a girl. And they're no strangers to the pro-life cause. Her husband started her on it when they lived in St. Paul, Minnesota, volunteering with Pro-Life Action Ministries there. She'd been praying and counseling in front of abortion facilities for about fifteen years already when she first heard of the 40 Days of Life campaign. After reading about the success of the fall 2008 40 Days for Life Campaign in other cities, Anita was thrilled to hear that another campaign would be scheduled for the next spring. *We just have to do this*, Anita thought. *Right here in Phoenix.*

Finally, on the last day to sign up ...

"It was 11:00 at night," Anita recalls. "We had to sign up by midnight. My heart was just pounding inside my chest, knowing that God was calling us to do it. My husband said, 'If God is calling you to do this, then sign up. He will provide.' So at 11:18 p.m. we signed up to bring 40 Days for Life to Phoenix."

As Anita soon discovered, Phoenix didn't have just one Planned Parenthood facility—it had twelve. "So I prayed hour after hour, day after day. I said, 'God, what do you want?' And every time I asked, I sensed him telling me, 'I want them all.' I'd say, 'What do you mean you want them all?' He said, 'I want the entire city.' *Well, of course you do,* I thought. He wants abortion ended in every single city."

So now Anita had her marching orders. What she didn't have was an army to march with her. One woman, even one family, could not stand and pray around the clock at twelve different facilities. She sent an email to everyone she could think of, inviting them to a meeting at her house, hoping some of them would volunteer. "I had people from the entire metro area from the east, the west, the north, the south. They came from miles away. Some people traveled an hour and a half to get to my house for this meeting about 40 Days for Life."

She presented her vision and the challenge they faced, then sat back to wait for responses. By the end of the evening, eight people had volunteered to be responsible for the campaign at eight different sites. Anita had written one email, and God multiplied it into eight new leaders!

Now she had volunteers to share the challenge. But none of those people had teams yet, either. "So they went back to their churches, back to their neighborhoods, and they just started finding volunteers. One woman with five children was six weeks from her due date for her sixth baby—and yet she took on the vigil at one of the sites and her mother took on a different site.

"Isn't it incredible how much God did with what little we had to start with? When we give him the little bit we have, he multiplies it. And how he multiplied the work of those of us who came to that meeting and volunteered what little we had! Those people are my heroes."

Anita has a long list of heroes who participated in that first Phoenix 40 Days for Life Campaign. "Kris Forbes was praying outside Planned Parenthood on President's Day when Planned Parenthood was closed for the day," Anita recalls. "A high school couple pulled into the parking lot and sat looking at the door of Planned Parenthood. They got out of their car, back into their car. Out of their car, back into their car. So Kris walked up and asked if they needed help. It turns out they were there to get the Morning After Pill. They wanted to make sure they weren't pregnant. Kris was able to direct them to a crisis resource center where they could get real help. What a blessing that Planned Parenthood was closed that day—otherwise, Kris wouldn't have been allowed to approach the car.

"Or Sister Mary Norbert, the principal of the school at St. Mary's in Phoenix. She is a perfect example of what can happen when we just make people aware of the presence of an abortion facility. When I started doing research I discovered I had been driving by a Planned Parenthood abortion site for ten years and didn't even know they were there. My church was only five blocks away and, as I spread the word, I learned that most people in my church were just as unaware as I was. When Sister Mary heard, she sprang into action. Each school day during a vigil she leads her students right down the sidewalk to that Planned Parenthood facility, leads the children in prayer, and then leads them back. People notice the kids walking back and forth and praying. Many have stopped to give a thumbs-up or to say, 'I didn't even know Planned Parenthood was here. I'll join you and pray with you.'"

Debbi Gambert and her husband are Phoenix volunteers who stepped forward despite their own life challenges. They have a son with special needs who requires twenty-four-hour care. Yet Debbi has done phenomenal work passing out information within the church. Debbi contacted the organization Priests for Life and their Silent No More Awareness Campaign (see chapter 7), and now those women come out weekly and pray in front of the Chandler Planned Parenthood for three or four hours.

I was particularly moved when I learned how Anita had continued to lead her local 40 Days for Life in the midst of a daunting challenge that has become all too familiar around our nation. I called her to see how she was doing.

"Well, God has allowed us to go through some trials—to

strengthen us, I think," Anita told me. "My husband is a real estate agent, but as everybody in the country knows, real estate has gone bottoms up. He now works at a restaurant making about one-sixth what he used to make."

Not surprisingly, the Ushers weren't able to make their house payments for several months. Their mortgage company was unwilling to work with them, and the house went up for public auction. "We got an eviction notice giving us five days to vacate. But God always takes care of us. Friends of ours had a vacant house." Another generous family offered to pay their rent in the new house. "God is just continuing to bless. We're very fortunate."

And yet, how many people, I thought as I listened, going through difficulties as severe as that, would immediately pull back from their volunteer activities and focus on themselves for a period of time? No one would have blamed them. Everyone would have understood.

But they didn't stop. In fact ...

On the day after they were evicted from their home, Anita was praying outside a Phoenix Planned Parenthood abortion center with one of her sons, who held a homemade sign encouraging mothers to choose life over abortion. A young couple drove into the parking lot, glancing at Anita and her son before parking their car near the door of the facility. But they didn't get out of the car, and it looked to Anita as if the couple was having a lengthy and animated discussion. The young woman kept pointing back to Anita and her son. Eventually the reverse lights came on, and the car backed out of the parking space and headed toward the exit. But before pulling out onto the busy street, the couple rolled down the car window to give Anita and her son a thumbs-up sign, thanking them for their witness. It had helped them to change their mind.

A life was saved that day because Anita and her family didn't quit when the going got tough.

But the loss of their home wasn't the only challenge the Ushers had to overcome.

"We were pregnant last September," Anita told me. "It was a little girl. We miscarried. Her due date was March 23. I feel the loss of that baby every day. As I approach her birthday I remember feeling her in my womb. I remember the doctor telling me she had died.

"As painful as it is to have miscarried my baby, how much more pain is there in the world because of the lies Planned Parenthood and other abortion proponents are telling women. After abortion, many people will feel loss every single day of their life because they made a tragic decision. And it will change their life forever.

"David." I could feel Anita's sense of urgency through the phone line. "That's why we have to be out there telling the truth to the people on the street, in the church, at Planned Parenthood, everywhere. So that these children will live, to have joy and to bring joy. We need to let people know there are other options, far better options."

I marveled at Anita's story. Her baby's projected birth date would have been March 23—the upcoming Easter. Easter, the very source of Anita's hope and mine. Because on Easter we celebrate the resurrection of our Savior, Jesus Christ, who is the hope of the world. Because of Jesus, we can all have hope, we can press on and finish the race strong.

So often I've had people ask, "What's the secret to the success of 40 Days for Life?" They're surprised to learn that it's not due to a marketing plan, organizational structure, leadership philosophy, or strategic use of the Internet, multimedia, and public relations. It's the thousands of ordinary people like Anita who by the grace of God are able to do extraordinary things, to overcome their challenges, so that they can speak up for those who cannot speak for themselves.

Ask yourself this question: *What excuses are holding me back from being everything and doing everything God wants me to be and do?* Now say, *If Anita can do what she has done, in the midst of seemingly insurmountable obstacles, I can certainly do what God is asking me to do.*

I think Anita can end today's story better than I.

"Anita," I asked, "as you endure these challenges, what gives you the hope to carry on?"

Anita didn't hesitate. "I hold on to the hope that someday abortion will be ended. God wants it to end, therefore it will end. He will use us. He will use the least of us, the ones who have nothing. So if you have no money and think you have no talent and therefore have absolutely nothing to offer, please understand that's not true. Never underestimate what God can do with your little. You have a little, he has a lot. He will use anything and everything you have, no matter how big or how little, and he will be glorified."

I have fought the good fight,
I have finished the race,
I have kept the faith.
2 TIMOTHY 4:7

God Almighty, having accepted your Son's sacrifice on my behalf, I in turn present myself to you as a living sacrifice. Thank you for deeming me holy and acceptable because of Christ's shed blood for me. I pray that you would help me to fight the good fight and finish the race. Use me as your vessel to rescue others who are perishing. Amen.

Devanie

David

At 6:01 p.m. on April 4, 1968, a shot fired in Memphis, Tennessee, attempted to silence not only a man but an entire movement.

That bullet ended the life of Dr. Martin Luther King Jr. But it failed to silence the civil rights movement, which pressed forward with renewed determination in a quest for equality and justice. Courageous social reformers refused to be silenced by the attack, and marched onward to the words of the great song, "We Shall Overcome."

On September 22, 2008, a different kind of shot rang out across Memphis—a legal attack meant to stop one person and silence a different movement.

The target of that attack was a eighteen-year-old homeschooled high school student named Devanie Cooper, and the legal action was intended to silence the 40 Days for Life movement in Memphis.

Devanie has more faith and courage than most people I have met, including those much older than she is. When she first learned about 40 Days for Life, she felt that Memphis needed such a campaign outside the Planned Parenthood abortion facility on the third floor of a downtown office building. That facility had aborted 2,305 babies the previous year, according to its annual report.

Devanie began to tell others in Memphis about 40 Days for Life and to share with them a vision for the difference a local campaign could make in the lives of people in their city. People told her again and again, "Are you kidding? We can't even get people to pray outside Planned Parenthood once a month. Do you really think you can line up enough people to pray twenty-four hours a day for forty days?"

Summoning her faith and courage, Devanie answered with a simple yes.

Nobody else shared her vision enough to volunteer to lead that first local 40 Days for Life Campaign, so Devanie signed up to be the Memphis campaign director. She didn't even have a driver's license, so her mother agreed to help transport her to planning meetings, campaign events, and the vigil site.

Devanie assembled a team of dedicated volunteers and, together, they began to prepare for their 40 Days for Life Campaign. When their plans were finalized, they publicly announced that their vigil would be held outside the office building that housed Planned Parenthood.

Word spread throughout Memphis. Soon the local 40 Days team received a threatening email from the owner of the building that leased space to Planned Parenthood.

The owner's message complained about "the financial consequences I will suffer" if the vigil proceeded as planned. He tried to pressure Devanie to move the 40 Days for Life vigil, telling her, "There are other abortion facilities in our area that are free-standing and dedicated for the purpose of abortion rather than our building, which is a multi-tenant building whose businesses would be hurt by such a vigil." He then leveled a threat of legal action. "I do not want to waste our resources on lawyers, and I am sure that is not what your group wants to do either."

Devanie and her team met to discuss the threat and how they should respond. They talked and prayed, and as they did, it became clear to them that their 40 Days for Life efforts were already having an impact. They collectively decided to press forward rather than buckle under this attempt at intimidation.

On September 22, 2008, two days before the first-ever Memphis 40 Days for Life Campaign kicked off, simultaneously with campaigns in 178 other cities across 47 states, Devanie discovered that the building's owner had followed through on his threat. Both she and her 40 Days for Life Campaign were under attack.

The owner filed a lawsuit against Devanie, three other volunteers on her campaign team, and our national 40 Days for Life organization. The legal complaint argued that Devanie's campaign constituted "a Nuisance to and upon the plaintiffs" causing "interference with economic advantage." The suit alleged that the Memphis 40 Days for Life Campaign "will adversely affect and otherwise impair Plaintiff's ability to attract new tenants to the Building and rent vacant space in the building." The lawsuit also claimed that Devanie's actions "will result in current tenants who would ordinarily renew their lease not renewing their lease."

The lawsuit demanded an immediate restraining order against Devanie and 40 Days for Life. It also demanded financial judgments against eighteen-year-old Devanie, her team, and our fledgling 40 Days for Life nonprofit organization "in an amount to be determined as compensatory damages."

Devanie and her team believed that the owner of the building was trying to silence them to avoid publicizing the fact that his company rented space to the largest abortion chain in America. He seemed worried that he would experience economic reprisal if that information became public knowledge.

So the Memphis 40 Days for Life team consulted with me. I put them in touch with the Thomas More Society, an amazing pro bono legal firm that has worked side by side with 40 Days for Life since our beginning.

Chief Counsel Tom Brejcha was furious when he heard about the suit. He encouraged Devanie—and us—to fight back against what he saw as a clear attack on constitutionally protected pro-life free speech. After we talked with Tom, Devanie told me that she and her team were not deterred and they were pressing forward with their campaign as planned. She also told me they were committed to fighting back against the frivolous lawsuit—and win.

On September 24, the Memphis 40 Days for Life Campaign began—and started to grow. More than 450 people participated in the peaceful prayer vigil outside the office building that housed Planned Parenthood. And as the campaign progressed, the legal battle grew hotter. I realized that I needed to travel to Memphis to support Devanie and her team, to prepare for the court battle, and to publicly call upon the building's owner to drop his suit.

On Day 27 of that fall's 40 Days for Life Campaign, I flew into Memphis and drove to the office building where Planned Parenthood continued to abort children.

As I pulled up, ready to speak at a press conference we had hastily organized, my cell phone rang. It was Tom Brejcha from the Thomas More Society. He had talked with the owner's attorneys, he said, and explained to them that he had argued pro-life free speech cases like this all the way to the U.S. Supreme Court on three occasions—and won in each of those cases. He explained that their case had no standing, and that he was asking the judge to dismiss the lawsuit.

The attorneys had quickly consulted with their client, and he had backed down and dropped his lawsuit. I thanked Tom for his help—and for the good news!

Instead of our planned press conference outside the building, we turned the gathering into a brief celebration and time of prayer. Then Devanie and I encouraged all the assembled Memphis 40 Days for Life participants to press on for the final thirteen days of the campaign and finish strong.

I flew home that evening very proud of Devanie and her team of dedicated volunteers. They could have backed down, they could have quit, and everyone would have understood. But they didn't. They were willing to press forward at great personal risk to protect the most fundamental human right—the right to life.

Five lives were saved from abortion during that Memphis 40 Days for Life Campaign.

And there was one more victory yet to come.

The following year, Planned Parenthood's lease came up for renewal. Due to all the controversy and negative publicity resulting from the campaign and from his ill-advised lawsuit, the owner of the building refused to renew the abortion facility's lease. Planned Parenthood had to vacate the building.

The organization immediately began searching Memphis for a new location to house their abortion operation. They found a building—right next door to Memphis Catholic High School—and began trying to secure a lease for the sixth floor. There was a tremendous public outcry against opening an abortion facility there, but Planned Parenthood started contract negotiations anyway.

On December 23, the company that manages that building sent out a letter to its tenants, announcing that Planned Parenthood's proposal had been rejected. "You are hereby advised," the letter read, "the negotiations for Planned Parenthood of Memphis to occupy the sixth floor have ceased and they will not be moving into our building. Several of you expressed reservations and concerns about the possibility of protests and activities regarding their occupancy. These concerns have been heard and reflected in our decision."

Like the gunshot in Memphis that killed Dr. King but failed to daunt the courageous civil rights activists who labored on in the cause he championed, the legal attack against Devanie Cooper failed to stop the 40 Days for Life movement in Memphis. It has continued to grow year after year, protecting many more mothers and saving more than thirty lives from abortion.

Devanie and her faithful volunteers persevered, and their steadfast spirit embodies the spirit of the song, "We Shall Overcome."

What I tell you in the dark, speak in the daylight;
what is whispered in your ear, proclaim from the roofs.
Do not be afraid.
MATTHEW 10:27–28

Lord, help me to be faithful and to overcome whatever challenges come my way as I seek to protect the well-being of God's people. I pray for your continued guidance and protection. May I be steadfast, unmovable, always abounding in your work, knowing that my labor will not be in vain. Amen.

A Little Drama

David

WHAT HAPPENS WHEN PEOPLE PRAY?

God hears and he answers.

He may give us exactly what we seek. Or he may give us something entirely unexpected that accomplishes his will so much better and so much more powerfully than what we'd intended that we can only stand back in awe and give thanks.

That's what happened at a 40 Days for Life vigil outside the Planned Parenthood location in Sioux City, Iowa, during the fall 2008 campaign. As usual, people had gathered to pray. Among the volunteers were Stormy and Mary.

Across the street from the abortion center was a fast-food restaurant, and sitting in the parking lot was a bus with Michigan plates. But the bus wasn't simply waiting for its riders to finish gobbling down their burgers and get back on the bus. They'd finished their burgers some time before. The bus was still sitting there because it was broken down. And it wasn't clear just how soon the replacement bus would arrive.

Sitting and waiting for a new bus was a drama team from a Christian school in Holland, Michigan. Among the players were thirteen children with disabilities.

As she waited, hoping the kids in the drama troupe wouldn't get too bored and begin to misbehave, the assistant director noticed the vigil across the street. Maybe this would be a way to give the kids something to do. And even if not, finding out would give *her* something to do. So she walked over and said, "Is this some kind of demonstration?"

Stormy quickly filled her in on 40 Days for Life and what the volunteers were doing there that night. She pointed out the abortion facility behind the fence and explained what they did there. Then she had questions for the assistant director as well. Who were the kids on the bus, and where were they from? What kind of trip was this? Where had they been, and what had they done there?

When Stormy found out who the kids were and what they did, she had an inspiration. What if the kids put on a play—right then and there?

It sounded like a great idea to the assistant director—for at least two reasons. For one, it would help keep the kids occupied and happy while the replacement bus was en route. Even cheeseburgers, fries, and Coke can keep kids happy just so long!

But there was a second reason. Before the drama team had left their school in their hometown of Holland, Michigan, their principal had told them something. "I don't know when or where, but I have a feeling that, sometime on this trip, you'll give one additional performance, something not listed on your schedule."

To the assistant director, it looked like this would be that performance.

"So they did it!" Mary said. "Right there, facing Planned Parenthood, these special kids and their friends re-enacted the Passion of Christ."

It was the perfect story to enact in that scenario. After all, to augment the prayers and efforts of volunteers standing against the evil of abortion, what could be better than a reminder of the sacrificial death of our own Savior. What better to remind us—and any onlookers and passersby that night—of the innocence of the babies killed through abortion before they had even taken a breath than a portrayal of the death of a sinless Jesus, who had breathed into each of us the breath of life at the Creation?

And to drive that point home even further, as Mary points out,

"The young man who portrayed Jesus had Down syndrome. He stretched out his arms and 'hung on the cross.'"

Another reminder. As Shawn mentioned in a previous chapter, many women and young couples choose abortion because their babies have been diagnosed while still in the womb with disabilities and handicaps. In some cases, that disability is Down syndrome.

Had his mother been so inclined, that young man who portrayed Jesus that night might have been himself aborted. But she chose life. And as a result, there he was, "hanging on the cross," his arms extended—and tears running down his face throughout the performance.

"I weep every time I watch them perform this," the assistant director of the drama team said. "Maybe it's because our 'Jesus' gets so emotional—every single time—that he can't stop crying."

And on this night, if he gave much thought to the circumstances and location of the performance, he'd have had even greater reason for his emotion.

"We're sure glad they were here that night," said Mary. "They were terrific! And they were so pleased to perform for people who respect all life. Their replacement bus arrived just after the kids finished their performance. They got lots of applause and thanks—and they each got a 40 Days for Life bracelet."

What an amazing and unexpected provision God made in response to the prayers of the volunteers on the sidewalk that night. I'm quite sure that none of them were praying, "Lord, please let a bus break down here tonight with a Christian drama troupe to perform a Passion Play right here to underline the high moral stakes of what we're doing." But God is creative enough to envision the answers that would never occur to us. The death of the innocent Lord and Savior—staged in front of Planned Parenthood, an organization responsible for ending hundreds of thousands of innocent lives every year. Performed by children with special needs, upon whom the abortion industry has declared open season. How powerful!

An unexpected answer to prayer. An unexpected joy.
A reminder of our hope.

> *This is what is written:*
> *The Messiah will suffer and rise*
> *from the dead on the third day,*
> *and repentance for the forgiveness of sins*
> *will be preached in his name to all nations,*
> *beginning at Jerusalem.*
> *You are witnesses of these things.*
>
> LUKE 24:46–48

Dear Jesus, what can I say in response to your sacrifice on our behalf? The pain you bore, the anguish of spirit—and you did it all so that we could be reconciled to your father. Thank you for daily reminding me of this, of all the benefits I have in life—and the life to come—because of that sacrifice, and of my privilege to bear witness to the world of all that I have seen. Amen.

A Statistic Named Leia

Shawn

HAVE YOU NOTICED HOW OFTEN THESE DAYS, IN DEBATES, IN media reports, and even among friends and coworkers, we argue issues not through logic, analogies, or real-life examples, but through statistics?

Statistics can help define sobering realities that demand a response. But when we boil everything down to facts and figures, everything—and everyone—can sound like a mere number. But people are not numbers. They are not mere statistics.

Consider the abortion statistics of California.

According to the Guttmacher Institute, there were 214,190 abortions in California in 2008, the most recently reported year. In Los Angeles County alone, there are forty-seven abortion facilities, and Guttmacher reports that each month those facilities are responsible for 1,287 abortions.

One of those forty-seven abortion centers is in La Puente, a suburb in East Los Angeles and the hometown of Yvonne Viramontes.

Yvonne is not only the mother of four beautiful children but also a tireless and relentless champion of the unborn. Yvonne has led five successful 40 Days for Life Campaigns.

The abortion center in La Puente was run by a woman known for managing five other lucrative California abortion facilities. She had a reputation for building up these businesses—increasing revenue. And that's what she was doing in La Puente.

Because of the manager's aggressive, businesslike approach, it seemed that the La Puente abortion center would be around for a very long time. So it was quite a shock when I got an email from Yvonne telling me the place was closing.

You'd think I would stop being surprised when God answers prayer, but this is California we're talking about. I knew the sobering statistics and seemingly insurmountable challenges faced by our local leaders even though California had more 40 Days for Life Campaign locations than any other state.

If you were looking for a lousy place to hold a 40 Days for Life vigil, the La Puente location would fit the bill. The driveway leading up to the building was extremely long. In fact, from the spot along the public right-of-way where prayer volunteers had to stand, you couldn't even see the abortion center. But Yvonne and her group had faithfully held five campaigns there, praying next to a busy street in the hot California sun. As a result, the owner had lost so many "customers" that she could no longer afford to stay in business.

It must have been humiliating for the abortion center director, but more importantly, it was a powerful witness to the simple fact that many potential abortion center clients are looking for help and solutions rather than to end the lives of the children growing inside of them. With Yvonne and her team lovingly offering that help, the owner could no longer make the profit needed to stay in business.

Yvonne planned a victory celebration in front of the closed abortion center and invited David and me to share the joy. We had gotten to know and respect Yvonne through her selfless work with the local 40 Days for Life Campaign, and there was no way we would miss this.

Unfortunately, after checking our calendars, we discovered that there was only one day on which both of us could fly to Los Angeles. And even on that day, the only way it would work was to do something no one in their right mind should do: We would take an early morning direct flight from Washington, D.C., to Los Angeles, participate in the celebration, and then take the red-eye back to Washington—all in the same day.

Exhausting? Yes. But worth it!

We even took a video camera to document the event and to film some interviews with the local volunteers.

When the owners had announced that the facility was closing, they meant it. They had packed up and left immediately. When we arrived, the building was closed and locked, but we could look inside all the windows because they had taken the blinds with them!

As we walked around the building, peering through each dirty window, the evil activities that had taken place in these so-called health centers became even more real for me. And it was gut-wrenching. The owners had left behind the tables equipped with stirrups where the women would lie to have abortions. *No one grows up wanting to lie on those tables*, I thought.

Staring with horror at this room where thousands of little boys' and girls' lives had ended, I wanted to find a way to show this place to the world—to demonstrate that the lives lost and the lives ruined were not just statistics. This evil goes on every single day on tables just like this in a nation where we are promised an inalienable right to life.

David and I lingered, sharing this sobering moment. Then we headed to the celebration to praise God with the volunteers who had stood in peaceful vigil outside this facility. We hadn't been there long when we heard Yvonne calling, "They're here! They're here!"

Who was here? David and I had no idea. But within minutes, we were introduced to a teenage mom and her baby daughter ... and then the baby's grandmother ... and then her great-grandmother.

Marcy, the baby's grandmother, described for us the day her eighteen-year-old daughter, Laura, had said, "Mom, I'm pregnant. But I have a solution. I'm going to have an abortion."

Marcy was stunned—and heartbroken—that Laura had decided so quickly to abort her baby. Marcy immediately called her mom and asked her to pray. Her mother, in turn, contacted a woman at church she thought might be able to help.

That woman was Yvonne Viramontes.

Yvonne telephoned Marcy and said, "I know this news has hit you hard, but have faith. We need to leave this pregnancy in God's hands."

At first that approach didn't seem to be working. Laura had already scheduled an abortion only days away! Marcy tried to talk her out of it. In fact, she even agreed to drive Laura to the abortion center, hoping that, on their way, God would give Marcy the words and provide the answer she was so desperately seeking before it was too late.

Meanwhile, Marcy's mother went to the 40 Days for Life vigil simultaneously taking place outside that very abortion center and begged for help, telling them that her granddaughter was going to have an abortion there that very day. The volunteers joined Marcy's mother in praying specifically for Laura and her baby.

As Marcy and Laura pulled into the facility's driveway, they noticed 40 Days for Life volunteers standing on the sidewalk, quietly and peacefully praying. When Marcy had parked and started to get out of the car, she heard Laura beginning to cry in the backseat.

Through her tears, Laura asked, "Why isn't God telling me what to do? Why do I feel so alone?"

All Marcy could say was, "He *is* telling you what to do—by your tears."

Laura confessed her fear that, if she gave birth to an out-of-wedlock baby, she would be letting her family down.

"If you have an abortion," Marcy replied, "you'll be hurting us far more."

Laura cried for thirty minutes, making no move to get out of the car, while her mom waited and prayed. Silence, sadness, and tears filled the car.

Laura became increasingly agitated with the 40 Days for Life volunteers praying down by the fence, just visible from the parking lot. She snapped at her mom, "Why are they praying so loud?"

Marcy looked out the window at the volunteers. They were at least fifty feet away, on the sidewalk. "Those people are praying silently," she said. "I can't hear them at all. Maybe it's God talking to you."

Those were the words. It was enough. Laura said it was time to leave. There would be no abortion. She couldn't go through with it.

As they drove past the 40 Days for Life volunteers on their way out, one of them approached the car and told Laura they would continue to pray for her and that she had made a courageous decision. "I can't find the words," Marcy told us, "to describe the amazing feeling of being so unexpectedly covered in prayer by so many people."

It is a rare moment when both David and I are left speechless. Just ask our wives. But as Marcy finished her family's story, we both shook our heads, unable to speak. Instead, we simply looked at these four generations of women and realized anew that abortion isn't about numbers. It's about people. And after decades of legalization, abortion isn't just a young person's struggle. It affects multiple generations, as in the family that stood before us that day.

In front of the now-closed abortion facility, Laura, the teenage mother, grinned and held up her daughter, Leia, the result of all that prayer. And Leia gave us a huge, perfectly timed smile. David and I got to take turns holding Leia, treasuring that precious experience.

Laura credits Yvonne's 40 Days for Life volunteers for saving the life of her daughter. As we were leaving, she said, "I love her so much. I can't believe I wanted to abort her. She's my world now."

The smiles on the faces of Baby Leia's loving family and the life in the healthy body of that baby girl are the reasons those 40 Days for Life volunteers endured the persecution and the heat to stand and pray in one of the most pro-abortion parts of our nation. They didn't get discouraged, and they didn't forget who they were fighting for. And on that hot July day they were able to see the results of their steadfast prayers in the life of a smiling baby made in the image and likeness of God. It had taken years of hard work by Yvonne and her volunteers, but it was worth it.

Those smiles, and the memory of the feel of that baby in our arms, reaffirmed to David and me—as we rushed to the airport, gobbling down an In-N-Out Burger—how right it had been to make this trip to Los Angeles even though by the time we boarded it was 2:35 a.m. Eastern time. We'd been up for almost twenty-four hours! We settled into our seats and promptly fell asleep.

Several hours later, when our plane landed in D.C., we talked about La Puente, and the one thing that struck us again and again was this: The beautiful little girl we'd held in our arms had been so close to becoming one of those 1,287 children aborted every month in Los Angeles County—and one of the 3,300 babies aborted every day in America. If that had happened, she *would* have been just a statistic, forgotten by the world except for the guilt and pain left behind for the mother and her family. But instead, being passed from arm to welcoming arm in front of a closed abortion facility, she radiated the love and joy of her creator. And the young mother who'd once thought she had no choice other than abortion now looked at her baby girl's beautiful smile and understood that her world would never be the same.

All the sacrifice that goes into 40 Days for Life—such as the years of standing and praying by Yvonne and her team, the prayers and temporary anguish of Laura and Marcy and their family as they struggled with their situation, the time and other resources devoted to the cause—is worth it.

Baby Leia's smile is all the reminder we need.

The statistics can show us the problem, but they can blind us to the humanity. Today, the blindfold is off, and we see a little girl named Leia.

The light shines in the darkness,
and the darkness has not overcome it.
JOHN 1:5

Father of mercy and grace, thank you for the gift of children. Grant that every fiber of my being may rejoice when a new baby is born into the world. Help me to be, for those newborn, a light shining in the darkness, welcoming them as I would welcome you. For whenever a new baby is conceived, another life to bear your image and another voice to praise and worship you is beginning. Amen.

Her Name Is Miracle

Shawn

SOMETIMES SITUATIONS SEEM SO BLEAK THAT THEY SEEM TO leave no room for hope. In the face of such circumstances, abortion may seem appropriate, responsible, urgent—even compassionate. But things are not always what they seem.

Take Rosa's story for example, which I first heard standing at a 40 Days for Life vigil on a sidewalk in Orange County, California.

Rosa was born in Mexico. In 1989, when she was nineteen, she married her longtime boyfriend, who lived legally in the U.S. and visited her regularly in Mexico. Two weeks after their wedding, the new couple came to the U.S., searching for their American dream. Like so many families, they struggled to make ends meet with sporadic work and meager income. Her husband found work on a night shift, eventually taking a second job. They had two children, and eventually moved into a home of their own. Finally, she believed, their family had a chance to live the American dream—her dream.

That dream was threatened when her husband's longtime drinking problem put them at risk of losing the house. It evaporated when Rosa went to a doctor for a prenatal physical, only to be told that her unborn child had a serious physical handicap. And to make matters worse, Rosa was diagnosed with diabetes.

"You should abort this pregnancy," the doctor told her. "This handicap is severe. For your own sake and for your family, abortion is your best option."

But Rosa did not believe in abortion. She decided to get a second opinion. After examining her, the second doctor told her the same thing. "I'm referring you to Planned Parenthood," he told her.

Devastated and broken, Rosa followed her doctor's instructions and scheduled an abortion at Planned Parenthood. When the day came, she drove to the facility, filled with fear, guilt, and grief. She knew this abortion was wrong, that the child inside her had value and dignity no matter what his or her handicap or circumstances. But Rosa believed she had no alternative; her husband agreed with the doctors about the abortion, and his drinking problem was becoming worse.

By the time they approached the driveway Rosa was trembling. She saw a group of people gathered outside the facility. Many had their heads bowed in prayer. Confused, she wondered what these people were doing there. She read their sign: *40 Days for Life*. She had no idea what that meant, but she was desperate for other options. She stepped out of the car and turned toward this peaceful group of people. Immediately her eyes locked onto the beautiful, smiling face of a volunteer named Alejandra—a face filled with light.

Only God could have brought these people together at this moment, in this location, and in these circumstances. Though I knew nothing of Rosa's story at the time, I had known Alejandra's for years.

As you know by now, when we conducted the first 40 Days for Life Campaign in College Station, Texas, in 2004, we had no idea it would start a movement that would spread beyond our community and around the globe and touch millions of lives. We were simply gathering in prayerful vigil to save lives and end abortion in our own hometown. But one thing led to another, and we launched our first-ever nationally coordinated campaign in the fall of 2007. One of the two California communities that took part was Orange County.

One of the people who helped to launch that first Orange County campaign was Alejandra Baker—one of the most joyful people I have ever met. When you're around her, it's impossible to be in a bad mood. Her love of Christ radiates, and it's no wonder she was able to recruit so many volunteers for her 40 Days for Life Campaign. Her light-filled eyes, her beautifully melodic Spanish accent, and her contagious smile make everyone around her eager to follow her lead.

One abortion center in Orange County seldom had people praying outside—except when 40 Days for Life was there. But Alejandra believed this facility needed a prayer campaign. The volunteers' prayers were heard and answered. Following the spring 2009 campaign, the facility's owners announced that they could no longer remain in operation and closed their doors forever. Alejandra was ecstatic! When she called David and me to share the news, her joy gushed through the phone line.

After this amazing news, Alejandra continued full speed ahead. She chose another Orange County abortion center and announced a new location for their next 40 Days for Life Campaign.

During the spring of 2011, I went out to visit Alejandra's team of volunteers. I had no idea what I was in for. When I pulled up in my rental car, I saw nearly two hundred people out front—and Alejandra running toward me. She greeted me with her typical smile and, speaking ninety miles an hour, said, "Quick! Quick! Quick! You have to meet as many people as you can before you speak!" I was just trying to keep up with her as she guided me through the crowd, introducing me to volunteer after volunteer.

When she introduced me to Marty and Graciela Marinoff, Alejandra glowed even more brightly. Marty and Graciela were holding a baby—Samuel, born a year earlier in the spring of 2010. In the fall of 2009, Samuel's mother had come to that same Planned Parenthood center for an abortion during a 40 Days for Life Campaign. Marty and Graciela were there when she arrived. They spoke to the mom and told her they would help in any way they could, and they meant it. That mom chose life for Baby Samuel.

Marty and Graciela backed up their words with action. They drove that young mom to doctor appointments and helped take her other children to school and other events. They helped put food on the table and even pay a few overdue bills. They supported her after she had the baby as well.

It was no wonder that, when Alejandra introduced me to them, this couple was holding the fruit of all their labor—this beautiful baby boy—in front of the very Planned Parenthood where Samuel had been scheduled to be aborted. They were smiling. Baby Samuel was happy. Marty appeared to be in his late fifties, with a powerful presence—strong, humble, wise, unapologetically faithful to God, with a strong sense of paternal authority each time he spoke.

"Shawn, have you heard about Rosa?" Marty asked me that day. His face grew intense and extremely serious. He pulled me aside so that we would not be overheard. "I want to tell you Rosa's story." And so I learned of Rosa's background and the journey that had brought her to this driveway.

I also heard what happened next. When Rosa stepped out of the car that day and turned toward the pro-lifers, Alejandra immediately recognized her look of desperation and approached her with the tender words the Orange County team have used so many times, telling her that she and the prayer group were there that day because they cared about her and about the unborn child she was carrying, and that they could offer her help and alternatives. That, of course, is exactly what Rosa was longing for. She leapt at their words, asking to know more. Alejandra called Graciela and asked her to pick up her and Rosa and take them to the closest pro-life clinic.

After that appointment, Alejandra and Graciela drove Rosa to meet with a physician in the Los Angeles area who specializes in pregnancies where the baby is severely handicapped. This pro-life doctor showed her a video of Nick Vujicic, a pro-life speaker with no arms or legs. After watching the video Rosa knew she could not abort her baby. She chose life.

"Shawn, it has been only a few weeks since the day we met Rosa," Marty went on, "but she's now receiving top-notch care. And you should see the joy this woman feels about her unborn baby, even though her baby is severely handicapped."

After Marty finished his story, I tried to gather my emotions, which wasn't easy. But I had to give a talk at the closing celebration in just a few minutes at a local church. As I stepped before the crowd, I was thanking God for these heroes who had stepped forward with such willingness to help a mother in crisis and save a life, and I was praying for Rosa and her children, thinking how much I would like to meet her someday.

Just as I wrapped up my talk, I was surprised to see Alejandra stepping to the front of the crowd with another smiling woman at her side.

"I would like to introduce you all to Rosa. Despite learning that her baby will be handicapped, and despite two doctors referring her for an abortion, Rosa chose life. She is now, in these difficult circumstances, putting her baby first." Alejandra stepped back

The crowd immediately jumped to their feet and began cheering and clapping. As they applauded, Rosa's eyes filled with tears; she gave a small, shy smile. I doubted that she had ever received similar affirmation in her entire life. As they cheered and Rosa blushed, I studied this woman. There was no doubt what I saw on her face—it was hope.

A few minutes later I met Rosa myself. She spoke very little English, but as I gave her a hug, tears welled in my eyes as well. I felt extremely humbled to talk to her, to share in that moment when she was receiving such love and affirmation from the prayer volunteers, to see the selfless love of Marty and Graciela, and to know that the unborn child inside of her, with whatever handicap he or she had, would be loved.

A few months later, I was in California for the West Coast Walk for Life in San Francisco and saw Alejandra at the 40 Days for Life Leader Workshop. I just had to know—"How is Rosa doing?"

"Rosa gave birth to a beautiful baby girl," she said. "The baby girl has no legs and has a cleft palette, but she is happy. Rosa's happy. Marty and Graciela have continued to help her get her life back on track. She's doing great."

My heart filled with joy. "What did she name her baby girl?" I asked.

Alejandra smiled. "She named her Milagros—Miracle."

And indeed, she is.

> *For now we see only a reflection as in a mirror;*
> *then we shall see face to face.*
> *Now I know in part; then I shall know fully,*
> *even as I am fully known.*
> *And now these three remain: faith, hope and love.*
> *But the greatest of these is love.*
>
> I CORINTHIANS 13:12–13

O God, our heavenly Father, give me courage and wisdom. Help me to realize that your divine Spirit alone can change hearts and minds so that all your human creatures may enjoy the fullness of life you intended for them. Amen.

There's No Place Like Home

Shawn

REGARDLESS OF WHERE IT IS OR WHAT DENOMINATION IT IS, *every* church has the lady who's involved with everything and everyone in the church, who seems to do more than everyone else. Everyone knows this woman—and everyone loves her.

When I lived in College Station, Texas, this woman at my church was Meredith Olson.

Meredith did missionary work. She helped the poor. She taught classes and led prayer groups. She was also the Respect Life coordinator at the parish and would go out frequently and pray at our local Planned Parenthood abortion facility. In fact, I'm sure there wasn't a week that went by when Meredith Olson, in her sixties, wasn't there praying for an end to abortion.

One day Meredith stopped by my office and told me about something that had happened to her that day while she was on the sidewalk praying. Someone driving by had heckled her.

If you've participated in any 40 Days for Life vigils, you know that incidents like this aren't unusual. Sometimes people drive by and show you their middle finger. (I guess if we wanted to give them the benefit of the doubt, we could assume they're just telling you you're number one!) Sometimes they scream at you or tell you to get a life.

On the day Meredith came into my office to tell me what had happened, the U.S. was still in the middle of the Iraq War and she'd been out there praying alone, as she often was, on a Friday afternoon.

"Shawn, a car drove by, slowed, and the man driving screamed at me, "Why don't you do something useful? Do something about the children in Iraq!"

Unlike that heckler, I knew Meredith's story and understood the complete absurdity of anyone telling Meredith she should do more for people on the other side of the globe. He was implying that Meredith wasn't doing enough for the children of the world. Little did he know that both Meredith and her husband had done more than he could imagine, more than most of us could imagine, for other parts of the world. Both had served the CIA as spies in the Soviet Union during the Cold War.

Meredith's husband, Jim, served in the CIA station in Moscow and later became chief of counterintelligence. They lived much of their marriage undercover and involved in espionage and covert action, always in danger from the KGB. Jim shares these experiences in his book *Fair Play: The Moral Dilemmas of Spying*. They raised their children in that environment. They devoted their lives to bringing peace to our world and eventually saw the end of the Cold War in the late 1980s. They're even featured in the spy museum in Washington, D.C.! So when Meredith told me what the heckler said, I almost laughed out loud at the rich irony.

But Meredith's face was very serious. I could tell that the driver's comment had bothered her. After all, this was a woman who wants to do everything for everyone, who rushed to help anyone in need. I could just imagine her standing there on the sidewalk, thinking, *Should I be doing more for Iraqi children?* But then Meredith leaned forward, her eyes determined, and I knew she was about to tell me what she had decided in the face of his challenge.

She looked at me and said very simply, "Today I can't do anything about the children in Iraq. But I can do something about the children here."

I have quoted Meredith ever since. She put her finger on something very important. Yes, abortion is a problem worldwide. But we can't save the world all at once. We have to focus locally—one woman and one child at a time. There is no place like home to make a difference in the world.

Jim and Meredith have lived all around the world; they each speak multiple languages. Their lives have been dangerous and exciting, and most who hear their amazing story of keeping their faith in the midst of such evil are inspired by these heroes. They know what it is to put their lives in harm's way for global problems. Yet their humble approach to fighting abortion is reflected in Meredith's simple comment. And her response challenges every one of us.

Abortion is a global problem with a local solution. We fight it at a local level.

And that brings us to Walker, Minnesota.

Walker is in northern Minnesota, the state with ten thousand lakes. Walker has a population of nine hundred—a small town, obviously, but that didn't stop them from applying to run a 40 Days for Life Campaign.

We asked them where they planned to hold their vigil. Most 40 Days for Life vigils are held outside surgical abortion centers, many of which are Planned Parenthood facilities. Others are held outside Planned Parenthood satellite offices that administer chemical abortions through RU-486 and refer for surgical abortions. But Walker, with only nine hundred residents, had neither—no abortion provider and no referral office. In fact, there wasn't one within a hundred miles. But the local volunteers still wanted to do a 40 Days for Life Campaign. They chose a central, visible location they hoped would bring awareness and prayer to their community around the issue of abortion: the county courthouse.

If they had no abortion provider, why did they need a vigil? It's easy to see why places like New York City, with the highest abortion rate in the world, or Los Angeles County, where 1,287 abortions take place every month, need a vigil (or several) and a strong local presence. It would have been easy for the people of Walker, Minnesota, to look at those cities and think, *Sure, abortion is an American problem, but not where we live. We live in quaint, beautiful, quiet*

Walker, Minnesota, where people vacation on the weekend up from the Twin Cities and Brainerd. Most of us have never even met some-one who has had an abortion!

Cass County, where Walker is located, in their last reported year had twenty-eight residents who left town to procure abortions elsewhere—in the entire year. At many of our vigil sites, there are twenty-eight abortions *every day*—or at least every week.

But the people in Walker don't live in Los Angeles, New York, Houston, or Chicago. And they wanted to do something about abortions in Cass County. Twenty-eight abortions in a year was twenty-eight too many for the people of Walker. Imagine if, instead, it had been twenty-eight teenagers dying from suicide or twenty-eight children dying as a result of drunk drivers. There would have been a universal outcry and calls for a major campaign to fight suicide or drunk driving.

How would the volunteers in Walker reach women like those twenty-eight? With a vigil in front of the courthouse.

Local 40 Days for Life campaigns have an option: They can hold their vigil twelve hours a day or up to twenty-four hours a day. You don't have to be a Weather Channel junkie to know that it gets cold in Minnesota. But that didn't bother the folks in Walker. They committed to a twenty-four-hour-a-day vigil outside their courthouse, holding peaceful signs and spreading awareness about the reality of abortion in their community.

And boy, did their campaign take off! Even with a population of only nine hundred people, they drew 1,328 participants! And a number of groups and churches throughout Cass County and the surrounding area pitched in to participate and support them.

That first campaign was so successful that they decided to do another, and another, and another. They did a 40 Days for Life Campaign every year after that. They took pride in the patch of dead grass where the Walker prayer volunteers stood outside their courthouse; it represented Walker's love for life.

During the winter of 2010, I was invited to speak at an event I will cherish forever. The dedicated people of Walker had generated so much interest and local support that they were able to create and staff a full-service pregnancy resource center; they could now offer free pregnancy tests and help to pregnant women in their region. They asked me to speak at their first banquet that spring.

I landed in Minneapolis and was picked up by a volunteer. As we drove up to Walker, I asked the driver, "What are those big white fields we keep passing?"

He laughed and said, "Those aren't fields. Those are the lakes."

The lakes were still frozen! It was April, for crying out loud! Boy, did I feel like a greenhorn in the frozen northern Midwest.

I was amazed at how much activity was taking place out on those frozen lakes. Walking, camping—and I saw a football game on a lake for the first time. It all gave a whole new meaning to walking on water.

After hearing the stories about Walker, I pictured the town as most of you probably picture it—no traffic signal but a four-way stop, maybe a gas station, the courthouse, and that's the extent of Walker. Well, it was bigger than I'd expected, and it was surrounded by beautiful lake resorts. Still, I assumed that because of the size of the town, there would be sixty, eighty, maybe even a hundred people max at the banquet.

I was blown away when I arrived in Walker and spoke in front of a crowd of 350 people at the first-ever banquet for their new pregnancy resource center. That was over a third of their population!

The center was already operational and had served a number of women. They even reported that they had saved a few lives. There was incredible excitement in that room about all they would now be able to do for the unborn and their mothers.

And it had all started when Beth Bohannon, the local 40 Days for Life leader in Walker, had felt the same reaction to the problem of abortion as Meredith had down in College Station, Texas. *I can't do anything today about the children who live far away. But I can do something for mothers and children in need locally—right here and right now.*

It's so easy to make abortion somebody else's problem, something the government should take care of, something this church or that church should take responsibility for. But as local citizens, as faithful believers, it is our responsibility to do something locally. Meredith Olson knew that. And Beth in Walker, Minnesota, knew that.

Walker has always been known for their lakes, frozen and unfrozen. But now they're known for something else. They're known for standing up for what is good in their local community. They're known for defending life, even when most people would look at their community and say there's no need. They took those twenty-eight abortions a year in their county personally, and the worn-down grass in front of their courthouse bears witness to their commitment and sacrifice. They did something about it, and God blessed that effort.

Abortion in your town, your county, your state, your country, and on your planet is the problem. You are the local solution.

Now is your time of grief, but I will see you again
and you will rejoice, and no one will take away your joy.
In that day you will no longer ask me anything.
Very truly I tell you, my Father will give you
whatever you ask in my name.

JOHN 16:22–23

Almighty Father, you are the author of life. It's easy to become discouraged as I see evil becoming commonplace around me. Remind me, when discouragement takes over, that you have promised to give us what we ask in your name. That gives me, and those of us who serve you, the capacity to change the world and trust you with the results. Let me use that privilege in such a way that the world may see you glorified. Amen.

Unexpected Welcome

Shawn

ANYTIME WE FIND OURSELVES ENGAGED IN SOMETHING NEW OR controversial, we face a certain level of fear. That's normal. Overcoming that fear takes a lot of prayer, a mustard seed of faith, and usually an action step.

This was true of Gerry Brundage in Sherman, Texas.

Sherman is a community about an hour north of the Dallas/Fort Worth area. In the summer of 2010, Gerry was feeling called to lead a fall campaign, what would be the Sherman area's first 40 Days for Life Campaign. He prayed about it and mentally accepted the challenge. But just as he was about to apply to host 40 Days for Life, Gerry—and these are his exact words—"chickened out."

Suddenly, it just sounded like too much work, too much sacrifice. He blinked. And then the opportunity was gone.

Gone, at least, until the following spring, when campaign applications opened again. This time, he found the strength to file his application. *No matter what,* he thought, *this is it. I'm going to do it.*

Thus Gerry launched a campaign that would change him and his community forever.

That change didn't take long. It began the first week of the campaign when the Planned Parenthood center manager walked out the front door, approached a female volunteer standing near Gerry, and said with great interest, "This is a 40 Days for Life Campaign, isn't it?"

Gerry was stunned. *Isn't she supposed to be hostile and angry?* he wondered. *She seems happy—almost glad to see us.*

What Gerry didn't know was that, while he'd been wrestling with the idea of hosting a 40 Days for Life Campaign, Planned Parenthood manager Ramona Trevino had begun struggling with her conscience to justify her work with Planned Parenthood.

Her job as manager of this Planned Parenthood facility had seemed like a very good thing to Ramona at first. It allowed her to spend a couple of days a week at home with her young son, the pay was good, and she liked the sense of satisfaction and accomplishment that came from being in charge of something she considered important.

But increasingly, as the years went by, something was becoming clear to Ramona, and it bothered her greatly. She had always justified her participation with Planned Parenthood by telling herself that her facility did not perform surgical abortions. But she found it harder and harder to deny that Planned Parenthood was America's largest abortion chain, responsible for the death of more than three hundred thousand unborn children each year.

She found herself, again and again, pressured to counsel women to abort and referring them for abortions. Planned Parenthood's primary interest, she finally admitted, was increasing their abortion numbers.

At about that time, Ramona started listening to Catholic radio—something Planned Parenthood would have likely never expected from one of its managers. Ramona had grown up Catholic, but as an adult she had drifted away from her childhood faith. Now she found that Catholic radio was giving her a number of things to think about, including the testimony of Abby Johnson.

Abby had been the director of the Planned Parenthood abortion facility that was the site of the first-ever 40 Days for Life Campaign in College Station, Texas. It was during the 40 Days for Life Campaign in the fall of 2009 that Abby quit her job and became an outspoken pro-life advocate.

Ramona was intrigued by Abby's story. As Ramona listened to the points Abby made about Planned Parenthood that had caused her to resign, she realized Abby was listing many of the same things that had been troubling Ramona. She felt like Abby was talking directly to her.

She also heard on the radio that a 40 Days for Life campaign was scheduled for the public right-of-way in front of Ramona's facility!

So when the day came that Ramona looked out her office window and saw volunteers bowing their heads silently in prayer, her heart leapt.

"This is a 40 Days for Life Campaign, isn't it?" she asked the volunteer.

After a few moments of shocked silence, the volunteer said, "Well, yes, it *is* a 40 Days for Life Campaign."

Gerry joined the conversation. "I'm the local coordinator here in Sherman, and this is our first campaign. It's good to meet you."

Ramona said, "I have to tell you something. Working here has really started to bother me. I've even thought of getting out."

This was all coming at Gerry awfully fast. The last thing he'd expected was to be enthusiastically welcomed by the facility director. "Have you heard of Abby Johnson?" he asked.

"Yes!" Ramona said. "I heard her story on the radio."

"Hold on a minute," he said. "I'll be right back." He walked a few feet to his car and picked up a copy of Abby Johnson's book *UnPlanned,* which had been released just six weeks earlier. He gave Ramona the book.

She took it home and read it. As soon as she'd finished, she came back to where Gerry stood praying on the sidewalk in front of her Planned Parenthood facility and said, "I can't do this any more. I have to get out. My conscience won't allow me to work in the abortion industry."

This was all new ground for Gerry, and he wasn't sure what to do. He wanted advice—quickly. He called me, and I put him and Ramona in touch with Lauren Muzyka, a member of the 40 Days for Life national team who lives in the Dallas area.

Not long after, I was on a plane to Sherman myself. I spoke with volunteers at the vigil, even gave a short talk on the sidewalk, but

I didn't get to meet Ramona in person. I later learned that she was sick that day and had wanted to meet me but couldn't.

A few weeks later, Ramona was ready to resign her job. She called me at a hotel in Carson City, Nevada, where I was staying in preparation to speak at a pro-life event. "I have the draft resignation letter," she said. "I want you to look at it." She emailed it to me, and it looked great. The only thing left for her to do was deliver it. I asked her to let me know when it was sent.

That afternoon, I waited to hear from her. And I waited some more. Then I started to worry. What if she had "chickened out"? She'd have had good reason—after all, she needed a job so she could help take care of her family. But I had a speech to prepare, so I turned my attention to it and turned the rest over to God.

Later that night, after my speaking engagement, I checked my phone and saw that there was a voicemail from Ramona.

"Shawn, I'm free at last! I can't tell you the weight I feel lifted off my shoulders! I am finally free and don't have to be embarrassed about telling people where I work. I am free!"

You could hear the joy in her voice. And like Ramona, I was ecstatic.

Ramona had turned full circle back to her faith. She had trusted God and was now soaking in the freedom that he gives the soul. She wasn't concerned about being without a job, or what her friends would think, or what those who worked with her at Planned Parenthood would think. She had proclaimed her freedom from all these things.

Great story, right? But that's not the end!

Ramona's conversion impacted her entire local community. After she resigned her position, month after month went by with Planned Parenthood unable to hire a replacement in the managerial position.

Starting with Day 1 of that first 40 Days for Life Campaign in Sherman, and continuing even after the campaign ended, business had been declining at this Planned Parenthood facility. It was struggling to break even, a problem compounded by the lack of a manager. Then the Texas legislature and Governor Rick Perry defunded Planned Parenthood of tens of millions of tax dollars across the state.

Something had to give. And on August 21, 2011, it gave.

Planned Parenthood of Sherman, Texas, closed its doors for good.

In part because one woman had a change of heart and had the courage to get away from the abortion industry, that Planned Parenthood facility is no longer operating in Sherman.

Gerry hastily organized a rally outside that office on the day it closed, and David Bereit flew in to participate and to speak to the volunteers. But the keynote speaker that day was Ramona Trevino. She thanked the people who had prayed—and loved—her out of Planned Parenthood. And she thanked God for closing the facility she used to manage.

I often think of Gerry's description of himself as "chickening out" in the fall of 2010. In retrospect, I don't think he chickened out at all. He'd felt the inspiration to bring 40 Days for Life to Sherman, and that was the right inspiration. But with prayer and reflection, he no longer felt a peace about doing it *at that time*. It wasn't God's time.

And now that we know what Ramona was going through during 2010 and its effect on her conscience—all of it unknown to Gerry, of course—it becomes clear that a spring 2011 campaign time frame was much more in sync with God's perfect will.

Today there's a large, well-staffed pregnancy resource center just down the street from where Planned Parenthood *used* to be—a free, local option for moms who don't know where to turn—again, in part because of one heart being changed.

After that spring 2011 40 Days for Life Campaign, if Gerry had wanted to lead a *second* 40 Days for Life Campaign the following fall, he couldn't have done it in Sherman. He would have had to go closer to Dallas to find the nearest Planned Parenthood office or abortion center! And in fact, he *has* now taken part in 40 Days for Life efforts in the Dallas area.

One step of faith, one mustard seed's worth, really can move mountains.

Gerry was hesitant at first to take that necessary first step. Who could blame him? But he took it—and just look what God did!

We may lack faith in the beginning and begin to sink just as Peter did when Christ invited him to get out of the boat and walk on the water. But we have to take that step, trust God, and know that with him all things are possible—even changing the most unpredictable hearts and minds.

> *"Truly I tell you, if you have faith as small as*
> *a mustard seed, you can say to this mountain,*
> *'Move from here to there,' and it will move.*
> *Nothing will be impossible for you."*
> MATTHEW 17:20

Lord, so often I commit my actions to you but do not trust what you promise to do with them. Too often I doubt the results you will provide from my tiny faith and simple actions. Please give me the humility to trust you with my small efforts and the courage to overcome my doubts. Amen.

The Other Georgia

David

My heart skipped a beat when I realized the email I was reading had been sent from the former Soviet state of Georgia. The realization that 40 Days for Life, a ministry born out of a few friends praying for God's intervention in the abortion crisis in one Texas town, is now a global movement still amazes me.

Most 40 Days for Life Campaigns thus far have taken place in the United States. But not all—in fact, we've had wonderfully encouraging campaigns in more than a dozen other countries, and 40 Days is continuing to spread internationally at a very rapid pace.

The day was November 22, 2010, and the email was from Carolyn Rice in Tbilisi, Georgia—a former Soviet state bordered by Armenia, Azerbaijan, Turkey, and Russia. Carolyn, we later discovered, is a transplanted South Carolinian who had connections in the former Soviet-bloc countries because of her father's business and who moved to Georgia for ministry. She fell in love with the country and felt called to stay. Carolyn's email shared her vision.

We would very much like to be able to register for the spring 40 Day campaign as early as possible, as we will need much time for translation.

Our team will be translating into two languages—Georgian and Russian, and we will share our Russian translation with the Russian-speaking population of other participating countries ...

We believe God has big plans for us and we really want to seek Him through prayer and fasting. Of course, we are doing some

191

of that already, but we want to join with our brothers and sisters around the world at the same time for the spring campaign.

We were, of course, thrilled at their interest. The situation in Georgia is unique—and frightening. According to reports from the World Health Organization and the abortion industry's Guttmacher Institute,[8] Georgia and its neighbors Armenia and Azerbaijan have the highest abortion rates in the world. Abortion is actually the most common form of birth control there. Surprisingly, most abortions there take place after marriage—although in the past decade the numbers of sexually active unmarried girls has increased sharply, resulting in increasing numbers of teenage abortions.

The figures from the Centers for Disease Control and Prevention are even more frightening: Abortions in Georgia average 3.1 *per woman*, highest in the world. And it's likely even worse than that, possibly even several times that number, according to local experts, who explain that abortions in facilities are underreported and many abortions are performed by private physicians.

In the months after Carolyn's initial email, it quickly became apparent that a 40 Days for Life Campaign in a former-Soviet-bloc, European country like Georgia would look very different from a campaign in the U.S., with our guaranteed freedoms. In March of 2011, I heard from Carolyn again:

We had a problem about our vigil and will make a final decision this morning about what to do. Last week we received permission from the Mayor's office to hold our vigil in front of Tbilisi Medical University. Then we went to meet the Rector to tell him what we are doing, and explain we are not protesting against the university but holding a peaceful vigil to pray for an end to abortion. The Rector was not available and we explained everything to his assistant ...

Over the weekend we received angry phone calls from the Rector saying we could NOT stand anywhere near his university and that he doesn't care about the permission we received from the Mayor. What he was saying revealed his assumptions that we would be blocking traffic, yelling with bullhorns, leaving trash and so forth (this is what happens when the opposition party holds political demonstrations) . . . He refused to calm down and listen to our explanation. He just yelled and hung up.

So we went back to the Mayor's office yesterday morning to ask advice or choose an alternative place. We don't want unnecessary conflict. The Mayor's office sent our request to the human rights department, and they gave us another letter saying we have the right to stand there or in front of Parliament, as long as we don't block entrances or traffic. Furthermore, the letter expressed their happiness that someone is doing this kind of project in their country.

Carolyn and her team decided to stage their vigil in front of the Parliament building on Rustaveli Avenue, in part because of its strategic location. Rustaveli is the city's main street, and they would be holding their vigil across the street from an Orthodox church and between a large school and the Pioneer Center, which holds many classes for young people.

With the location settled, next Carolyn and her team needed to sign up volunteers. They were hoping they'd have enough for a round-the-clock, forty-day vigil, and by the time the vigil began they had at least two volunteers for every time slot—and often several more!

The vigil began, and ministry opportunities abounded. First, there were the children. Carolyn's team was able to obtain plastic fetal models at eight different stages of development, ranging from seven weeks up to seven-and-a-half months, and children on their way to school would spot the models and drag their sometimes-reluctant mothers along to see them. Girls would cradle the models like dolls. The message was not lost on these young hearts and minds—these were babies, not blobs of tissue.

While the kids played with the models, counselors would engage the adults who'd accompanied them. This was when the dual role of the vigil in Georgia became clear. Yes, they were there to make a statement against abortion. But they were also there to provide outreach and encourage healing among women who had already had many abortions. The emotional scars from those abortions were visible in the haunted eyes of many of the women who stopped.

"Women would come by and say, 'Oh, how many abortions I've done!'" Carolyn explained. "We would see their tears and their pain and have an opportunity to offer them the healing we know is available through Jesus Christ. So we gave out lots of brochures about our healing program."

One of the surprises of the program for Carolyn and her team was how many men responded—and in a variety of ways. Not all men, of course—many hurried past the display, insisting that abortion is a women's issue. But Carolyn recalls handing one man a brochure and telling him that men have a lot to do with a woman's decision to abort. As he began to read of post-abortion hurt in men, tears came into his eyes. Soon he and Carolyn began to talk.

"My wife and I already had four sons," he said. "And then she got pregnant again. We could not afford to feed one more. I was angry —but mostly because I was frightened. I insisted on an abortion. Afterward, my wife didn't seem to suffer from it."

Or did she simply hide her pain from him? Carolyn wondered.

"But I thought about it often," he said. "Some days I couldn't get it out of my mind, what we had done. I thought I was the only man who had these feelings—and now—" he waved the brochure—"you tell me that other men feel this too!"

Carolyn was able to guide him toward opportunities for counseling and healing.

"One of our participants," Carolyn continued, "is a very godly Christian man. Before he became a believer, two girls got pregnant by him, and both had abortions. He said he just felt it was their problem. After coming to Christ, he sought out those girls and deeply apologized for using them sexually and then abandoning them. He said he often wonders about his babies—realizing now that they were his own flesh and blood as well as that of his girlfriends, and how impossible it seems now that at the time he just thought of it as 'their' problem."

Other men volunteered to hang around the vigil site long into the evening, after their own time slot had long passed, as a safety measure for the women who prayed there at night. And, as Carolyn said, "We were so thankful to have some godly men who stood in the evening hours who talked with young men—some teenagers, others university students in their early twenties—about their relationships with unmarried girls."

There was heartache as well as encouragement. "I have also grieved so much," Carolyn explained, "as I heard women who came with their sons or daughters talking right in front of their children about how they wanted to abort them, and how difficult it is for them now to have these children. These lovely children constantly hearing about how they are unwanted! I try as often as I can to use the little Georgian I know and tell them that they are precious, planned for, and beloved by God. Valuable beyond measure. Oh how I pray that we can change this culture of death into a culture of life. We also regularly have street children coming by, getting their little dose of love for the day. So many desperate needs, and so few of us."

How effective was the vigil in Tbilisi? Since it wasn't held in front of an abortion facility, providing help for women arriving for their abortions, its impact is a bit difficult to gauge in numbers—although Carolyn and her team do know their effort saved the lives of at least four precious Georgian babies that otherwise would have been aborted. But this vigil may have had even wider-reaching impact in other ways.

Because of its site in front of the Parliament building, reporters often stopped for a story. Carolyn was interviewed by one of Georgia's major television stations. That same station also interviewed a woman who had been helped by a post-abortion healing program. So the word of what they were doing got out to a nation woefully uninformed about the true nature of abortion and the alternatives to it.

"One of our biggest successes with 40 Days," Carolyn insisted, "is uniting churches. We had at least some participation from every denomination in Tbilisi, and many people commented on what an important step this was. It was really unprecedented."

It was also a crucial first step in bringing the message of life to a region of the world where that message is sorely needed. "I've talked with people from Spain, Azerbaijan, Iran, Holland, Germany, and other countries," Carolyn said. "So who knows where the message may spread!"

So today, join us in praying for Carolyn Rice, her co-laborers in Tbilisi, and the men, women, and children wounded by abortion in the far-off country of Georgia—as well as the many millions more who are negatively affected by this crisis around the world every single year.

Just as the sun illuminates the entire world, may the light of hope in Christ pierce the darkness of abortion in every nation.

He said to them: ..."But you will receive power
when the Holy Spirit comes on you;
and you will be my witnesses in Jerusalem,
and in all Judea and Samaria,
and to the ends of the earth."

ACTS 1:7–8

Dear Lord and Savior, Earth is a huge planet, with billions of people, and it's easy to be daunted by the prospect of combatting abortion in all the places where it's practiced around the world. Remind me, when I feel overwhelmed by the task, of people like Carolyn Rice. There is a motivated, energetic army already on the ground, waiting for the call, everywhere this battle must be waged. Help more people in every nation answer that call. Where the need is greatest, that is where you have provided most abundantly, and I thank you. Amen.

Jakai

David

FROM THE VERY BEGINNING OF 40 DAYS FOR LIFE, I HAD A SECRET wish: I wanted to meet at least one baby whose life had been spared from abortion because of 40 Days for Life.

Many local 40 Days for Life volunteers have had this privilege. But my role is different—I travel from city to city, encouraging leaders, training and encouraging volunteers, and speaking at pregnancy resource centers and right to life events, to community leaders, to the media. I rarely stay at one 40 Days for Life event for more than a few hours before moving on to the next city or town.

By the time we'd been conducting national 40 Days for Life Campaigns for two years—from 2007 until 2009—my wish had still not yet come true. I had traveled to hundreds of cities and spoken to tens of thousands of people across dozens of states. I had spent many nights away from my family. And when my wife, Margaret, and our children traveled with me, we had eaten far more drive-through fast food than any human should, and we had stayed in far too many cheap, dingy hotels for too few hours of sleep.

Every time I heard a story of abortions averted, babies saved—whether I heard it in person, by telephone, or by email—I thanked God. I treasured each victory of life over death. But my heart still silently ached to *meet* that one baby saved, that one mother restored, through the sacrifices of so many.

When the spring 2009 40 Days for Life Campaign was nearing its end, I stopped at home to see my family briefly before heading back out on my final road trip of the campaign. On my last evening home, Margaret and I finally had the chance for a few uninterrupted moments together after I had finished packing for my departure the next morning. I took her hand, led her to the couch, and we eased down for a quiet conversation.

"Margaret, I'm tired," I said. "I'm running on fumes. And I really wish I didn't have to leave you and the kids tomorrow."

Margaret has an amazing ability to read my heart and prompt me to open up. She sensed my exhaustion and prompted me with a few questions about the trip so far. She listened intently as I described the volunteers I'd met and the amazing events I'd seen unfolding in city after city. Watching her eyes light up, my energy grew with each story, and before long we were marveling at how God was moving across the nation through 40 Days of Life.

Then Margaret, her mission accomplished, grew quiet and serious, and in her gentlest voice she assured me, "David, this is what we've been called to do. You need to finish this campaign strong."

Restored and affirmed, I left early the next morning and drove to events in Connecticut, then New York State, then worked my way through Pennsylvania. I stopped in Harrisburg on Day 38 of the campaign. The night I arrived, I was scheduled to speak at a banquet for a pregnancy resource center. I would visit the 40 Days for Life vigil site early the next morning.

At the banquet, just before I was to speak, the host introduced a woman to share her testimony of how this pregnancy resource center had helped her—and her baby. As the woman stepped up to the microphone, I could see her hands shaking as she looked out over the large audience, trying to find her voice. But the faces in the audience were warm and smiling, and finally, voice shaking a bit, she told her story.

Months earlier, facing an unexpected pregnancy and feeling scared and desperate, she scheduled an abortion at the Harrisburg abortion facility. On the day of her appointment, she parked her car, walked from the parking lot down the sidewalk, and was just opening the door of the facility to go in when she glanced out toward the street and saw a few people praying there.

One of those people quietly praying was a woman named Karen.

Karen was participating in her very first 40 Days for Life Campaign. For years, as a post-abortive woman, Karen had thought, *I can't go out there and tell people not to do something I did. I can't tell them not to have an abortion when I aborted my own child.* But on that particular day, she'd felt that she *needed* to go. So she stood there, praying, holding a simple sign.

As that mother was opening the door of the abortion center that day, the face she saw was Karen's, and the sign she read was Karen's sign: **My abortion hurt me.**

The two women's eyes met.

Across the yard that separated them, Karen said to her, "There are better choices than the one you're about to make. I will help you."

That was all it took. The mom slammed the abortion facility door shut and ran down the sidewalk and into the public right-of-way. She fell into Karen's arms, tears streaming down her face. "I need so much help," she sobbed.

"Karen and the other 40 Days for Life volunteers took me to the local pregnancy resource center that day," the woman said from the podium that night. "And the Christian community surrounded me—people I'd never met before. They supported me through my pregnancy and the birth. And even after my baby was born, they continued to help me." The woman had found her voice by now. No longer trembling, she beamed, and the audience beamed back.

"Now I'd like you to meet my little baby boy. I named him Jakai."

In the back of the room a woman stood with Jakai in her arms. She carried him up onto the stage and laid him in his mother's arms. There wasn't a dry eye in the house. People stood and applauded this mother for having the courage to say yes to life even in difficult circumstances. I clapped along, of course. But at the same time I was applauding God, who was, tonight, responding to my longing to meet a child saved from abortion through the efforts of 40 Days for Life. It was all I could do to collect myself and steady my voice so that I could address the crowd after this mother shared her courageous testimony.

When the program ended, the excited crowd pressed in on me. By the time I'd spoken to everyone waiting to speak to me, the volunteers were stacking the chairs and tables. I scanned the room and thought I'd burst with joy when I saw that mother move toward me, baby Jakai in her arms.

"Mr. Bereit!" she called as she approached. "Thank you. Thank you for what 40 Days for Life has meant to me. And thank you for what it has meant for Jakai."

I just shook my head. "It wasn't me. It was Karen. It was the local volunteers. It was the Holy Spirit. I've never even *been* to Harrisburg before."

Smiling broadly, she simply said, "Wouldn't you like to hold little Jakai?"

She laid her beautiful, smiling, precious baby boy in my arms. As proud and happy as that mother was that night, I don't think she had any way of knowing what that moment meant to me, or how long I had waited for it, as I felt little Jakai's weight in my arms.

As I held him, I realized how close he'd come to being an abortion statistic. What if people hadn't been praying that day? What if Karen hadn't overcome her worries and gone out with her simple sign? What if there hadn't been a 40 Days for Life? What if there hadn't been a pregnancy resource center around the corner? What if Christians hadn't been willing to support Jakai and his mother? The answer to each of those questions was the same: If not for faithful people willing to pray and then put their faith into action—*people just like you*—then this little boy would not be alive today.

Jakai's brown eyes twinkled as he studied my face. This was the moment I'd been awaiting for more than two years. Holding this little guy was worth everything I had gone through—the challenges, the greasy fast food and shabby motel rooms, the persecution, the lost sleep, and the long, lonely miles. All worth it in that instant.

If you haven't yet had the incredible blessing of holding a boy or girl in your arms, a child made in God's image and likeness, who is alive because of you—then I pray that one day you, too, will get to experience that amazing blessing. Then you'll also know—it's worth it.

For you created my inmost being;
you knit me together in my mother's womb.
I praise you because I am fearfully and wonderfully made;
your works are wonderful, I know that full well.

PSALM 139:13-14

Heavenly Father, thank you for knitting me together in my mother's womb, and for doing the same for every member of our human family. Never let me take for granted the gift of children, all of whom are fearfully and wonderfully made in your image. Make me a faithful steward of these precious lives so that each generation might be raised in the nurture and admonition of the Lord. Amen.

Deep in the Heart of Texas

Shawn

"DOES MY BABY HAVE A HEARTBEAT?" THE TENDER-HEARTED Texas woman asked the nurse this question while she was lying on a surgical table, vulnerable, just moments before her abortionist was about to begin.

And she asked this question "deep in the heart of Texas."

The *Roe v. Wade* case, the lawsuit that launched the 1973 U.S. Supreme Court decision that made abortion legal in the United States, also originated in Texas. Who would have dreamt at the time of that landmark case that the story of abortion in America would lead, thirty-five years later, right back to the Lone Star State, to the birth of 40 Days for Life, which now offers new hope to so many communities around the world?

Since 1991, two-thirds of all abortion facilities in America have closed. Yes, you read that right! Local movements, including the proliferation of pregnancy resource centers offering free alternatives and assistance for women, have made huge strides in providing real resources for women and their children during and after pregnancy. In fact, pregnancy resource centers now outnumber abortion providers three to one in America today.

As great as this news is, there is some bad news as well. These trends influenced Planned Parenthood to begin building massive abortion facilities in large metropolitan areas. The first of this size, in Aurora, Illinois, a suburb of Chicago, was built in 2007 (see Day 10), followed by another in 2008 in Aurora, Colorado, just outside of Denver, where tens of thousands of square feet are dedicated to abortion. And the largest to date, in Houston, Texas, is the focus of today's story.

I was invited to a meeting in early 2007 with Joe Pojman, executive director of Texas Alliance for Life, and other Texas pro-life leaders. In June 2006, Planned Parenthood, using a different name, had purchased a six-story bank building right in the heart of Houston. Only after the purchase was completed was it discovered that it was Planned Parenthood that had acquired the building, and that their intention was to turn that huge bank building, all six stories, into a late-term abortion facility in the Lone Star State.

Joe, who has a PhD, is normally calm and soft-spoken. But I'll never forget his words as he described the size of this new facility: "This is Auschwitz coming to Texas."

Looking at what would become the largest abortion facility in the western hemisphere at 78,000 square feet, one couldn't help but feel overwhelmed. And consider the location: down the street from the main campus of the University of Houston, and one mile from Texas Southern University.

The third floor is an ambulatory surgical center for all abortions, including late-term abortions up to twenty-five weeks.

With Planned Parenthood's history of racial targeting for abortion and population control programs, it's no accident that the facility is located in a predominantly minority neighborhood. Houston is made up of super-neighborhoods, and this facility is right where three predominantly Hispanic neighborhoods and one African-American neighborhood meet.

Planned Parenthood announced that their goal was to open this facility in the fall of 2009. The coming of the largest abortion facility in the hemisphere is a call for prayer and action. And Christine Melchor responded to that call.

Christine had been in the pro-life movement for decades, and many in the Houston area knew her. She often prayed at the local Planned Parenthood abortion facility. As director of the Houston Coalition for Life, she had led several 40 Days for Life Campaigns over the past few years.

She immediately began rallying groups across Texas and beyond, including Texas Right to Life, based in Houston and led by Jim and Elizabeth Graham, two pro-life heroes. They helped Christine and other leaders raise awareness through media and other outlets.

As through these efforts word spread of the true nature of the still-being-renovated facility, contractors and subcontractors began to back away from the project. A six-story bank building needs a lot of remodeling to turn it into a medical facility suitable for licensing to perform late-term abortions. Because many of those contractors and subcontractors bailed out, the opening date was postponed from the fall of 2009 to January of 2010.

This movement resisting the opening of the Planned Parenthood facility received national media attention with the assistance of evangelical leader Lou Engle of The Call, an organization that holds massive prayer rallies, usually in stadiums across the country and on the National Mall in Washington, D.C. Year after year, The Call sponsors some of the largest Christian events in America, attracting from fifty thousand to two hundred thousand participants, many of them under the age of twenty-five, to gather in prayer and fasting for our nation.

When he became aware that the largest abortion facility in the hemisphere was being built in Texas, Lou decided to hold a solemn assembly in 2010 in Texas on the anniversary of the *Roe v. Wade* decision.

That rally brought ten thousand people—Catholics and evangelicals—to the Catholic Charismatic Center across the street from the six-story facility in Houston still being renovated into the abortion facility. A number of speakers rallied the huge crowd, including one speaking for the first time in an open venue—Abby Johnson. Abby had resigned from her position as a facility director with Planned Parenthood just a few months earlier. Before her resignation, she'd been expected to occupy an office in this new abortion facility in Houston. I joked with Abby after her speech that her new office was probably being turned into a janitorial closet!

The momentum from the rally helped push the opening of the facility back *again*—from January 2010 to May 2010.

We suspect Planned Parenthood had picked this particular location for their abortion facility because the bank was in a huge parking lot right off the Gulf Freeway, which meant very limited access for prayer vigils and very little likelihood that anything else could be built nearby. They would have had good reasons for being concerned. At their previous location in Houston, a crisis pregnancy center had been built right next door, drawing a lot of "business" away from Planned Parenthood—and saving a lot of lives. In addition to the strategic location of the new facility, they fenced it off with a huge wrought-iron fence. It seemed that they'd thought of everything to ensure that previously successful pro-life strategies just wouldn't work this time.

So that's when Christine and her team got creative.

There was, she and her team finally decided, only one way to put a pregnancy resource center near this massive Planned Parenthood facility—and that was to put it on wheels.

Christine raised hundreds of thousands of dollars to purchase a state-of-the-art, 40-foot mobile medical clinic equipped with everything needed to professionally offer women real alternatives. The modified bus had the equipment to provide pregnancy testing and ultrasounds, as well as to support an on-site medical staff. It even had plasma TVs, visible from outside the bus, showing high-definition footage of life in the womb. And because of its mobility, it could be positioned where women would arrive at it first, before they got to the Planned Parenthood megaplex.

Christine's courage and the support of the Houston Coalition for Life, Texas Right to Life, and Texas Alliance for Life provided an effective response and attractive alternatives to an overwhelming and daunting late-term abortion presence in one of the most conservative cities in one of the most conservative states in America. As a result, hundreds of lives have been spared from abortion. Here are the stories of just a couple of them.

During the spring 2011 40 Days for Life Campaign, a young woman scheduled an abortion and drove into the new Houston Planned Parenthood facility. She noticed the people praying along the perimeter and holding 40 Days for Life signs. One of the signs showed the picture of a baby at eight weeks' gestation in the womb. The young woman went inside, but she couldn't get that picture out of her mind as she lay on the abortion table. At the very last moment, she asked the nurse, "Does my baby have a heartbeat?"

Thanks be to God, the nurse answered truthfully. "Yes, your baby does have a heartbeat right now."

Yes, your baby does have a heartbeat. The words penetrated her mind, then her heart. She remembered seeing the huge mobile clinic parked just outside where she lay. She got off the table, went out to the 40 Days for Life volunteers, and soon found herself on another table—the ultrasound table in the mobile clinic. She was so overcome with emotion that she wept, her hands covering her eyes. But she managed to peek out when the nurse told her the image of her child was on the monitor, and her tears quickly turned to tears of joy. She couldn't believe what she saw on the monitor—her own living, moving child, its little heart beating. She wanted no abortion now, and the 40 Days for Life volunteers connected her with all the help she needed.

Another woman had had an ultrasound at the Planned Parenthood facility the week before her scheduled abortion, where she had asked whether the baby would feel any pain during the abortion. They had, of course, told her one of the most egregious lies perpetuated by the abortion industry—that the fetus would feel no pain. And when they turned on the sound of the fetal heartbeat, they told her to cover her ears.

But when she drove into Planned Parenthood's parking lot on the day she was scheduled for her abortion, she saw a young woman standing on the street simply praying. The image was a powerful one for her, and she couldn't shake it from her mind. Still uneasy about the possibility of her baby feeling pain during the procedure, she decided to visit the mobile clinic. She was shocked to see, on the ultrasound monitor, her baby jumping and moving around, complete with arms, legs, a body, and a head. After her Planned Parenthood ultrasound the week before, they had given her a picture that showed just a circle within which she couldn't make out the baby at all. They'd also told her, when she asked, that the fetus was not moving.

Through the grace of God, she decided to continue her pregnancy and have her baby.

If the mobile clinic had not been there in front of the Houston Planned Parenthood facility, this unborn child might very well have been aborted. Thank God that Christine was not overwhelmed or intimidated by the sheer size and power, as well as the uncompromising agenda, of the largest Planned Parenthood facility not just in America but in the western hemisphere. Thank God, too, for an approach as simple as meeting the problem where it is, right where the abortions actually happen, no matter what you have to do or how creative you have to get.

As of the writing of this book, if you visit the website for the Planned Parenthood Center for Choice Ambulatory Surgery in Houston, Texas, you will see this warning on their site: *At times there may be protesters outside of the health center. We suggest you avoid interaction with them.*

We can see why. Some Texas mothers, when given loving alternatives, compassionate help, and the opportunity to discover the truth of the life within them, choose to embrace that little life. Praise God!

When hard pressed, I cried to the LORD;
he brought me into a spacious place.
The LORD is with me; I will not be afraid.
What can mere mortals do to me?

PSALM 118:5−6

Lord, thank you for the grace to defend life and to stand strong when others may ridicule or oppose me. May your peace fill my soul, especially when I am called to endure the opposition of others, and may I become more like your crucified and risen Son. Amen.

Take It Personally

Shawn

FEW TOPICS IN OUR CULTURE TODAY ARE MORE HOTLY DEBATED, more divisive, than abortion. Do some people take abortion too personally?

Pro-life advocates see abortion as losing one of our own. A baby lost in a family. A missing seat at the dinner table that can never be replaced. A might-makes-right decision inflicted on a defenseless human. We take abortion personally because it involves our brothers and sisters, created by God, our Father.

On the other hand, those who support abortion see the pro-life stance as an infringement on a personal right to do what you wish with "your own body." Their assumption is that we can defend the baby *or* the mother—not both.

Today's story blows the lid off that assumption.

To a lifelong Texan, the weather in May in Helena, Montana, is *cold*!

My first-ever trip to Helena came in May 2010, when I spoke at a local pregnancy resource center's banquet. When I left Texas, it was 95 degrees. When I landed in Helena, it was a downright chilly 42.

We'd had 40 Days for Life Campaigns in Helena before, but neither David nor I had had a chance to visit the city. So I had never met Margaret Foster, the woman who'd brought 40 Days for Life to Helena and who had led three successful 40 Days for Life Campaigns. At this banquet, I was introduced to Margaret and her husband, and I immediately felt as if she were part of my family. Her smile lit up the room, and it felt as if her eyes could see right into a person's soul.

As I chatted with Margaret that night after the banquet, I heard one of the most unbelievable stories I have ever encountered through 40 Days for Life.

The people who take up the challenge of leadership in 40 Days for Life usually have profound personal reasons for accepting this burden. In Margaret's case, she felt called to bring 40 Days for Life to Helena because of the pain abortion had caused in her own family.

A few years earlier, Margaret had learned that her sister had experienced five abortions. That affected Margaret quite deeply. She saw everyone as family, and she took abortion personally. The pain she experienced when she found out she'd never have the chance to meet five of her nieces and nephews because of abortion became the motivation she needed to get involved in the pro-life movement.

She had to do something, and when she heard about 40 Days for Life, she realized that this was what she must do. She led the first-ever 40 Days for Life Campaign in Helena and two campaigns after that as well, besides encouraging 40 Days for Life Campaigns in other Montana cities.

This book is filled with stories of the many blessings 40 Days for Life volunteers see, and David and I have heard many, many more than that. But not everyone involved in 40 Days for Life personally witnesses positive, tangible results, and that can be extremely discouraging.

In her years leading 40 Days for Life in Helena, Margaret prayed. She worked. She sacrificed. But she didn't see the results she hoped for.

She didn't let discouragement shake her rock-solid faith nor alter her contagious joy. Still, she was undeniably frustrated that she did not know of one single baby who had been saved from abortion as a result of the 40 Days for Life effort in Helena.

Margaret never gave up; she assured her team that their prayers were being answered somewhere. And she prayed that eventually she would get to meet just one of those saved babies!

One day Margaret got an unexpected and disturbing phone call. Her unmarried granddaughter was pregnant. Such phone calls always elicit a conflicting array of feelings: concern for the pregnant, unmarried family member and her future, concern for the unborn child, concern about family relationships. But this phone call had news more definite and dire: Her granddaughter was scheduled for an abortion at Planned Parenthood at 2:00 p.m. on Friday of that week, the only day of the week abortions were performed there. As soon as she hung up, Margaret began praying for her granddaughter, and she called her team and invited them to join her.

During the campaigns, Margaret takes the 6:00 a.m. shift at Planned Parenthood every day. She prays that her prayers will impact every person who visits Planned Parenthood for an abortion. But this week, abortion Friday would have a new meaning—someone in her own family was scheduled for the loss of the precious gift of life.

Friday was already a busy day, but Margaret quickly arranged a prayer gathering at Planned Parenthood. It was a cold and blustery morning, but fifteen to twenty prayer warriors gathered to beg the Lord for a miracle. They prayed for about an hour before Margaret had to go to her job at a local adoption agency. It was a morning filled with emotion but also with trust in the Lord no matter what would happen.

The telephone rang at ten minutes before noon. The voice on the other end of the phone was Margaret's daughter-in-law, who said, "We're going to have a baby!" Their prayers were answered in Helena that morning. Not only did the 40 Days for Life volunteers have their first known saved baby, but Margaret would have a new great-grandchild! Margaret left work immediately to share her joy, encouragement, and comfort with her granddaughter—and thanksgiving that her granddaughter and the precious gift of life within her were loved and supported by family and community.

Margaret had been faithfully praying for so long for that first save. Her team of volunteers had been praying and looking for the same thing. And after all that time, the first save of the Helena,

Montana, 40 Days for Life Campaigns was Margaret's great-grandson. Her own flesh and blood—her great-grandson, who would be born the following summer—had been saved from abortion.

Margaret had wanted so badly for God to bless her campaign with a mother changing her mind about abortion. But she'd never imagined that the baby saved from abortion when that day finally came would be her own great-grandson.

Margaret had had no idea—but God had.

Her great-grandson was the first. But in the time since, Margaret has seen more evidence of her prayers being answered. Other babies have been spared from abortion in Helena because of the efforts by her and her team.

During the spring 2011 campaign, the local team learned that a young woman named Kim had chosen life for her child—thanks to the campaign kickoff rally!

Kim had confided to a coworker that she was pregnant, and although she was uncertain what to do, abortion was high on her list. Her coworker calmly pointed out that there were other choices that would be much better, both for her and her baby. She then invited Kim to attend the 40 Days for Life kickoff event.

At the rally, Kim picked up information about the city's pro-life resource center and arranged an appointment. The counselors there offered her an ultrasound, and seeing her baby moving on the monitor made a tremendous impression. Kim decided to parent her baby.

During those early campaigns, Margaret could have become discouraged. A person of lesser faith might have given up. But anyone who knows Margaret or has spent time around her has seen her faith, her dedication, and her love for the unborn. Once I got to know her, it became clear why God had picked this woman for this difficult but joyful story.

—

A year and a half later, I returned to Helena to speak at a statewide Culture of Life Conference. And who do you think was there to greet me at the airport? A smiling great-grandmother, Margaret Foster, treating me as if I were family with a big hug and gifts—including chocolate and wonderful salty food (treats I really didn't need but gratefully received—and ate!).

Looking at Margaret's smiling face, my thoughts went to her young great-grandson and the legacy of love he'd been given. Her efforts on behalf of the unborn in Helena helped save his life. But it's clear that Margaret has loved *all* the women and babies she has encountered as if they were her own flesh and blood. She has loved them as Christ loved them. She has loved them as we should all love them.

Why can't we?

Maybe it's our pride. Or maybe it's our fear of letting down our guard. Maybe we mistakenly assume that every woman who aborts a child had really felt she had choices and had deliberately decided she really *wanted* that abortion. Or maybe it's because we just don't believe that that woman walking into the abortion facility is our problem.

Our culture tells these women they have a choice, and that whatever choice they make is up to them. But our culture does this because far too many of us refuse to see them as Margaret Foster sees them. We don't see them as Christ sees them. We don't see them as family. We see them as strangers, people we don't want to be bothered with, people we don't want to be responsible for.

Margaret's story reminds us who those women are aborting.

When you hear that abortion is a personal choice that impacts only the mother, tell those who believe that about Margaret Foster, who was inspired to do something about abortion in her community after learning she was missing five nieces and nephews in her own family—and about how God used her efforts to save her own flesh and blood.

Abortion impacts generations. But so does selfless love, like the love Margaret Foster had for strangers and for her own family. Thank God she took abortion personally!

Then the Lord said to Cain,
"Where is your brother Abel?"
"I don't know," he replied.
"Am I my brother's keeper?"

GENESIS 4:9

Lord, you alone are the giver of life. Your Word tells me that you know every single hair on my head, and that you take my life, and all of our lives, personally. You became one of us to save us. Help me to empty myself and take all attacks against human life personally, because the littlest and least of these are my brothers and sisters in Christ. Give me the grace to see you in everyone and to not judge the value of human life based on the circumstances of worldly judgments. Help me to take abortion personally and to trust you to give me the strength to be my brother's keeper. Amen.

Milwaukee's Dan Miller

Shawn

"SURE, I REMEMBER HOW I FIRST GOT INVOLVED IN 40 DAYS FOR Life. Somebody invited me."

Dan grew up on a farm. Even if he hadn't told me that, I would have guessed it. He's a big, burly, Midwestern man, about six-foot-seven, with a heart of gold and an open, honest face. When I met him he was already a remarkable leader of 40 Days for Life in Milwaukee. He had witnessed 161 saved babies during 40 Days for Life Campaigns and had met five of them, including a baby with a severe genetic disorder, whose story, among others, you are about to read. I was visiting Dan's campaign in fall 2010 and was amazed at all they had accomplished, including putting a crisis pregnancy center across the street from the abortion facility.

Touched by the thought that a simple invitation from a friend had put Dan on the pathway to saving lives and helping women, I said, "So, you wondered if this invitation was the Lord calling you?"

"No!" Dan said. "I told my friend, 'No way! I'd rather have all four wisdom teeth pulled *without* anesthetic than go there.'"

As you can see, Dan has a way with words. So I'll let Dan tell you the story himself.

My name is Dan Miller. I know that Shawn wants me to get to the good stuff fast, like the guy who came after us with a boa constrictor—you should've seen Shawn's eyes when I told him that one! Or how my leg was crushed hydraulically—not in the line of pro-life work! But I think I'd better start at the beginning.

I first heard about 40 Days for Life in 2007 from Mike Frisby. I met Mike on a six-month mission trip to Trujillo, Honduras, at an orphanage called Finca del Niño. But it wasn't until 2010 that my friend, Tim Dunne, invited me to pray with him on February 17, 2010, at a 40 Days for Life vigil in front of Wisconsin's largest abortion center, right here in Milwaukee.

I said no. And I meant it! I had a lot of fears about the pro-life movement, and my greatest fear was getting arrested. Back in the early '90s, before 40 Days even existed, I had prayed in front of this same abortion facility. In those days, some pro-lifers would block access to the abortion center with a car or a human pyramid. The idea was to disrupt the facility as much as possible, and you just knew somebody was going to get arrested. I was so repelled by it that I never went back after that. I would even avoid driving past it.

Tim could see that I had no idea how 40 Days really worked. So he told me about 40 Days—their commitment to peaceful, public prayer vigils, and their emphasis on showing love to the women walking in and out of the centers, and to the workers too. I liked that they were the last sign of hope for the babies about to be aborted and also the first sign of mercy and forgiveness to the women coming out. That blew me away.

Tim knew I couldn't use the excuse that I was too busy. I'd had an accident in which I had crushed my leg. It involved a six-hundred-pound refrigerator and the hydraulic lift on a front-end loader. After being laid off for about six months, I'd begun to heal. My doctor told me the best thing I could do for my rehabilitation was to walk and stand. And that's when Tim sprang his 40 Days invitation on me. Sneaky, right?

So Tim convinced me. Well, probably God did, through Tim. And during 40 Days, that's basically all you do besides praying—walk and stand. The doctor would have been happy to see it.

My first day was a Wednesday. At the time, I didn't know that all 40 Days for Life spring campaigns begin on Ash Wednesday. I also didn't know that this abortion facility was pretty much closed for business on Wednesdays. Only a skeleton crew of employees came in and out that day, not dressed up in their work smocks or anything—probably doing paperwork or something.

I thought, *This is great. This campaign is going to shut this place down in no time.* But, of course, the facility was basically closed that day.

When I showed up the next day, I was wearing my Ray-Ban shades. And I thank God that I was wearing them, because all I did that day was cry. I felt like I was virtually getting trampled in the stampede of women on their way in to abort their babies. We stopped counting after thirty-five.

I think that's when Christ turned my fears into conviction. I could see that this kind of prayer had to happen all the time. We joked that it's too bad the campaign is called 40 Days for Life. It should be called 365 Days for Life! But it's funny how God works. He answered that prayer too. Sidewalk counseling in front of this particular abortion facility turned into a full-time, year-round vocation for me.

I confess that at first I had no understanding at all of what kind of evil we were dealing with. When people talked about this being a spiritual battle, I shrugged that off as exaggeration. I knew that abortion was evil, but it was a *remote* evil. I didn't see it happening.

Then one day during the campaign I took a break. Usually I'm on the sidewalks nine to ten hours a day during a campaign. I was sitting in my car, resting, and I noticed that the employees of the abortion center had propped open both sets of doors—inside and outside. I didn't see any trucks coming with a delivery or anybody approaching in a wheelchair, so there was no obvious reason to have both sets of doors propped open. It was a very hot day. Then a breeze came up, and I could tell it was moving through the abortion center. They were airing the place out.

My car was lined up with the breeze exiting the facility. The smell that hit me that day raised the hairs on my neck. I knew that smell. It was the rotten stench of blood and death.

When we were kids growing up on the farm, my dad would make us clean the slaughterhouse. We used bleach and other cleaners that were supposed to get rid of the smell, but it never did—not completely. And I figured, that was the problem they were facing on a super hot day. Maybe people were complaining about the smell. Since then, I've talked to women who, after changing their minds and coming out of the abortion center, said to us, "That place is awful. That place smells."

Another time on the sidewalks I was there with a small group of mostly women. A man approached us, and there was something odd about the way he was walking. We couldn't tell what it was right away, but then he pulled it out in the open—he was carrying a boa constrictor! So we thought, *Maybe it's a pet—he certainly wouldn't use that snake to attack us.* But that's exactly what he did. No one was hurt, but it was an awful scene.

So for me, the evil in that place isn't abstract. It's very real. You can smell it—the stench of death. And with the help of guys like "snake man," you can feel it. But amidst the evil, we have witnessed miracles.

God showed us our first save on August 3, 2010. Since then, he has shown us 251 more, 161 of them during 40 Days for Life Campaigns. I could talk for days telling you all the stories we've heard and experienced on the sidewalks. I'll tell you just one—the most recent one, which touched me like I have never been touched before.

A young Latino couple came to the abortion center, Estrella and Martin. Thank God, they came on a Monday when it was closed. It was February 27, 2012, around 4:00 p.m. Estrella was about eighteen weeks along in her pregnancy. They knew that their child was a boy, and they were heartbroken because their unborn son had been diagnosed with Trisomy 18. I knew nothing about Trisomy 18, but they told me that all of their medical caregivers were telling them to spare their child a short life of misery and just have him aborted. They had already gone for a second and a third opinion on their baby's condition, each report the same as the one before. If the abortion center had been open, they would have at least gone in to see what their options were—after all, that's why they'd come. Experience has shown me that they only really suggest one option once you're in that place.

So with the Spanish I had learned working at that little orphanage in Trujillo, Honduras, I started to counsel them the best that I could in their language. The Holy Spirit filled my mouth with words I had forgotten I'd even known. God helped me convince them to let God take control. They were scared—so uncertain of what to do. I'll never forget them telling me, "We don't have any family here. We have no one to lean on." I said, "We're your family now."

Somehow, God convinced them during that conversation that one more opinion wouldn't hurt. With the help of many, many pro-lifers here in Milwaukee, we had built a crisis pregnancy resource center directly across the street from the abortion center. I walked them over there to the Women's Care Center. I said good-bye and let the Women's Care Center take over—and then I began to pray in ways I had never prayed before, a really deep prayer.

At the Women's Care Center, unknown to me, they were referred to a pro-life OB/GYN doctor in the Milwaukee area, where they received free prenatal care. Don't you just love hearing that? Estrella and Martin were so thankful that we met on the sidewalks that two weeks later they invited my wife, Janine, and me to witness the birth of their son.

I said, "You mean you want us to come to the baby shower?"

They said, "No, we want you in the delivery room when he's born."

Wow. We really *had* become family.

I had never witnessed a birth. But on July 7, 2012, that same pro-life doctor delivered a baby boy to Estrella and Martin with my wife and me in the room. The baby was just so beautiful. I was in tears. *Everybody* was in tears.

Because he had Trisomy 18, we didn't know whether he would

live, or for how long. I think the longest Trisomy 18 babies last is maybe ninety days—in fact, about half don't live beyond a week. So immediately after he was born, Martin held out a bottle of holy water and asked me to baptize his son, Martin Jr. As if witnessing the birth of their son hadn't been blessing enough, I had the privilege of baptizing him! Janine and I held Martin Jr. for quite some time. He had many visitors, both family and friends. We left later that night.

Six hours and fourteen minutes after Martin Jr. was born, we got a message from his father that Martin Jr. had taken his last breath. I couldn't help but think of my promise to them when we first met. Janine and I had indeed become their family throughout their pregnancy—and so had the whole pro-life community. Everyone made sure Martin Jr. was given a proper Christian burial at no expense. Everything was donated. Estrella and Martin were awestruck that complete strangers would help them through all of this, from pregnancy right through the funeral. I think the experience was a beautiful thing for their family, drawing them closer to one another. It made their marriage stronger and strengthened their faith. Mine too! Estrella and Martin plan to join us on the sidewalks this fall, to help us save more babies.

I've talked to pro-lifers who have been doing this for twenty years and still have not witnessed a save, so I know what an honor and privilege it is when it happens.

In my time on the sidewalks, there have been so many young moms and so many stories that have touched me personally. And I have deep respect for the mothers who have the courage to come back and tell us their stories. It's not easy to say, "I was contemplating abortion. But I chose life." One of those mothers who came back, Stephanie, had a son. My wife and I are now the very proud godparents to her son.

The real hero of my story, though—besides God, of course—is my wife, Janine. She's been my greatest supporter during this journey. She could tell you how, with God's help, I've gone from somebody who was lukewarm about abortion, a pro-lifer who just wrote checks, to somebody with pro-life convictions so deep that they took me to the sidewalks. Without Janine and my faith in Jesus Christ, none of this could have happened. Absolutely none of it.

> *For God did not give us a spirit of timidity,*
> *but a spirit of power,*
> *of love and of self-discipline.*
> 2 TIMOTHY 1:7

God Almighty, you mark my path, but often I don't know where that path will lead. Give me a spirit of power to trust you as I walk that path toward destinations I don't know. Why you put me in certain positions at certain times I don't know, but lead me, your child, with love so that I may be used for your greater glory. Amen.

Across the Pond

Shawn

ENGLAND WAS ABOUT THE LAST PLACE ON OUR MINDS WHEN David and I launched the first 40 Days for Life Campaign in Texas in 2004. We gave England nary a thought when 40 Days for Life went nationwide in 2007. All that changed in 2010 when, out of nowhere, this peaceful and prayerful approach was introduced to one of the most secular cities in the West—London, England—by a young, proper British gentleman named Robert Colquhoun.

Robert is in his late twenties, well educated and well spoken. After university he and a friend went to Canada on National Evangelization Teams (NET). It was a formative year for Robert, during which, as a missionary, he saw the power of the gospel at work. Canada hosted the first international 40 Days for Life campaign, and it spread rapidly due to the faith and courage of pro-life Canadians willing to endure extreme weather and persecution to save lives. Canada has now held twenty-five individual 40 Days for Life Campaigns in seven provinces, from Halifax to Calgary to Vancouver and even Winnipeg. It was in Ottawa that Robert first encountered a 40 Days for Life Campaign when he saw a group of about fifteen people praying close to the Canadian Parliament.

"I had never seen anything like that before," Robert said. Even so, he didn't think much about it until about six months later when he returned to the UK and remembered what he'd seen. Looking up 40 Days for Life online, Robert stumbled upon a talk given by David. "Watching this video on YouTube, I felt that God was calling me to start a 40 Days for Life Campaign here in England. I had to do this —I couldn't say no."

There were good reasons for Robert's sense of urgency. In the UK alone, there are around two hundred thousand abortions every year. Since the Abortion Act 1967, there have been over seven million abortions in England.

But if he were to start a 40 Days for Life program in the UK, Robert wanted to do it where it would have maximum impact. So he made the courageous decision to move to London. "I took a risk in faith and committed myself to the campaign," Robert said, "trusting that I would be able to find a job and a place to live in London. Amazingly, the very first day I got to London, I found a job."

As a new resident and with no money to his name, Robert signed up London, England, for the country's first-ever 40 Days for Life Campaign.

Despite his initial enthusiasm, Robert was not optimistic. "At the beginning, I believed the campaign would be a failure. I was filled with doubts. Would I be able to motivate enough people to pray in public in Britain? Do enough people care about pro-life issues?"

Robert had stepped out in faith, and it was his faith that sustained him. As word spread, Robert was pleasantly surprised. "I discovered that there were many people who were passionate about the issue, yet didn't have the means to express it. 40 Days for Life would provide those means."

For that first campaign, Robert chose one of the first abortion facilities in England, a notorious Marie Stopes abortion center in central London, named after a eugenicist who used to write love letters to Adolf Hitler. The organization named after her performs sixty thousand abortions every year in Britain and receives millions of pounds from the Department of Health. In Britain, the taxpayer funds an abortion every 3 minutes and 20 seconds, or 489 abortions every day. With an abortion costing between £520 and £1610, this means that £100 million is spent on abortions every year. Perhaps it's not surprising that Britain has the highest rate of teenage pregnancies in Europe, considering that abortion is free to them and readily available.

If Robert needed evidence of the immense power of prayer, even in a city that has turned so far from God, he got that evidence on Day 2 of the campaign when he and his team saw the first baby saved!

It happened this way: Marie Stopes International does not allow children into their centers, so a boyfriend waited outside with two children as his girlfriend went in to have an abortion. Intrigued by the presence of the prayer volunteers, he asked them what they were doing. After just a few minutes of conversation, he rushed into the facility and rescued his girlfriend and unborn child.

That was the first baby saved in England as a result of 40 Days for Life, and many more would quickly follow. Not long after, a young man stopped his car, jumped out, and shook the hands of the volunteers, thanking them. "If you hadn't been here, my girlfriend would have gone ahead with her abortion," he said.

Another woman who chose life wrote one of the volunteers a note. "Thank you from the bottom of my heart, I am lucky to have a friend like you."

As the campaign continued, word spread rapidly throughout England of this forty-day vigil that had originated in America. To his amazement, Robert received a letter from the Vatican acknowledging his 40 Days for Life Campaign and informing him that Pope Benedict XVI would be praying for him.

As awareness and enthusiasm spread, Robert knew that something else would come with it—persecution.

The volunteers experienced frequent verbal abuse from passersby, including students throwing buckets of water over them and even abortion proponents waving satanic symbols in an attempt to intimidate them. Hecklers shouted anything and everything…

You're just wasting your time—there is no God!

You hypocrites—what about the millions of starving children around the world?

You're doing the work of the Devil!

Why aren't you praying for the twenty thousand back-street abortions every year in Pakistan?

I have a perfect right to have sex with men I dislike so much there's no way I'd want to bear their children.

I don't need *your prayers, and I don't believe in your evil God!*

And even a first for a 40 Days for Life Campaign:

Smoking kills as much as abortion!

Robert wasn't deterred by persecution or resistance—not when interest in 40 Days for Life was increasing across England beyond what he would ever have imagined. After the success of the first campaign, Robert began organizing multiple 40 Days for Life Campaigns in London for the next season, including one at the largest abortion facility in England—British Pregnancy Advisory Service (BPAS), located in Bedford Square.

The most dramatic moment at that campaign came when Bishop Alan Hopes courageously joined the volunteers and led five hundred attendees in prayer. A mob of three hundred pro-abortion protestors arrived to shout at the prayer volunteers and the bishop. But the volunteers simply continued praying—many of them on their knees. That day was a first for a 40 Days for Life Campaign. Fifty police were present to protect the prayer vigil—never before had so many police been needed at a 40 Days for Life event.

The British national media began giving 40 Days for Life lots of attention, with feature stories in *The Guardian, The Daily Telegraph*, and on BBC, among other media outlets. Unfortunately, the media described 40 Days in not particularly flattering terms as an American-style protest, one that began in that center of the Wild West—Texas.

But it gave Robert a chance to broadcast the message. In fact, he was asked to debate the head of the largest abortion provider in England—Ann Furedi, the head of BPAS—on national radio with an audience of four million listeners! In that debate, Robert calmly described the peaceful mission and lifesaving focus of 40 Days for Life. But the goal of the abortion industry was to cast Robert and his volunteers as villains, so Ann Furedi's only response to him was to politely say, "They can take their love somewhere else." You have to admit, the British have a way with words.

Not all media were hostile—the newspaper *The Daily Telegraph* printed a huge expose revealing that some abortion facilities in the UK were agreeing to sex-selection abortions. This quickly developed into an international story that left the abortion industry reeling. Doctors lost their jobs, and the government promised a national investigation led by the Care Quality Commission. That investigation revealed that fourteen hospitals were pre-signing their forms—a shortcut that bypasses important safeguards.

The publicity motivated Robert's volunteers—but it motivated others as well. During the third round of 40 Days for Life Campaigns in England (involving vigils in five cities), the "Kamikaze cyclists" appeared—cyclists who purposely rammed their bicycles into 40 Days banners and boxes.

It started on the first day of the vigil when a lady in her twenties repeatedly drove her bicycle into the easels holding the banners, overturning them, while shouting at the top of her voice, "You are scum! Get lost! Shame on you!"

"A week later," Robert said, "another cyclist stole one of the easels, then waved it mockingly at us from a safe distance. Strangely, the easel and its banner were returned a day later. Did the cyclist feel remorse?

"During the rest of campaign, comedians delivered sacrilegious and derogatory jokes, and more water, eggs, and horse dung were thrown at our volunteers. Our sign was destroyed by angry cyclists passing by, and the level of abuse and obscene language rose to a level that made one wonder how mannerly we really are in England.

"But none of these shenanigans stopped us from concentrating on the prayer vigil."

The phenomenal success of the 40 Days for Life Campaign in England finally enticed David and me to fly over before the spring 2012 campaign to meet in person this Robert we had already grown to love from thousands of miles away. When he picked us up at the airport, it was as if we had known him for ten years rather than knowing him from afar for only two.

Abortion proponents in the British media describe him as "hostile and dangerous." But Robert is a mere thirty years old, with blue eyes, glasses, and a baby face. His humble nature, perfect manners, and courtesy are typical of everything we Americans love about our friends "across the pond." During our visit, Robert worked us to the bone, taking us to London, Birmingham, and Manchester to speak at six different events, followed by a banquet at Canterbury Cathedral where we saw firsthand why people have responded to Robert: He's a leader. In a nation with a tradition of providing brave leadership when most are losing hope—think of names like Churchill and Wilberforce—Robert inspires peers and elders alike and has brought together groups and leaders who hadn't worked together before.

The real movement of 40 Days for Life in England did not start in Texas. It didn't start in the U.S. It didn't start with David or me. It started when Robert responded to the Holy Spirit. As a result of his faith in the face of difficulty, many babies have been saved, hearts have been changed, and this so-called "American protest" has prayerfully opened hearts that many in England thought were closed.

40 Days for Life Campaigns have now spread throughout England with Robert's guidance and leadership—including in Brighton, Birmingham, Manchester, Milton Keynes, Oxford, and Southampton.

When you ask Robert what hope he has for England, he has a ready answer.

In 1989, Communist governments began to collapse in Eastern Europe, leading to the collapse of the Soviet Union. If I'd told you in 1982 that Communism would be over within a decade— you would think me either a lunatic or deeply deluded. Yet we know that with the *domino effect*, we can have the same impact here in the United Kingdom! Abortion will end, and when it falls, what an *almighty* fall it will be. On my knees I say: Whoever, wherever you are, get a 40 Days for Life Campaign going in your local community in order to save lives, inspire hearts and minds, and impact eternal souls. This is a life-saving initiative that has the ability to transform your community and build hope among people.

William Wilberforce, Gandhi, the Civil Rights Movement, Solidarity in Poland, and 40 Days for Life are all individuals or are composed of individuals that have at heart a common goal: the ending of injustice in society.

Today, we have the opportunity to make history. With prayer and faith, we can *move mountains.*

"Truly I tell you, if anyone says to this mountain,
'Go, throw yourself into the sea,'
and does not doubt in their heart
but believes that what they say will happen,
it will be done for them."

MARK 11:23

Dear heavenly Father, help me to see my effort on behalf of the unborn as part of a grand tradition of fighting injustice. You ask your followers to intercede for the widow, for the fatherless, for the oppressed, and I strive to follow that exhortation when I intercede for the unborn. Empower me to invest my time and energy in that battle. Bless my effort, and that of my co-workers on behalf of the unborn, so that today's worldwide pro-life movement has a lasting and profound effect on saving lives. Amen.

Surrounded

Shawn

*Jesus answered …"the reason I was born
and came into the world is to testify to the truth.
Everyone on the side of truth listens to me."*

"What is truth?" retorted Pilate.

JOHN 18:37–38

PILATE'S QUESTION STILL HAUNTS OUR WORLD TODAY. "WHAT IS truth?"

Pilate and Jesus were on the battlefield of the truth war on the day of Jesus' arrest and trial, surrounded by an angry mob screaming out for Pilate to put Jesus to death. Pilate asked about the truth, but seemed completely unaware of the truth that he was standing face to face with the Son of God. So he gave in to the cries of the mob and went from questioning the Truth to executing the Truth when he gave the order to crucify Jesus.

At first reading, it might appear that truth, when surrounded by its enemy deception, lost the battle that day.

I know the feeling. I often stand on the frontlines of the battle between truth and deception, between life and death, and see how the moral relativism of our culture has taken us to the point where basic logic and fundamental truths have no more weight than mere opinions. In that culture, deception saturates our lives. Turn on the TV, and deception travels the sound waves and surrounds you in your own living room.

Listen in to the CBS news program *60 Minutes*, aired on August 8, 2010.[9]

60 Minutes: "Do you believe you are taking lives?"

Abortion provider: "No, I don't. I think one has to decide when life begins. I think that my belief is the unborn child is a parasite. It has no rights. Science has not been able to come up with an answer. Religion has not been able to come up with an answer. I think the only answer to when life begins is when the mother's heart says it begins."

60 Minutes: "How many abortions do you do a year?"

Abortion provider: "Just under two thousand."

60 Minutes: "Do you feel uncomfortable about the work that you do at all?"

Abortion provider: "No, not at all."

60 Minutes: "Is your god happy with your work?"

Abortion provider: (smiles) "Yes, she is."

Those words are the words of Leroy Carhart, MD.

Carhart is one of only a small number of abortion providers in America willing to carry out late-term abortions (those over twenty weeks' gestation)—and he does them very aggressively. He has devoted time and money to the legal fight over late-term abortions at both the state and federal levels.

In 2010, when Nebraska became the first state to ban abortions past twenty weeks, only one person in the state had been performing abortions beyond that point—Leroy Carhart. Apparently unwilling to abandon his "specialty," Carhart decided to find someplace else to operate his late-term abortion business. The East Coast provided just the opportunity. One of its most notorious late-term abortion centers had just gone out of business.

On February 18, 2010, the FBI raided Kermit Gosnell's abortion facility in Philadelphia. On the strength of the evidence discovered in that raid, Gosnell was charged with eight counts of murder. His victims? Women on whom botched abortions had been performed, as well as babies born alive but left to die. As of this writing, Gosnell awaits trial and his abortion center—the prosecutor called it a "house of horrors"—was shut down. Though all pro-lifers were appalled by what we learned about his facility, it was a great relief to know that this late-term abortion facility was no longer open for business.

In business terms, however, that left a huge vacuum in the market. No other provider in the region was offering late-term abortions even though they were legal there. So Leroy Carhart set up shop in Germantown, Maryland—not far from Washington, D.C., and Baltimore, and about a three-hour drive from Philadelphia. He announced that he would do not only first- and second- but even third-trimester abortions.

Many people in Germantown weren't happy to hear that news. Abortion hadn't been a forefront issue for many people in the community before. But now, church and civic leaders were rushing to oppose Carhart's presence in their otherwise peaceful community.

The local response was inspiring. Two young men, Mike Martelli and Andrew Glenn, decided to host a 40 Days for Life Campaign outside Carhart's new Germantown business. Thanks to their leadership, volunteers eagerly stepped forward for an around-the-clock prayer vigil. And to double that good news, 40 Days volunteers in Nebraska planned a simultaneous campaign outside Carhart's office in Bellevue, Nebraska, where abortions up to twenty weeks were still done regularly. As news of these vigils spread, pro-life advocates around the country surrounded both events with prayer.

I was scheduled to speak at the kickoff in Bellevue. The following day, David Bereit would speak at the opening of the campaign in Germantown.

On March 5, 2011, I stood in the cold outside of Leroy Carhart's Nebraska facility, trying my best to encourage the prayer volunteers even as we all knew that the abortionist was performing abortions inside. The battle lines seemed clearly drawn that day. Truth had deception surrounded. But I was troubled that, though surrounded, deception was "winning" inside that facility.

Heading to my hotel room for the night, I was unable to think about much besides Leroy Carhart. I was discouraged. Even if I counted the prayer volunteers there in Bellevue, added those gathered in Germantown, and then added our prayer supporters around the globe, weren't we still outnumbered by those all too willing to allow the deaths of the unborn? Who surrounded whom?

The next morning at the airport, I sat down in the boarding area and checked my watch. Five in the morning. I thought of an Irish priest I knew who once said, "Not even God is awake at 5:00 a.m." I smiled, knowing that while God was awake, I was still struggling to get there.

But someone else was awake as well. I noticed a man approaching in the distance. My heart dropped. *I don't believe this*, I thought. There, walking straight toward my gate, was Dr. Leroy Carhart.

I admit it—I hoped he wouldn't see me. If he did, how could he *not* recognize the guy in the 40 Days for Life shirt who had been giving a speech on the sidewalk outside his building just the day before?

But when boarding for my flight was announced, he and his wife got in line—to get on *my plane*! He was just a few steps ahead of me, so I realized that we would probably be seated in the same section of the plane.

But would you believe the same row? Would you believe that my seat on that plane was right between Leroy Carhart and his wife?

I sat down between them. Carhart at my left elbow, his wife at my right. Now *I* was surrounded!

His wife, clearly having no idea who I was, began to chitchat with me. Carhart pulled out his phone and sent her a text. She read the text, glared at me, fiercely shuffled her magazine, and turned away toward the window. As we sat in silence, I remembered times Carhart had publicly described himself as "at war" with the pro-life movement. He often referenced violence against abortion doctors, and it sounded as if he believed the stereotype that all pro-life people are in league with such violence—a stereotype that particularly grieved me, given our commitment at 40 Days for Life to peaceful vigils and care and concern for abortion workers.

By the time we took off, both Carhart and his wife had fallen asleep. And that's when it dawned on me. I'd been given a rare opportunity.

Never again, most likely, would I be sitting so close to this man. Shouldn't I spend this time praying for him? So I did. And as I did, I realized how blessed Carhart was to have so many people—in both Nebraska and Maryland—praying for him. This man's occupation—and his attitude—could easily generate anger. But in both locations, what he was receiving was not anger but prayer. He had no idea of that, of course, but it was true just the same. I may have been surrounded on that plane, shoulder to shoulder in fact. But in the wider view, we were all three surrounded by prayer.

As I prayed, my entire perspective shifted. I knew that when this plane landed, I'd be driving home to our three children and my loving wife, six months pregnant with our fourth baby. As always happens during that very best part of my day, I'd be greeted at the door by excited kids and kisses and hugs. I was going home to spend Sunday with family—a slice of heaven. Carhart, on the other hand, was on his way to his late-term abortion facility in Germantown, the site of gruesome work. I could not imagine the life he was living. And so I prayed all the more.

When we finally arrived at our destination and de-boarded, Carhart stared at me for a moment and then walked off. I imagine he assumed he and his wife were finally free of me. But I knew the truth: He was still surrounded by prayer and would soon see David and the Germantown prayer force gathered at his Maryland facility. God was on the move. Ultimately, truth would win.

I began this story by talking about Jesus' trial. On the surface, it looked as if truth lost that battle. After all, Jesus was marched from the trial to his gruesome death. But we know the battle was God's to win. In Romans 8, verses 31 and 32, we read:

What, then, shall we say in response to these things? If God is for us, who can be against us? He who did not spare his own Son, but gave him up for us all—how will he not also, along with him, graciously give us all things?

At Jesus' trial, Pilate didn't control the outcome. God did! God *willingly* gave his only Son for us all. He had a far greater plan in the works than anyone could have possibly imagined.

From that perspective, Carhart's role and God's role in the battle over abortion look very different. Though Leroy Carhart is a powerful national figure in the abortion industry, with shocking numbers of abortions performed, his move to set up a late-term abortion facility in Germantown stirred the prayerful response of Mike Martelli and Andrew Glenn.

Their response has borne much fruit. For the first time, their community came together on behalf of the pro-life effort, awakening thousands to the little-known fact that in Maryland, abortion is legal up to the minute before birth. Yes, it has been heartbreaking for Mike, Andrew, and the other volunteers to see pregnant women, the shape of their bodies revealing that they are carrying babies near term, walk into Carhart's abortion facility, knowing they are about to pay him large sums of money to end the life of their fully-formed, unborn children. But they report to us that it has also been amazing to see the reaction of the thousands of people who have worked to save so many lives that otherwise would have been lost. They have now opened a pregnancy resource center—right across the street from Carhart's abortion facility—offering women free alternatives to abortion! Babies' lives have been saved during their 40 Days for Life Campaigns. During a recent 40 Days for Life kick-off event in Germantown, David Bereit was blessed to meet one of these babies—and his mother—in person. The mom thanked the volunteers at the rally for their dedication and prayers, which she credited with saving her son's life and sparing her from a lifetime of regrets.

Each child who perishes as the result of abortion—whether aborted in the first trimester or the third—reminds us how vital it is to stand as witnesses and to pray. In the United States alone, every twenty-four seconds another unique, irreplaceable child is lost. That is the gruesome reality. Even so, Andrew, Mike, and the thousands in Germantown give us all hope. They serve as an example of what can be done when abortion, in its ugliest form, arrives in our own towns. They remind us how vital it is to speak truth and to act against an injustice such as this.

When we act, lives are saved.

Do not be overcome by evil,
but overcome evil with good.
ROMANS 12:21

Dear Lord, today I lift before you Leroy Carhart and his colleagues who perform late-term abortions. He does not know your truth. Believing a lie, he has spread deception and death through his words and deeds. I pray for your truth to invade his life and the lives of other abortionists. You have us all surrounded, Lord! Your truth will win in the end. Build my confidence in you, and help me to not only see you at work but to be part of the work you are doing. Amen.

The Webcam Storm

Shawn

SUE THAYER WORKED FOR PLANNED PARENTHOOD IN STORM Lake, Iowa, for seventeen years. By today's standards, that's a long time with one company. When I first heard Sue's story, I couldn't decide which was more bizarre—why she got hired or why she got fired. I'll let you decide.

Sue had applied for a job with Planned Parenthood for the same reason some other women do: She had always believed that Planned Parenthood's mission, as they regularly asserted, was to offer health care for women and to prevent abortions, and those were both causes Sue wanted to invest herself in. On the day of her hiring interview, she was asked a simple question: *Do you believe in abortion?* Her answer was simple and honest: *No, I do not.*

As she drove home after the interview, she assumed that, despite their stated intention to *prevent* abortions, she may have just ruined her chances for a job with Planned Parenthood. That was because some Planned Parenthood facilities in Iowa, but not all, performed abortions.

To her surprise, Sue soon received a call from Planned Parenthood of Greater Iowa informing her that she was hired! And the particular center where she soon went to work did not perform surgical abortions. Before long, Sue became the manager of this affiliate, and for the next seventeen years she did all she could to shower warmth and care on each client she encountered, naïvely believing what she now describes as "Planned Parenthood's big lie"—that the organization was striving to prevent abortions.

236

Over time, the affiliate under which her office was managed began to institute a few changes. First, at a few of their locations, they began to distribute the RU-486 abortion drug, also known as a chemical abortion. RU-486 is a series of two pills. The first pill poisons the baby and ends its life. The second pill, taken twenty-four hours later, forces the mother's body into contractions. RU-486 pills have been widely used over the last decade in Europe and the United States. Even so, Sue found U.S. Food and Drug Administration reports that more than a dozen women had died from complications due to RU-486. She also noticed that the RU-486 pills were sold to customers for about the same price as surgical abortions. Since Planned Parenthood didn't have to pay the physician as much as they would for a surgical abortion and they didn't need to be staffed to care for the women during and after the abortion, Planned Parenthood made a much larger profit for administering RU-486 than for surgical abortions, all while putting women's lives at risk.

In my work with post-abortive women, I've often heard the emotional scars of RU-486 described. Most women take the pills at home, often in secret. These women, often in tears, later tell how they passed the baby in the bathroom, all alone. The cramping and pain, the amount of blood, the actual delivery of the tiny fetus, and the aftereffects are frightening for many women, made worse by their secretive isolation in the days that follow.

Although Sue was very uneasy about the chemical abortion pills that would soon be distributed through the regional Planned Parenthood affiliate, she continued with her job at the small, rural office in Storm Lake. Her parent company, Planned Parenthood of Greater Iowa, under the leadership of a woman named Jill June, was already one of the fastest-growing, largest Planned Parenthood affiliates in America.

And then, late in 2007, Sue, as facility manager, caught wind of a new twist on saving money and "increasing efficiency" in providing abortions. She heard that Jill June had come up with a new idea while watching a crime show on television, an idea that would eventually change the abortion industry—the webcam (also known as telemed) abortion.

A webcam abortion allows for a woman to receive the RU-486 abortion pill in a Planned Parenthood office *without a doctor on location*. The doctor can be in a different city, even a different state. The doctor speaks to the patient through a webcam for only a few minutes, never examining the patient in person, and with no doctor-patient relationship. An ultrasound of the mother's uterus is performed by Planned Parenthood personnel, not necessarily medically trained, and the results are transmitted electronically to the doctor. After approving the RU-486 abortion, the doctor simply hits a button from his remote location that opens a drawer miles away inside the rural Planned Parenthood facility where the mother is sitting. In that drawer are the RU-486 abortion pills. Thus the abortion is administered without even the doctor's presence.

Jill June decided to debut this new procedure in Iowa—first in Ames but eventually in Storm Lake as well. As the time grew closer for Sue's facility to start webcam abortions, a knot formed in her stomach. When a state-of-the-art 4D ultrasound machine was delivered to her Storm Lake facility, Sue knew that she would soon be forced to take a stand that would end her employment. Sue had no medical training of any kind, and she wanted no part of aborting children.

As the day of her ultrasound training grew closer, the knot in her stomach grew larger. She depended on the income from her job. She felt secure in her job and didn't want to leave. But neither did she want to play a part in what she saw as an abhorrent method of Planned Parenthood increasing their abortion revenue and profits at the expense of desperate women whose health and lives would be put at risk. Finally, recognizing that the turmoil she felt was her conscience's way of warning her against an immoral act, Sue knew what she had to do. She didn't have to wait long.

As each facility implemented webcam abortion, they were given a goal for the number of abortions they were expected to perform. At every Planned Parenthood meeting Sue attended, the topic was the importance of increasing their abortion numbers and how web-cam abortions could do just that while increasing their bottom line. From the moment Planned Parenthood announced their plan, Sue had been voicing concerns and asking questions, becoming increasingly vocal in her opposition.

It came as no surprise, then, that after seventeen years of service, Sue Thayer was fired by Planned Parenthood of Greater Iowa.

Sue went home hurt and shaken but knowing she had done the right thing by speaking up. It was December 2008. A few weeks later, the Storm Lake Planned Parenthood facility began providing webcam abortions.

Sue invested herself in her children and home. Over time, as she reflected about her time at Planned Parenthood, Sue sought God's forgiveness through prayer and found healing.

"God has a way of nudging us into action," Sue explains today. "Sadly, I had become very adept at ignoring his gentle encouragement for me to speak up. I kept thinking that somebody else would 'fix it.' After two years, I'm sure he got tired of me going my own way. Finally, in the summer of 2011, I could no longer remain silent."

Sue called a meeting with a small group of friends and told them about the webcam abortions Planned Parenthood was providing. She joined a small group of fledgling pro-lifers, and they began to brainstorm how to get out the word.

Sue remembered hearing, in meetings she'd attended while she worked at Planned Parenthood, about one particular pro-life organization that had effectively thwarted their abortion efforts in city after city. The group was 40 Days for Life. So Sue went to our website and learned how to register for a 40 Days for Life Campaign. With no idea how they'd ever pull off a forty-day vigil, she signed up to lead a vigil outside the facility she'd worked at for seventeen years.

David and I had never heard of Sue Thayer. We knew only that a new city, Storm Lake, Iowa, had joined our fall 2011 campaign.

Sue's group received our comprehensive training materials and campaign tools and got to work. As she excitedly told friends and family of plans for the vigil, she was met with baffled stares and disbelief. What about her former coworkers—some of them friends who admired her gumption for speaking up, some of them ex-friends who had taken offense at her stand against the webcam abortions? How would they feel working inside while she was holding vigil outside? And what would neighbors think? Storm Lake was a small town, and most people knew she used to work there.

"What happened over the next weeks and months was nothing short of a miracle!" Sue now tells others as she shares her passion for 40 Days for Life. "God honored our efforts in a mighty way! Every single minute of the vigil was filled! Brothers and sisters in Christ who had never even met were regularly praying together! We actually had worship, several times, on the sidewalk directly in front of the very facility where I had worked! Bible study groups came, youth groups came, families came, whole schools came! Early on, fear had gripped me at the very thought of standing up and speaking and praying. By Day 1 of the vigil, God sent an amazing calm that I knew came directly from him. But along with the peace, he sent a holy boldness, a courage that I had never experienced before."

God showed up, as he does every time. Sue stood outside and waved to her former coworkers, while meeting new staff members. She prayed for every family affected by each person who entered and left the center, workers and clients alike. And Sue watched in amazement as the steady stream of volunteers came to stand and pray.

Sue didn't know it yet, but a storm was brewing over Storm Lake—a God-storm. And Planned Parenthood was feeling its effects. Client numbers were decreasing. And that meant abortion revenue was falling.

Meanwhile, back in D.C., word of Sue's story reached us. A former manager of a Planned Parenthood center was leading a 40 Days for Life vigil? And we hadn't heard until now? We were ecstatic! And that was *before* the unbelievable development that would show us that this storm in Storm Lake was really the work of the Holy Spirit!

I'll never forget getting the news from Iowa. "Shawn, did you hear about Storm Lake, Iowa? Sue Thayer's facility? Planned Parenthood just announced that they're closing it!"

It sounded too good to be true. But when we investigated, sure enough, Planned Parenthood had announced that the facility would close on March 1, 2012—right at the start of the next internationally coordinated 40 Days for Life campaign. Sue invited us to attend a celebration in Storm Lake on that day. David and I agreed we couldn't miss it.

We flew to Iowa in the freezing rain. It was 28 degrees when we landed, and we rented the only car available—a red Ford mustang convertible—and drove to Storm Lake. As we got out of the car, Sue ran toward us, a big smile on her face, gave us huge hugs, and said, "I feel like I've known you guys forever"—even though this was in fact the first time we'd met face to face.

I got to meet Sue's kids that night at dinner and discovered another beautiful layer in her story—several of her children are adopted! Here I was speaking to the adopted children of a former Planned Parenthood manager who had led a 40 Days for Life Campaign that ended up closing her former workplace of seventeen years. Only God!

Webcam abortions, which Planned Parenthood continues to provide, are a frightening reality in the culture of death allowed by the laws of our land. They are a dangerous new trend we must now contend with as we champion the life of the unborn. But we must remember that though technology may be powerful, nothing is more powerful than the will of God, and nothing more inspiring than the human heart that longs to do good because of the urging of the Holy Spirit. Sue's faith and courage give us a map of how to end abortion in our communities.

As Sue Thayer told me her story, she said, "I was caught by surprise by the greatness of our Lord and the limitless love he lavishes on his children."

I, too, am "caught by surprise"—over and over again.

See, I am doing a new thing!
Now it springs up; do you not perceive it?
I am making a way in the wilderness
and streams in the wasteland.

ISAIAH 43:19

Lord, forgive me of my sins and give me the strength to repent, accept your forgiveness, and work to amend this world. As the world finds new ways to sin against life, remind me that there is no heart you can't turn and no conscience you can't penetrate. Help me to bring your joy and love into the wasteland so that life may be restored. I ask this through Christ our Lord, amen.

DAY 38

The Pink Shoe
from Down Under

David

"YOU HAVE STIRRED UP MORE PUBLIC OPPOSITION THAN ANY other visiting speaker in the history of the Australian pro-life movement!" My new Australian friend, a prominent Christian leader there, pumped my hand vigorously, grinning from ear to ear as he declared this "good news" in his wonderfully thick Australian accent.

I had to laugh as my wife, Margaret, and children, Claire and Patrick, looked at him quizzically. They were clearly mystified that he spoke glowingly of opposition as if he were awarding me a medal of honor. I could almost hear them thinking, *Why is public opposition a good thing?* Especially given what they'd witnessed firsthand just a few days before.

"Really, guys," I said, "he just gave us a great compliment. Think about the planning and effort the Australian abortion advocates invested in protesting the events during our visit. If 40 Days for Life weren't so effective, why would they have spent so much energy trying to disrupt us? And just look at what their protests accomplished—God used their attempts at shutting us down to provide widespread media coverage. Now more Australians than ever know how they can get involved to save lives! When Jesus said, 'Blessed are those who are persecuted because of righteousness, for theirs is the kingdom of heaven,' he really meant it. We have been blessed!"

My family and I were nearing the end of our whirlwind trip to

Australia in the fall of 2012—one of my most memorable 40 Days for Life trips ever. And I still have the most unique souvenir I've ever brought home from such a trip—a sparkly pink ballet shoe!

That's right—a pink ballet shoe.

Let me explain.

My very first contact with this Australian came when Chantel —our administrative coordinator doing her best to help me stay on top of a flood of emails—told me of a man named Warwick Marsh, who'd left multiple messages trying to get in touch with me. From the moment we finally connected long-distance, I realized this was a man after my own heart and clearly a man after God's own heart too.

"David, Australia needs a miracle," Warwick announced to me over the phone, "just as America does. That's why we get on our knees and start with God, because we know that with man, ending abortion is not possible. But with God, all things are possible."

Thanks to the many intercontinental emails and phone calls we had over the next several weeks, comparing notes on the effectiveness and progress of various ministries and pro-life initiatives around the globe, Warwick and I became friends. A tireless advocate for the family in Australia, Warwick was awarded the father of the year award by the parliament of New South Wales. He has had roles in many ministries. He has served as a leader in the Australian Heart Ministries and the Fatherhood Foundation; held membership on the National Day of Thanksgiving Management Board; was convener of the National Prayer Council; and was founder of the Australian Christian Values Institute. The list goes on and on. But the thing that impressed me most about Warwick Marsh is that he's a man who loves the Lord with all his heart, and he loves his family. In nearly every conversation, he talks about his wife, Alison, and his five children.

Thanks to the extraordinary collaboration of nearly every national and regional pro-life group in Australia, my family and I were invited in 2012 to conduct a busy speaking tour across Australia.

Warwick planned my itinerary and prepared me well for the trip. "David, when it comes to abortion, Australia is following in America's footsteps—and, unfortunately, in the footsteps of the whole world. About one hundred thousand babies are killed in Australia each year, snatched from the mother's womb, which should be the safest place in the universe for a little baby. In America, you have federal laws and state laws—here in our country, most abortion falls under the state laws. In Victoria, the abortion laws are some of the worst in the world, next to China. On the signature of two doctors, abortion can be carried out right up to nine months! In Victoria and other parts of Australia as well, babies have been literally born alive in the course of an abortion, then left to die."

I was amazed to learn how energized the pro-life movement in Australia is in the face of these horrific conditions—and how many people God had called to the cause of life "down under." Starting in 2009, 40 Days for Life had already spread to seven Australian cities: Brisbane, Melbourne, Sydney, Perth, Adelaide, Tweed Heads, and Hobart, Tasmania. Excited to meet these campaign leaders, Warwick, other co-laborers for life—and, to be honest, also excited to see koalas, kangaroos, and other Australian wildlife up close—my children, my wife, and I boarded planes for our twenty-three-hour journey to the opposite side of the globe.

We landed on August 21 and fell immediately in love with the people and the land of Australia. Determined to make the best use of my time, Warwick had planned an intense coast-to-coast itinerary. We first visited the Sunshine Coast, then Brisbane, then the capital city of Canberra, then on to Melbourne, and then to Hobart. Given the workload and time-zone changes, my family then returned to Sydney while I continued on to Adelaide and Perth and finally rejoined Margaret and the kids in Sydney before returning to America on the third of September.

In those eleven days, God peeled back my American blinders and gave me a big-picture view of just how beyond my comprehension, how complex, how global this movement—God's movement to save the unborn—truly is. Over and over I encountered

Australians who told me they had been pro-life for years, but—and here they sounded like me when I was a bit younger—they hadn't known what to *do* about it. They kept thanking *me* for starting 40 Days for Life, a model of public, peaceful prayer vigils they could easily implement and that was now growing exponentially in their country. Of course, as you know from the first chapter of this book, 40 Days for Life had not been my idea at all. It was God's idea. At one of my many meetings with the Australian pro-life leaders, I had to set the record straight:

> I wish I could tell you it was some brilliant strategic plan. It wasn't. It was literally four people praying for one hour that launched what has now become a worldwide movement. Shawn Carney and his wife Marilisa, Emily, and I were sitting around an old, beat-up wooden table in College Station, Texas, frustrated about the abortion crisis in our community, not knowing what to do. Finally out of desperation we said, "We need to pray and take those words of 2 Chronicles 7:14 seriously: 'If my people, who are called by my name, will humble themselves and pray and seek my face and turn from their wicked ways, then I will hear from heaven, and I will forgive their sin and will heal their land.'"
>
> So we prayed for one hour. During that hour, the first thing God put on our hearts was the time frame of forty days, because throughout biblical history, over and over again, God brought transformation throughout the world in forty-day periods. From Noah on the ark, to Moses on Mt. Sinai, to Jesus in the wilderness, to the apostles' time with our Lord following his resurrection, over and over again we see transformation. Looking at the crisis of abortion in our world today, we *need* some transformation. That's where we sensed we should begin. That was the birth of 40 Days for Life.

As we approached the end of the tour, in just eleven days I'd spoken to over 1,200 people at thirty-five events and meetings, including members of Parliament, religious leaders, and nearly all of the key leaders of the Australian pro-life movement; reached hundreds of thousands of people through newspaper, video, web, and radio; and filmed a full-day training seminar for 40 Days for Life leaders to be used to expand 40 Days for Life to dozens of new sites across Australia. This tour had activated, reactivated, and encouraged many pro-life leaders and volunteers who'd been on the verge of giving up. By the grace of God, it had brought an unprecedented level of unity, cooperation—and even healing—to the Australian pro-life movement. God had set the stage for the 2013 Australian National Day of Prayer and Fasting, which, for the first time ever, would be focused on the sanctity of life. And God had laid the groundwork to launch a major expansion of 40 Days for Life across Australia in 2013 and beyond.

But the trip wasn't quite over yet. God had another surprise in store for me.

It was September 1, the final Saturday evening of our trip. I was to speak at a banquet in Sydney for New South Wales Right to Life. Right after I was introduced, two young women jumped up from a table in the back of the room. They began yelling, "This is for the women!" One of them threw a pink, sparkly ballet shoe at me. (It missed.)

That was the cue for ten more people to burst into the room, chanting slogans in support of abortion. They ran around the room throwing glitter on banquet attendees and distributing brochures depicting Mary and Baby Jesus along with "prayers" demanding that abortion be affordable and accessible and that pro-lifers "keep their vitriolic nonsense to themselves." Then they ran to the front of the room and locked arms around the podium, intent on shutting down the event. One young lady was yelling into what looked like a toy megaphone, which thankfully failed to work.

In the first moments, I was stunned by the sudden barrage. But as their dramatic protest unfolded before our eyes, I found myself mostly saddened. Judging from the anger and hatred in the eyes of these young people, some of them likely had experienced the pain of abortion in their own lives. They had no idea how God was calling people all over the globe to "speak up for those who cannot speak for themselves"—to intervene for the unborn and to help women and men wounded and scarred by the violent act of abortion—people, perhaps, just like them.

I did the only thing I could think to do—pray. I asked the audience to bow their heads and join me in praying the Lord's Prayer. The audience stood and bowed with me, reciting the prayer Jesus gave us. Then we prayed for all women and men harmed by abortion, that they would find healing and experience love and compassion from pro-lifers, without judgment or condemnation.

After about ten minutes, security guards were able to remove the abortion advocates from the room without incident, and our event continued—with the audience even more motivated than before.

As if that wasn't enough excitement, just two days later on Monday morning—the very day we were to fly home—I spoke to sixty college students from the University of Notre Dame (Australia) and the University of Sydney at a breakfast. Desperately trying to disrupt us once again, three dozen abortion advocates organized another protest outside our planned meeting site.

We simply moved our event half a block away to avoid confrontation, and they never figured out that they were protesting an empty room.

Sydney's largest newspaper covered the twin protests, and that's how we learned that one of the most prominent feminists in Australia was among those protesting on Monday morning. Thanks to her notoriety and the substantial media coverage she attracted, even more people, more churches, and more silent and passive pro-lifers who longed to *do something* about abortion—but never knew what to do—learned of 40 Days of Life and discovered that they could make a lifesaving difference.

Today, that sparkly pink ballet shoe sits on my desk, a constant reminder of my trip across the sea to the Land Down Under where our sisters and brothers on the opposite side of the globe are praying and fasting, standing in peaceful vigil, and conducting grassroots community outreach—just like we do here in the States. And the sparkly shoe serves as a reminder that, in spite of persecution, their faithful efforts, like ours, are changing hearts and minds, saving lives, and impacting eternal souls.

> Can you fathom the mysteries of God?
> Can you probe the limits of the Almighty?
> They are higher than the heavens above—what can you do?
> They are deeper than the depths below—what can you know?
> Their measure is longer than the earth
> and wider than the sea.
>
> JOB 11:7–9

Almighty Father, give me the humility to accept any persecution or discomfort for your sake. The sufferings your followers experience here on earth are so small compared to what you endured for us on the cross. Help me to seek your holy perspective to look beyond myself and see the injustice of abortion as a worldwide crisis and you as the worldwide answer. I praise you for the many faithful leaders around the world whom you have lifted up to protect your innocent children in the womb. I ask this through Christ our Lord, amen.

DO IT ANYWAY!

David

YOU HAVE NEARLY COMPLETED YOUR FORTY DAYS OF STORIES AND prayer. I hope that in the stories in this book you have discovered what Shawn and I are witnessing every day—that God is moving all over the globe, demonstrating his love in such a way that lives are saved, hearts are changed, and whole communities are transformed!

Before you end your experience, take a moment to remember what is at stake. Ask God to help you understand the true cost of fifty-four million children—and that's just in America—who have perished under the so-called banner of choice. Think about the women whose hearts have been wounded by abortion and those at risk of making a decision for abortion—the worst decision in their lives.

As Shawn and I have shared just a few stories from the journey we've had over these last few years, it's clear that doing God's work, following his path, answering his call, isn't going to be easy. There will be decision points for you along the way. You may want to flee—I did! There will be days when you may not want to do the work God calls you to do. I have felt that way.

Do it anyway.

That is why the pro-life movement is as effective as it often is today—because of people who simply decided to do it anyway, whether or not they felt like it. And that is how I believe that, ultimately, we will win this battle for life—by each of us doing it anyway. We have all benefited from a great legacy of prayer that went before us. And in the stories in this book, you witnessed God's answers to many of those prayers. But he has more answers in store for the future, and I believe *you* will be a part of God's answers. That may make you nervous.

Do it anyway.

In this book, you've read stories about my wife, Margaret, about her praying as a child outside abortion centers with her family in Corpus Christi, Texas. It wasn't convenient or fun or comfortable. But Margaret, her family, and many more of God's people did it anyway, and they watched as, one by one, every standalone abortion facility in Corpus Christi went out of business.

You read about Lauren Gulde, a nineteen-year-old church secretary who heard the news that Planned Parenthood was building an abortion facility in her hometown of College Station. *I don't know what to do, but something should be done*, she thought. Nervous and uncertain, she called some friends and said, "Let's have a meeting. I haven't got a clue how to go about this—but let's do it anyway."

You read about how my wife, Margaret, and I responded to that invitation, attended that meeting, and later found ourselves praying at the site where that abortion facility was being built. I didn't want to be there. But it was there on the sidewalk that God began to convict my heart, telling me that I had a bigger role to play. Before I knew it, I was chairman of the board of the fledgling Coalition for Life. I resisted. "I've never been on the board of anything. I don't know anything about pro-life work." But I did it anyway.

I hit a point when I wanted out. But God used the words of a speaker named Joe Scheidler, who talked about overcoming our fears and doing it anyway—even when we don't feel like it. The next thing I knew, rather than quitting the pro-life cause, I quit my day job in the pharmaceutical industry instead and took on the full-time role of leading Coalition for Life. Margaret and I were both terrified. We did it anyway.

I was inspired by a schoolgirl named Lacey. I haven't told you her story yet. She was a sophomore at a high school in my town of College Station, Texas. Planned Parenthood, at that time, had a presence in high-school classrooms, pushing their philosophy through "comprehensive sex education"—which by their own internal measurements by Louis Harris & Associates,[10] a polling company, has been proven to increase sexual activity by 50 percent in the students who go through it. Lacey started a petition among her classmates, saying to the school board, "Please kick Planned Parenthood out of our schools and away from our classrooms." Some teachers signed on. One weekend, thirteen churches passed around Lacey's petition, garnering over 3,300 signatures.

At the next school board meeting, Lacey went before the school board. Her voice was cracking. She was clearly terrified. She presented the 3,300 petition signatures and said, "On behalf of my friends who are prey to this organization, Planned Parenthood, please get them out of our classrooms. Please get them away from us." Because Lacey had faith, because she overcame her fear, because she did it anyway, the school board resolved to kick Planned Parenthood out of the classrooms and keep them away from children from then on. Lacey was young and scared, but she did it anyway, and she inspired me to keep on keeping on.

Next came 40 Days for Life. We had a decision to make. We had never done anything like this before. It was overwhelming. It was terrifying. We didn't know whether we would be able to pull it off. But when we realized lives were at stake, that souls were at stake, we did it anyway.

You heard the story now of how that turned out—how city after city heard about 40 Days for Life and wanted to do their own campaign. Soon, in cities across the United States and now across the globe, thousands upon thousands of people were participating in forty days of prayer and fasting, forty days of peaceful vigil, forty days of community outreach. Post-abortion healing programs like the one in Charlotte are springing up. Pregnancy resource centers like the ones that "sandwich" the abortion center in chapter 21 are offering real hope and help for women in crisis. Pro-life laws are being passed in record numbers. And all of this happens for only one reason: People are willing to do it anyway.

To date, we have now seen 2,210 40 Days for Life Campaigns conducted in 481 cities across all fifty American states and fifteen other countries. More than half a million people have participated in 40 Days for Life Campaigns. As of this writing, we have confirmed reports of 6,749 babies who had been scheduled for abortions but whose mothers changed their minds because of the people praying outside.

We've seen twenty-five abortion facilities go out of business during or after a 40 Days for Life vigil was held in the public right-of-way outside. We mentioned only four of them in this book, even though all twenty-five are beautiful stories. But frankly, forty days isn't enough to tell you all the stories of what God has accomplished through this movement! We'd need at least a year, probably much more.

Each and every 40 Day campaign happens because of a local leader who was scared, who faced a lot of challenges, but who did it anyway. One result of the campaigns I don't believe any of us expected was the exodus of seventy-five abortion workers who experienced conversions and left the abortion industry as a result of people praying outside. You know Abby Johnson's story and others that have been shared in this book. Each of these courageous people was afraid, but they took the leap. They did it anyway.

What does all of this mean for you today?

It means now is the perfect time for you to discern your role.

Could you pray more than you've been praying in the past—even if it doesn't seem like the perfect time? Please, do it anyway! Pray for the babies. Pray for the mothers. Pray that those on the other side of the fence will have a change of heart and join us, where they can offer real hope and healing to women in crisis and find healing for themselves.

Maybe the next step for you is to educate yourself more about the sanctity of human life so that you can help to educate others.

Maybe you're a high school or college student. If so, you and your friends and peers are in the crosshairs of the abortion industry. You can be a spokesperson for the unborn, helping your friends understand that one-third of your generation has been aborted, and that as survivors of the abortion crisis, you and your peers need to be courageous and turn the tide for life.

Maybe the next step for you is to volunteer with a pregnancy resource center. Maybe you're meant to be a counselor, a shoulder someone can lean on at a time of need. Someone to encourage them when their family, their boyfriend, and everybody else is telling them to abort. Even if you fear inadequacy, do it anyway. Help a mother choose life.

Maybe your role is to participate in 40 Days for Life. Two campaigns take place every year—one in the fall, beginning in September, and one during the Lenten season, beginning on Ash Wednesday. Maybe you're supposed to *lead* a campaign. Even if you've never been out on the streets to pray in front of an abortion facility, even if, like me, you have such fears as, *What will people think? What will people say?* do it anyway!

Maybe you could be a prayer vigil volunteer or a sidewalk counselor lovingly reaching out and offering alternatives—not just for forty days, but 365 days a year. Yes, you'll have frustrations. Yes, some of the people you talk to will still choose abortion. But do it anyway!

Maybe your gifts suit you to get more involved in the political process—to help a candidate or promote a specific piece of legislation and by doing so help change the laws of the land. Maybe you should run for office. Don't you agree that we need more God-fearing men and women in the political process?

Maybe your call is to speak to youth about the gift of chastity, to tell them that God gives us this beautiful gift of sexuality with instructions. If we follow those instructions and use that gift within the context of marriage between a husband and wife, it will be life-giving. But if the instructions are ignored, it can be devastating. That's not a popular message! You'll have young people roll their eyes and look at you like you're from Mars. Do it anyway!

Maybe you need to seek healing from your own past abortion or to help a friend to do the same. It's uncomfortable to bare your soul and acknowledge your sin, and sometimes it's just as hard to help somebody else do that. But do it anyway.

Is it easy to do it anyway? No, it's not. But it's worth it.

Do you remember the story of Baby Jakai? How I longed to meet just *one* of the babies saved through 40 Days for Life. I heard the stories. I saw the pictures. But after years of working in 40 Days for Life, I had not met a single one of those children. Until I went through Harrisburg, Pennsylvania, where his grateful mother laid Jakai in my arms as his little brown eyes twinkled. He giggled. How close had Jakai come to being an abortion statistic? What if people hadn't been praying that day? What if that pregnancy resource center hadn't been there? What if people hadn't been willing to do it anyway?

I held little Jakai in my arms, thinking that, if it weren't for people just like you, terrified, uncomfortable, out of their comfort zone but willing to do it anyway, little Jakai would not be alive.

"For I know the plans I have for you," declares the LORD, "... to give you hope and a future."

JEREMIAH 29:11

We are a part of God's plans for good, right here on earth. In fact, I believe we're at a tipping-point moment in history. How is God going to give us the "hope and a future" part of that verse? I truly believe the mechanism God will use to provide that hope and a future is you.

So get involved—or more involved—in this world-changing work. Even if you're scared, even if you're uncomfortable, even if you're stretched beyond your comfort zone, do it anyway. Do the work you are called to do. And look forward to hearing those beautiful words one day when we meet our maker, "Well done, good and faithful servant."

Now to him who is able to do
immeasurably more than all we ask or imagine,
according to his power that is at work within us,
to him be glory in the church and in Christ Jesus
throughout all generations, for ever and ever! Amen.

EPHESIANS 3:20–21

Heavenly Father, you can do immeasurably more than I can ask or imagine. I offer myself to you completely, no holding back. Show me what to do, Lord. I open myself to your power at work in my life and through my life to others, as you will. Give me your strength and perseverance to do whatever you would have me do—and to do it anyway, no matter the challenges. Lord, I am willing. Amen.

The Rest of the Story

David

"DAVID, I JUST HEARD THE LATEST ABORTION NUMBERS FROM THE Planned Parenthood abortion center here in College Station. Two thousand children have died. Man, I'm frustrated. Our Coalition for Life has been praying and working for five years, but the abortion numbers are going *up*, not down. Are we fighting a losing battle?"

My friend, David Arabie, was clearly frustrated, and so was I. It was the summer of 2004. My wife, Margaret, and I were hosting a dinner at our house for married couples who had assisted us in putting on a marriage preparation retreat through our church. One of the young couples in attendance was the Arabies, David and Monica. Shortly before I blessed the meal and we started dinner, David pulled me aside to vent his concerns.

He went on to complain that the church seemed to be largely silent and apathetic about abortion. He asked me why, as Christians, our actions didn't reflect the urgency of stopping what had become the leading cause of death in our nation—abortion. I didn't have an answer for him, but I certainly identified with his disillusionment.

Five years earlier, Margaret had coaxed me to my first pro-life meeting, a turning point for me and for the pro-life community in College Station. That was the night Coalition for Life was born. I felt called to the new ministry, and I felt myself becoming more and more committed to its mission. Before long I quit my job and signed on as the full-time executive director.

But the past two years had been frustrating—we'd lost ground, lost volunteers, and frankly, I was so discouraged I had considering quitting, though I'd told no one but Margaret.

As David Arabie confided his frustrations to me, something mysterious happened. First, as we spoke about the babies dying, the women who'd been wounded, the audacity of Planned Parenthood to impose itself on our community and build a growing market for its deadly services, our passions were fanned from dying embers into bright flames—even though we'd previously been speaking the language of commiseration and discouragement! Looking back, of course, I see that the Holy Spirit was stirring our souls.

Then my friend said, "David, if we really believe that abortion kills innocent children and wounds women—and men—then we should stand in peaceful vigil outside that facility for twenty-four hours a day—bearing witness to the injustice going on inside and offering hope and help to those at risk of making a tragic decision."

A twenty-four-hour vigil outside an abortion center? My first thought was, *That's crazy!* But I kept that thought to myself, and David and I joined the other couples to begin our dinner.

Later that night, I had trouble going to sleep. David's idea kept rattling around in my mind.

The next morning, I went into the Coalition for Life office and met with three other people—Shawn, Marilisa, and Emily. That was the day of the hour of prayer around the wooden table—the hour of prayer I described in the first chapter of this book, the hour of prayer that birthed 40 Days for Life.

Because of my conversation with David Arabie the night before, a portion of our prayer time that day centered on the "crazy" idea of a twenty-four-hour-a-day vigil outside the local abortion facility. As a result, that idea became one of the three components of 40 Days for Life.

Shortly afterward, I called David Arabie and invited him to meet with us at the office. When he arrived, I told him we were prepared to follow through on his idea of an around-the-clock prayer vigil. To test his commitment to his own idea, I asked when *he* would be willing to pray outside the abortion center.

His answer stunned me. David pledged to be at the vigil from 11 p.m. to 7 a.m.—for *each* of the forty days.

David made good on that commitment, coming out to pray each night with a passion and intensity I had never seen.

An active participant in the Knights of Columbus, David recruited many of his brother Knights to join him out on the sidewalk for what they ended up calling the Knight Shift of 40 Days for Life. Some nights there were more than twenty young people praying together there because of David's dynamic leadership.

David Arabie, as you can see, was crucial to the start of 40 Days for Life.

Not long after that first 40 Days for Life Campaign, my family moved from Texas to the Washington, D.C., area. For the next few years, I had no communication with David Arabie—until I received a surprise email from him at 2:22 in the morning on November 7, 2007, three days after the completion of our first nationwide campaign.

David's email message—which I share here—opened my eyes to the "rest of the story" behind David's idea, his commitment, and his passion that helped to launch 40 Days for Life in the first place:

> David,
>
> This is a long email. I know how busy you are. But I have been thinking about this stuff for about 43 days now and thought I should share it.
>
> Congratulations on the completion of the National 40 Days for Life campaign. I got a call from Columbia Magazine, the Knights of Columbus national publication, and the conversation reminded me of the beginning of this whole thing.
>
> How many people will spend their entire lives yearning for a sign that God is with them? We had a couple of ideas, combined them over a dinner party and a meeting at the Coalition for Life office in 2004 and then 40 Days for Life started, all in a matter of weeks. We watched God, plain as day, mold that project in front of our very eyes. And now it's changing the world.
>
> I have thought, thousands of times, how did I get in the middle

of that? I had been at Texas A&M for almost four years before we met. I didn't even know where the abortion clinic in College Station was before July of '04. I am a carpenter. I cuss like a sailor and I party too much. Not so much anymore. But definitely then.

Then we did 40 Days.

After it was over it became apparent that I wasn't called to pro-life ministry in the same way you and Shawn are. Abortion is the greatest evil we face, so of course we pray and support its demise in every way.

But other than the miracle of 40 Days, I never felt called to be a part of the ministry except when I brought the idea of 24 hours' presence to you in the first place.

This is how it happened. I don't think I ever told anyone the details.

My dad entered the last stages of his long fight with cancer on Memorial Day weekend '04. He began hallucinating and such. During this time he prayed nearly all of his waking hours. Doctors said he would be gone in days. So I stayed with him.

It wound up being two months before he passed away. In those months, he was rarely the man I knew as my father. But he said he loved me all the time, several times per conversation. After a couple of weeks he would say, on a daily basis, "Let's pray to end abortion."

After several prayers to end abortion in one day, I asked, "Let's pray to heal your cancer, or ease your pain."

He said, "NO! We are praying to end abortion."

And then he told me a story that explained why.

He shared that as a young man, he hadn't wanted any children because he had a genetic nerve disorder that he feared might be passed along to them. Then he found out that he had gotten a girl pregnant.

He convinced her to have it "taken care of." He paid the money ... and then she stood him up for the abortion appointment.

He didn't speak to her for weeks, but later they married.

He said, "Here it is twenty-five years later, and the baby I wanted to kill is by my side at my deathbed."

I was not upset at all about any of the circumstances

surrounding that trip to the abortion clinic. I was upset that he had to struggle with that guilt on his deathbed, instead of all the great times we had in my wonderful childhood. I just wanted to talk about the good times. I wanted to thank him for teaching me how to throw a ball and how to hunt. How to be a man and stand up for what you believe. I wanted to thank him for everything he had done for me, for making me who I am.

But he was carrying the burden of a near miss.

Julius Allen Arabie died shortly thereafter, in July of '04.

I decided right then that I was going to do something drastic. I mentioned the idea of a 24-hour presence at an abortion facility to clergy and fellow Knights and a bunch of other people. Originally I figured we were just going to stand there until it closed, and then go to the next one. And I didn't even know who "we" was.

Everyone tried to temper the idea. "Why don't you just cover a few of the hours the clinic is open," or something of the sort.

Not you. The Lord was moving in you, because you knew we could do it.

You made my harebrained idea practical by putting a timeline on it, and making it repeatable and marketable. You gave me an outlet in the Coalition for Life, and a microphone to help convince people we could do it.

And then you were given an outlet to spread the word to the rest of the country.

I am sorry for the length of this email. I just wasn't sure if you knew that part of the birth of 40 Days.

Monica and I often think about the example you and Margaret have set for us. My daughter Nicollette is almost 2 now and when I open the door she runs full speed to meet me with a hug.

Thank you for everything. And again, congratulations.

David Arabie

For David Arabie, the crisis of abortion became *personal*. And because he took it personally, David proposed an idea that, when seasoned with an hour of prayer around a wooden table, led to the birth of 40 Days for Life.

Now you know the rest of the story.

One individual who took the abortion crisis personally, combined with fervent prayer, is what fueled a worldwide movement that is—by the grace of God—changing hearts and minds, saving thousands of lives, closing abortion centers, helping workers to leave the abortion industry, and impacting eternal souls.

Now it's your turn.

As you pray, and make this personal, what will God do to change the world through *you*?

I am the vine; you are the branches.
If you remain in me and I in you, you will bear much fruit;
apart from me you can do nothing.
My command is this: Love each other as I have loved you.
Greater love has no one than this:
to lay down one's life for one's friends.
JOHN 15: 5,12,13

Heavenly Father, thank you for inviting me to join you in this great work you are doing around the world. I may not have been a "near miss" like David Arabie, but I recognize that abortion personally affects every one of us. Friends and family members have been scarred. Children have been lost. Families have been torn apart. Our cities and nations have been ravaged. Lord, I can do nothing apart from you. I lay my life down for you to use. Show me what you want me to do in response to this crisis. And may my commitment to love others—the unborn, their mothers and fathers, abortion workers, legislators and my fellow pro-life advocates—pour from my life in such a way that they are all drawn closer to you and personally experience your sacrificial love for us all. Use me, Lord, to help make this moment in history the beginning of the end of abortion. Amen.

Acknowledgments

As you have discovered throughout the pages of this book, 40 Days for Life would never have existed—let alone accomplished anything—were it not for God's blessing. So we first and foremost give all the praise, honor, and glory to God almighty, and to his Son, our Lord and Savior, Jesus Christ. Had it been based on man's ability alone, this endeavor would have been impossible, but, as we have learned time and time again, with God, *all things* are possible.

Additionally, we want to acknowledge the many people who invested time and energy to help make this book a reality, as well as those whose tireless efforts have contributed to the growth and worldwide impact of 40 Days for Life.

Wes Yoder at Ambassador Agency, you were the first person to ever propose the idea that we should write a book about 40 Days for Life—even though we initially laughed at your suggestion. Your inspiration, leadership, and expertise throughout this process have been invaluable. Thanks also to Gloria, Maria, Emily, Sherry, and your entire team for believing in us, for giving us a platform by enthusiastically representing us as speakers, and for supporting this effort long before 40 Days for Life grew into an international movement.

Cindy Lambert, you are an amazing writer. Working side-by-side with you throughout this process has been a tremendous blessing. We feel that it was divine intervention that brought us together when you were working on former Planned Parenthood director Abby Johnson's book *UnPlanned*. It was certainly unplanned that our paths would cross—but we're sure glad they did. When the three of us had lunch in Fredericksburg, Virginia, we both expressed how much we wished we could have you, and your gifts and talents, involved in writing this book. Thanks for surprising us by agreeing to take on this project, thanks for believing in us, and thanks for not giving up on us during the crazy process of assembling this book.

Dave Lambert, our editor, and the whole Somersault Group, thanks for using your many years of experience in the publishing world to make this endeavor possible. You went above and beyond the call of duty in every way to deliver a polished and professional finished book.

Whoever said you can't judge a book by its cover clearly never saw the great cover design that Matt Lehman came up with for this book on such short notice. Thanks, Matt.

We must give a shout out to Fr. Joseph Fessio at Ignatius Press, who at the West Coast Walk for Life in San Francisco stopped us in the crowd of forty thousand people to ask point-blank when we were going to "finally" write this book. Thanks for the encouragement. Your prompting was a key factor in convincing us to actually get started on this project.

Thanks to the many local leaders and campaign participants who have shared thousands of 40 Days for Life stories with us over these past five years. Though we unfortunately couldn't fit them all in this book, know that we treasure your reports of what God is accomplishing through your faithful efforts. For those whose stories are featured in this book, thanks for allowing us to track you down to gather details and for allowing us to use your name to highlight your courageous work.

Abby Johnson, thank you for writing such a beautiful Foreword for this book. What an unbelievable, but wonderful, journey these last few years have been. Thanks for continually being open to the promptings of the Holy Spirit—even when it has completely rocked your world. We appreciate you and treasure your friendship!

To the hundreds of faithful people who have taken the leap of faith to apply and lead a 40 Days for Life campaign in your community—you are our heroes. The long hours, thankless efforts, emails, phone calls, church visits—not to mention the persecution you have endured—cannot be measured in this world, but they will be in the next. You have collectively recruited more than 550,000 volunteer participants to pray and fast, stand in peaceful vigil, and engage in community outreach—making this the largest, longest, and fastest-growing internationally coordinated pro-life initiative in history. As we travel to your cities and see you in action, you continually amaze and inspire us. We love you!

For the hundreds of thousands of people who actively participate in local 40 Days for Life campaigns, know how much we appreciate your speaking up for those who cannot speak for themselves. Your tireless dedication provides great hope for the future, and demonstrates to the world that abortion's days are numbered.

God has blessed us with an amazing board of directors. Jim Olson, Carmen Pate, and Amber Dolle, you've been with us since day one and we treasure your guidance and leadership. John Siedhoff, Joyce Zounis, Haywood Robinson, and Dave Sterrett, we're so glad that you joined the team and took this organization to a whole new level. And Barney, thanks for helping to get us off to a great start. We appreciate all of you!

Our 40 Days for Life national team members are second to none. You kept this movement alive and growing simultaneously in hundreds of cities around the world while seeing the drama and challenges behind the scenes of this book project. Erin Shircliff, thank you for your detailed research and enthusiasm for the book. Lauren Muzyka, thank you for spending countless hours on the phone with local campaign leaders and for being an inspiration to so many people at times when this work has been overwhelming or discouraging. Chantel Poisel, thank you for transcribing much of this book from our spoken words—despite David's hour-long run-on sentences. Your professional attitude and punctuality amaze us. Thanks for enduring our comments about Argos, Indiana!

For the unsung hero of 40 Days for Life (just ask all of our local leaders), huge thanks are due to our communications director, David Brandao, along with his wife Barbara and their children. God was watching out for 40 Days for Life when you decided to join this crazy new initiative when it had no money and a highly unpredictable future. Your willingness to work full-time for a year without pay is beyond astonishing, and this effort will forever be indebted to you. Thank you for grounding both of us when needed (which is frequently) and for running to the frontlines whenever duty calls. Now, can you help us get logged in?

To the donors whose support has enabled 40 Days for Life to save lives and make such a powerful impact in hundreds of cities, thank you. Your sacrificial financial contributions got us through difficult times and your ongoing generosity is helping to spread the hope of 40 Days for Life around the world. We appreciate you more than words can express.

To the board, staff, and volunteers at Coalition for Life in Bryan/College Station, thank you for getting this all started. When things began to grow beyond the Brazos Valley, thanks for your willingness to freely allow 40 Days for Life to launch as an independent effort that could spread the impact of Aggieland around the world. We'd especially like to express our gratitude to Emil and Clementine Ogden for making so much of this work possible. Gig 'em!

40 Days for Life is a relative newcomer to the pro-life movement, and we stand in awe of the many courageous people who have selflessly advocated on behalf of human life for decades. We applaud your dedication and are continually inspired by your example. We are humbled and honored to co-labor in the Lord's harvest field with you.

We have been blessed to work in partnership with nearly every national, state, and local pro-life organization over the last few years. We deeply respect the marvelous work of pregnancy resource centers (now exceeding three thousand in number and counting!) Right to Life groups, adoption services, prayer- and church-based ministries, youth outreach efforts, research, education and advocacy organizations, post-abortion healing and awareness ministries, and legal, political and legislative groups. Our movement is made up of many parts, but we truly are one body, united around a common objective. We are proud to work side-by-side with you.

Though there is not space here to name the hundreds of pro-life organization leaders who have helped 40 Days for Life, we want to give special mention and thanks to Fr. Frank Pavone of Priests for Life, Kristan Hawkins of Students for Life of America, Marjorie Dannenfelser of Susan B. Anthony List, Joe and Ann Scheidler of the Pro-Life Action League, Lila Rose of Live Action, and Eva Muntean and Dolores Meehan of the West Coast Walk for Life for selflessly championing this effort.

We owe a huge debt of gratitude to many members of the clergy. We have been deeply inspired to witness the courageous and compassionate leadership of local pastors, ministry heads, denomination leaders, bishops, archbishops, and cardinals. Through your words and actions, you have truly shown what it means to be a good shepherd of God's flock.

We greatly appreciate the numerous Christian media outlets and organizations that have helped to spread the word about 40 Days for Life far and wide. Special thanks to the National Catholic Register, EWTN, Focus on the Family, Baptist Press, the American Family Association, CBN, Bott Radio Network, Salem Communications, Relevant Radio, the Catholic News Agency, WorldNetDaily, Life News, and Life Site News.

We are grateful for our amazing lawyers, Tom Brejcha and Peter Breen, at the Thomas More Legal Society in Chicago. You guys have kept us—and our local campaign leaders—out of trouble more times than we can count. Thanks for the wise counsel and for your friendship.

Thanks to the Carney family and friends in Virginia and Texas. For my parents and the huge support from my siblings April, Jake, Josh, and Jason. To the best in-laws anyone could ask for, thanks for raising such a woman of God, for your sacrifices, and for allowing her to marry me. To my brothers-in-law who are like blood brothers. For my best friend Chris, his wife, and his parents. For the Irish priests who taught me in high school how to live my Catholic faith with joy and courage. Fr. Michael Doyle, Fr. Anthony McLaughlin, and Fr. Morgan White did for me what all good priests do—they led me closer to Christ.

Thanks to the Bereit family and friends in Virginia, Texas, and Pennsylvania. For my mom in heaven, I miss and love you. For my dad, thanks for being the best example of a father anyone could ask for. Much love to my brother, Mark, and his family. For my "other" mom and dad, Walter and Helen, thank you being such wonderful in-laws. I appreciate you raising such a remarkable woman, and for instilling strong faith and a pro-life conviction in Margaret. Your encouragement of our work gives us great strength. To our friends in Aggieland—we miss you! To our Virginia friends, thanks for providing such a wonderful community that supports our faith and family.

Finally, enormous thanks are due to our amazing wives and children. Like all things we commit to with your support, this book took far more time and effort than we originally told you it would. Margaret and Marilisa, thank you for first getting us involved in the pro-life movement, and for standing at our side throughout this whole adventure. You truly are our strength. Claire, Patrick, Bridget, Bailey, Seamus, and Bernadette, you inspire us every day and remind us why we press on in what Pope John Paul II called, "the most important work on Earth." We are involved in this work to ensure that the world you grow up in is better than the one we grew up in. Thank you for your love, support, and example. We couldn't do any of this without you.

Notes

1. The Planned Parenthood facility was actually built in Bryan, Texas, and covered the entire area, including College Station. But since the two cities are usually thought of together as the Bryan-College Station Metropolitan Area, which is a mouthful, we're going to simplify things throughout this book by referring to the entire area simply as College Station.

2. Testimonials taken on 8/21/2012 from: www.priestsforlife.org/postabortion/postabortiontestimonywomen.htm

3. issuu.com/actionfund/docs/ppfa_financials_2010_122711_web_vf?mode=window&viewMode=doublePage

4. bit.ly/11pm8DB

5. Abby Johnson with Cindy Lambert. *UnPlanned* (Chicago, Illinois: Tyndale House Publishers, Inc., 2010) pp. 4–6

6. Adapted from Ephesians 3:20–21

7. References for Day 20: Planned Parenthood of New York 2010 Annual Report, www.plannedparenthood.org/nyc/files/NYC/PPNYC_Annual_Report_2010_online_version.pdf

    Ross Douthat, "The Media's Abortion Blinders," *New York Times*, February 4, 2012. http://www.nytimes.com/2012/02/05/opinion/sunday/douthat-the-medias-blinders-on-abortion.html?_r=1

8. Anglicans for Life website, www.anglicansforlife.org/content/european-country-georgia-has-highest-abortion-rates-world

9. References for Day 36: Kliff, Sarah. *Newsweek* "The Abortion Evangelist" August 14, 2009

    60 Minutes: "The Front Line (Abortion Story)" sixtyminutes.ninemsn.com.au/stories/7940584/the-front-line

    Testimony of Leroy Carhart, MD, July 1997: www.texasrighttolife.com/whatsnew/abortionists_testimony.html

    KVUE News Austin, Texas. November 5, 2009. www.kvue.com/home/Abortion-doctor-Am-I-killing-Yes-I-am--69294137.html

    Kermit Gosnell arrest: www.slate.com/articles/news_and_politics/the_back_alley/2011/02/what_happened_to_the_women.html

10. Study cited in George Grant, *Grand Illusions: The Legacy of Planned Parenthood* (Franklin, Tennessee: Adroit Press, 1992) p. 32. Download of *Grand Illusions* available at www.exodusbooks.com/Samples/entrewave/13103Free.pdf

DAVID BEREIT (right) is national director of 40 Days for Life. Since launching 40 Days for Life, he has spoken extensively across the United States and around the world, inspiring audiences as large as seventy thousand people. His work has been prominently featured in the media, including coverage on CNN, ABC, NBC, CBS, Fox News, HBO, hundreds of radio programs, and over one hundred newspapers across the country, including *The New York Times*, *The Washington Post*, *Los Angeles Times*, and *USA Today*. David has received many prestigious awards, including the Henry Hyde Life Leadership Award, the Students for Life of America Defender of Life Award, and the Walk for Life West Coast St. Gianna Molla Award for Pro-Life Heroism. David is a graduate of Texas A&M University with a degree in biomedical science. He is married to his best friend Margaret, and they reside in Virginia with their two children.

SHAWN CARNEY (left) is campaign director of 40 Days for Life. Starting in college as a volunteer for a local pro-life organization, Coalition for Life, Shawn became its director and then helped launch 40 Days for Life. He is one of the youngest and most sought after pro-life speakers in America, and regularly addresses audiences coast-to-coast and internationally. Shawn's work has been featured in hundreds of media stories including Fox News Channel's *The O'Reilly Factor*, *The Laura Ingraham Show*, *Drudge Report*, and *Focus on the Family*, and has produced and hosted award-winning documentaries for the Eternal Word Television Network (EWTN). Shawn graduated from Texas A&M University, having studied history and philosophy, and is currently working on a master's degree in theology from Franciscan University of Steubenville. He lives in Virginia with his wife, Marilisa, and their four children.

David and Shawn are exclusively represented by Ambassador Speakers Bureau. To book either of them to speak, visit: www.AmbassadorSpeakers.com or call 615-370-4700.

You've read the book ...
now, join the movement!

40 DAYS FOR LIFE ™

Go to: www.40DaysforLife.com

Enter your name and email address to:

- Receive the latest stories, breaking news, and updates of what God is accomplishing

- Find the 40 Days for Life campaign nearest to you

- Discover how to bring 40 Days for Life to your town

- Learn about the many other lifesaving efforts and organizations which work collaboratively with 40 Days for Life

- Understand how God can use *you* to change hearts and save lives ... right where you live!